# A GUIDE TO SMART GROWTH

## Shattering Myths, Providing Solutions

Edited by Jane S. Shaw and Ronald D. Utt

Preface by The Honorable Malcolm Wallop

The Heritage Foundation
214 Massachusetts Avenue, NE
Washington, DC 20002
800.544.4843
*www.heritage.org*

The Political Economy Research Center
502 South 19th Avenue
Suite 211
Bozeman, Montana  59718-6827
406.587.9591
*www.perc.org*

Digital Imagery  © 2000 by PhotoDisc, Inc.
Background cover image courtesy of Rick Harrison

ISBN 0-89195-088-5

# TABLE OF CONTENTS

# PREFACE

Since the time of the Pilgrims, we Americans have held a compellingly romantic view of nature. Inspired by the celebrations of Thanksgiving, by the idea of manifest destiny, and by the adventures of Daniel Boone and Lewis and Clark, we tend to view nature as a static paradise that will remain forever unchanged. Old growth forests are forever old, and new growth forests are forever changing without change.

Can anyone doubt that many Americans today still pine for space, expansive views, and cloudless skies, themes evoked by the once-popular song, "Home on the Range": "Oh, give me a home where the buffalo roam, and the deer and the antelope play, where seldom is heard a discouraging word and the skies are not cloudy all day." They pine too for surroundings that are crime-free, lightly taxed, and fully served.

The closer Americans come to achieving this goal, however, the more resistant they are to sharing it. Their descriptions of those who come in search of the same qualities of life are never flattering, usually hostile, and always defensive. Whether they are new arrival, early settler, or hereditary family, they oppose many of the changes brought on by development and growth.

When landscapes change and our romantic views are disrupted, something visceral happens. Conservatives and liberals alike protest what has come to be known as sprawl. "Smart growth" is the new political catchword, although its definition is far from clear.

In contemplating the rapid pace of development occurring in many communities, it behooves us to recognize that the demand for one's own place to live has not diminished, nor have quarrels over how to meet that demand and yet build nothing more. Short of some national program of mandatory birth control, combined with the requirement that we live on top of each other, no simple answer exists.

Americans began leaving their cities as their surroundings were changed first by rule, then by law, taxation, crowding, and increased danger. Liberated by the automobile, Americans located where their needs were met with shopping centers, new schools, new churches, and open spaces, with corridors of access to their places of work. As others became attracted to the same types of amenities, developers responded to market demand by building more. Counties and urban planners built roads and services, and ever more Americans were attracted. The suburbs grew.

Some of this growth was spurred on by the declining quality of life in the cities. As judges began to dictate permissive policing procedures toward panhandlers, gangs, and other intrusions to street life in cities, the nuisance factor drove shoppers, diners, casual strolling couples, and movie patrons to privately owned malls. On private property, they could avoid such nuisances. Shopping was safer and there was abundant parking. Soon, the malls became what downtown used to be. Young and old, couples, families, friends, and individuals could be found shopping, strolling, dining, resting, and movie-going. They are casual, happy, and safe.

As markets continued to respond to the changing consumer preferences, sprawl emerged. The treasured visually appealing qualities and conveniences began to disappear—as often as not by the misguided good intentions of county or state planners attempting to maintain rural character through such tools as single-use requirements. Seeking to avoid the problems of urban America, planners imposed the separation of retail and commercial districts. The zoning rules and requirements resulted in the use of more and more land, which dictated more roads and dissipated any sense of community. State and local officials plowed on in the earnest belief that their decisions were the keys to the new kingdom.

As these changes were taking place, highways became crowded. Taxes increased. Services diminished. There was the oft-repeated claim of the loss of wildlife—though studies will demonstrate that in some cases the new surroundings actually enhanced habitat for wildlife from the days of intensive farming. What was once near heaven now seemed more like hell on some days. As is the way with us in modern times, the solution seemed to be to close the gate.

Meanwhile, governments tried to enlist public support for subsidizing mass transportation. More often than not, however, the new bus and rail routes did not serve the needs of commuters. They were lightly used and often failed. Even President Clinton has acknowledged this. In announcing that the Administration would drop the price level requirement of automobiles for those seeking to qualify for food stamps, he recently noted: "Too often, the public transportation does not go where recipients need to go!"

The supposed cures pose their own problems. Some farmers, for example, have found that their property has been rendered uneconomic by the high tax burdens and targets of complaints from crowding neighbors who complain of the noise or smells. They are not allowed to sell their land because of regulations that are designed to maintain open space and keep development within urban boundaries. City, county, state, and federal officials all say that there isn't enough money to compensate property owners for values denied. In effect, they are saying, "Constitution be damned."

The changes known collectively as sprawl, and the attempts to stop them, raise a myriad of questions. Can Americans be dissuaded from urban flight? Can the desire to close the gate—the NIMBY ("not in my back yard") syndrome—be addressed without property rights transgressions or heavy-handed dictates from central government? Can we protect property values without denying property rights?

And what about those left behind? As America's population grows in numbers and in wealth, many minorities are just now able to afford escape from the confines of ill-run cities with high crime rates, high taxes, and low services. Are we to tell them the party is over?

This splendid little book will help us answer these questions. It is a cogent examination of the history and consequences of the search for space, air, views, schools, and safety that has resulted in suburbanization. It explodes some myths as it examines the effects of suburban growth on wildlife and nature. It contrasts the results of big government–imposed "solutions" with those of local initiatives and private-sector creativity. It explores the failures and successes of efforts to restore core values and quality to inner-city life. It should become the handbook for those officials who seek to maintain both quality of life and the access to it by those who are just now rising to afford it.

A variety of successful private-sector and local initiatives are examined here. They are contrasted with little-recognized but monstrous experiments in government growth management, such as in Portland, Oregon, where home prices are soaring beyond reach and mass transit attracts minimal use. Or Atlanta, Georgia, where the federal government through the Environmental Protection Agency asserts its authority over local zoning boards and laws.

There are answers that work without violating property rights. There are answers that work by more efficiently using countryside space while maintaining highly valued views and environments. There are answers that work by improving inner-city neighborhoods, with restored policing, city parks, and other amenities. They are found in market-based solutions. As Portland discovered, you can fence the homeland, but it does not diminish the demand for places to live and access to jobs.

The proposals here go a long way toward implementing efficient, environmentally sound, and constitutionally qualified resolutions to the vexing problems of today and satisfying the demands of a growing population to live in grace. That, after all, has been the American dream. Government has yet to enforce its will and arrive at grace. Perhaps the local citizens whose job it is to satisfy both the market's demands and the future's quality can find the path to do both within these pages by trusting in the ingenuity and judgment of an exceptionally decent populace we call Americans.

—*The Honorable Malcolm Wallop*

# ACKNOWLEDGMENTS

A project of this scope is never possible without the contributions of many people. The authors of the chapters, of course, deserve special thanks for what we consider to be some of their best and most innovative work. The energy and insight they devoted to this project will ensure that this book makes an important contribution to the debate over sprawl. Understanding the process of suburbanization and then crafting effective market-oriented, innovative solutions to the problems that communities encounter will address Americans' concerns and still allow them to pursue their dreams.

We gratefully acknowledge Senator Malcolm Wallop's thoughtful preface to the book. Senator Wallop was the ranking Republican on the Energy and Natural Resources Committee during his tenure in Congress.

*A Guide to Smart Growth: Shattering Myths, Providing Solutions* is a collaborative publication of The Heritage Foundation and the Political Economy Research Center (PERC). Under Edwin J. Feulner's leadership, Heritage constantly reminds us that principles do matter and that policymakers should strive to achieve the ideal. We thank Stuart M. Butler, Heritage's Vice President for Domestic and Economic Policy Studies, and Angela Antonelli, Heritage's Director of the Thomas A. Roe Institute for Economic Policy Studies, for helping to ensure that this book became a reality.

We also appreciate the support of PERC's Executive Director, Terry L. Anderson, who saw the value of broadening PERC's analysis of environmental issues to include issues of suburban growth. As with all activities at PERC, Monica Lane Guenther, PERC's Administrative Director, helped this project go smoothly.

Finally, we would like to thank the capable staff members of The Heritage Foundation who finely tuned these pages for publication. We especially thank Managing Editor Janice A. Smith and Senior Editor Richard Odermatt for their editing talents and oversight. We also thank the staff of Heritage's Publishing Services Department: Ann Klucsarits, Director; Thomas J. Timmons, Deputy Director; and Michelle Fulton Smith, Senior Layout and Design Specialist. It has been a pleasure to work with such a professional group of people.

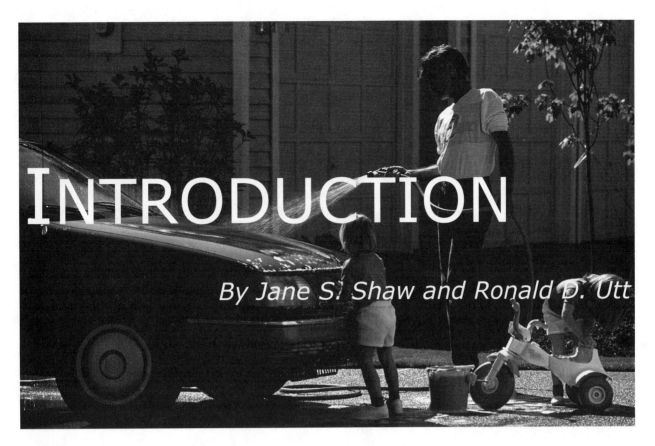

# INTRODUCTION

*By Jane S. Shaw and Ronald D. Utt*

F ew Americans realize that the suburbanization of America began in earnest in the late 19th century as a lifestyle meant to free the well-to-do from the crowded central cities that then bore the brunt of the industrial revolution. As the 20th century got underway, architects and designers gave artistic coherence to this emerging trend. The Craftsman movement in New York, the Arts and Crafts style in California, Frederick Law Olmsted's influence on suburban site planning, and Frank Lloyd Wright's focus on suburban houses all validated life in garden-like settings outside the cities. Suburbanization accelerated in the decades after World War II as prosperity and demographic shifts made suburban living an affordable imperative.

Today, many Americans find themselves questioning the impact of 50 years of sprawling suburban growth and are searching for ways to reshape and redirect their communities. Their search, critically considered, is the subject of this book.

Encouraged by a loose coalition of environmentalists and suburban residents, and given a compelling sense of purpose by anti-growth theorists, the movement to control growth scrutinized by Steven Hayward in Chapter 1 is beginning to influence development strategies in many states and communities. The most obvious manifestation of the trend is the rising number of growth-control initiatives on the ballot and anti-growth candidates running in local elections. Between 1996 and 1998, state and local ballot measures related to land conservation increased by 50 percent to 240, and nearly three-quarters of these passed. In the off-year elections of November 1999, local candidates running on growth-control platforms often scored substantial victories against incumbents.

In recent years, many state legislatures—notably in Georgia, Florida, Maryland, Oregon, and Pennsylvania, to name just a few—have enacted a series of measures to preserve land, limit growth, and/or provide greater planning authority to regional governments to help them curb or redirect suburban development. John Charles in Chapter 9 and Angela Antonelli in Chapter 10 report on such efforts in Portland, Oregon, and Atlanta, Georgia.

Recent public opinion polls confirm the trend. In late February 2000, the Pew Center for Civic Journalism reported the results of five public opinion surveys showing that issues such as sprawl, unfettered growth, and traffic congestion had edged out more traditional issues such as crime, the economy, and even education. Nationwide, the poll found that 26 percent of respondents cited sprawl as their community's top problem, higher than any other issue. In Denver, 60 percent of respondents shared such concerns, while 47 percent did so in San Francisco.

Perhaps sensing this emerging groundswell of concern over the pace and quality of suburban development, the Clinton Administration in early 1999 proposed a "Livable Communities" agenda in the President's budget, and urged Congress to enact legislation that would provide communities with more money to acquire and preserve undeveloped land and to allocate additional funds to relieve traffic congestion, among other provisions. Although the President's proposal was released with considerable fanfare, and the Vice President promised to make it one of his top issues of concern, the idea of a federal growth-control initiative failed to garner much public support. It has since—at least temporarily—largely disappeared from the national policy debate, including those surrounding the heated presidential primary campaigns early in 2000.

The failure of growth-control and land-use initiatives to make any headway at the federal level is a tribute to the American electorate's ability to distinguish between issues appropriate to the national government and those best left to local decision-making. This is as it should be. Given the diverse nature in which residential and commercial growth, or the lack thereof, can affect a community, top-down, one-size-fits-all solutions are of limited value.

Yet the concern has increased, not declined, on the local level. In distinctively different ways, nearly every major urban area is attempting to address growth-related issues. Of course, problems confronting a distant suburb where farmland and woods are giving way to development are markedly different from those of an older, close-in suburb whose growth problems manifest themselves through intense "in fill" that contributes to higher population densities, worsening air pollution, and traffic congestion. For some suburbs, and most central cities, the problem is not so much that there is too much growth, but that *there is none at all.*

Although there appears to be an emerging agreement in favor of local solutions, there is widespread disagreement on what those solutions should be, and some of the disagreement involves contradictory solutions for which there is no middle ground or point of compromise. Critics of suburban growth have split into factions such as New Urbanists, Main Streeters, advocates of the metropolitan agenda, and proponents of smart growth.

Some want to preserve their community largely as it is and argue for a moratorium on any new growth or for strict limits on how fast it can proceed. Those that seek these objectives tend to favor such proposals as rigid growth boundaries and high impact fees. Others have a more modest agenda, wanting to preserve more open space while still allowing for growth. These citizens favor flexible growth boundaries, comprehensive planning, higher density development, greenbelts, and public purchase and preservation of undeveloped land.

Still others simply want to reshape the development that is taking place in their communities into something more attractive than today's typical suburban development. Citizens in favor of this objective often encourage developers to build "traditional communities," as Donald Leal discusses in Chapter 8, while others argue for large lots to preserve a community's rural character. Others may seek to maintain a higher quality development by excluding less attractive and less expensive high-density housing units, such as townhouses and apartment buildings, and argue that such housing may undermine a community's rustic character. Such restrictions also work to exclude the less affluent residents.

Other issues complicate these competing visions and different approaches. A widespread hostility targets automobiles, shopping centers, strip malls, and retail establishments clustered anywhere other than in a traditional town or city center. America's love affair with the automobile has been vilified by urban planners and other growth-control advocates for most of the postwar era, and their concerns, ironically, are shared even by many motorists who decry the worsening traffic congestion they confront in metropolitan areas.

Opponents of sprawl and automobile dependence urge the construction of more public transit systems and fewer highways, but as Wendell Cox notes in Chapter 4, transit's share of the commuting market has been shrinking steadily over the postwar era, and transit systems have failed to attract new riders even when commuters are offered modern, attractive light rail systems. Apparently, many Americans believe that public transit is a commuting solution for their neighbors, but not for them.

Likewise, many Americans complain about the artificial nature of most shopping centers and the tacky appearance of strip malls, but they continue to flock to them in droves, bypassing older city centers and traditional downtowns even in communities where centralized retailing is still a viable option. And while many urban planners and growth-control advocates oppose single-use zoning practices that concentrate commercial activities in one section of a community and homes in another, homeowners have shown a decided preference for the peace and quiet of commercial-free, housing-only developments.

Indeed, consumer opinion polls continue to show an overwhelming preference for single-family detached housing on ample lots in a suburban setting. Nonetheless, there is room for improvement. In Chapter 5, Samuel Staley discusses some of the community development problems attributable to current zoning practices and suggests a number of reforms that will provide citizens with greater flexibility to accommodate alternative growth strategies.

Efforts to ameliorate the less attractive side-effects of rapid surburbanization are relatively recent. In part, these problems reflect nearly two decades of uninterrupted economic growth, which has allowed more and more people to live the American Dream and become homeowners in better communities with safe streets and good schools. Like any nascent problem-solving effort, the search for solutions will find many dead ends and take several wrong turns, but through trial and error American communities ultimately will find the appropriate path to the quality of life they are seeking.

This book is an attempt to help that process along. One way is to separate myth and misrepresentation from the true nature of the suburbanization process, and to evaluate the pros and cons of many of the solutions that have been suggested and even imposed. Likewise, an understanding of the causes of suburbanization and sprawl is essential to crafting responsive solutions.

In reviewing the extensive (and growing) literature on the subject of suburbanization for this book, we could not help but be struck by the extent to which questionable or marginal "causes" for "sprawl"—Federal Housing Administration (FHA) mortgages and interstate highways are among the most notable—are widely accepted by critics of the suburbs. Yet other more compelling factors, such as rising incomes and a growing population, are largely ignored, as Ronald Utt details in Chapter 7. Similarly, we also realized the need to put into proper perspective the alleged harmful effects of suburban growth on the environment, as Jane Shaw does in Chapter 3, in reviewing the growing evidence of the compatibility of nature and residential development.

This book attempts to sort through the many factors commonly cited as contributing to sprawl and evaluate the significance of each. By focusing on the most significant factors, communities can adopt workable solutions, which the authors have provided in each of the chapters.

We should emphasize that we do not consider the solutions offered to be in any way conclusive or comprehensive. We live in a dynamic society subject to constant and often surprising change, a point made clearer by

Richard Stroup in Chapter 2, in which he contrasts the benefits of a market-driven search for solutions with the more rigid and coercive proposals that many smart-growth advocates want to impose upon communities. We are confident that, over time, ingenious citizens, enlightened leaders, creative builders, and innovative architects will puzzle through these common problems in a dynamic process that only the free market and a democratic society can provide. From this process even more effective solutions will emerge to provide Americans with communities that more closely fit their hopes and dreams.

# THE SUBURBANIZATION OF AMERICA

## By Steven Hayward

Ever since the first European settlers landed on the East Coast 500 years ago, American communities have been sprawling across the landscape. Yet the phenomenon of sprawl—and the suburbanization of land on the outskirts of the city—is neither new nor uniquely American. The etymology of the English word "suburb" can be traced to the 14th century, when the term appeared in Chaucer's *Canterbury Tales*. Bad planning, it seems, was a problem then as well: "Medieval English suburbs," notes Professor John Stilgoe of Harvard University, "grew haphazardly, stretching ribbonlike along the main roads leading to town gates."[1] Evidence of sprawl in colonial America (and the precursors of modern real estate developers) is found in newspaper advertisements of 18th-century Boston and Philadelphia, in which landowners on the existing urban fringe offered to subdivide their property for "House Lotts."[2]

Public concern about sprawl is also not new. Peter Nivola of the Brookings Institution points out that the drafters of a 1929 New York Regional Plan worried about development that "proceeded indiscriminately into areas which are predominantly rural in character." The planners observed: "Urban growth outside the city" takes on "forms that do not harmonize with and may be injurious to the central community."[3]

Today, sprawl has become a national concern and a political issue, highlighted frequently by Vice President Al Gore when discussing his "livability agenda." Sprawl used to generate the most local or state concern in the fast-growing states on each coast, especially in California

**Notes:**

1. John R. Stilgoe, *Borderland: Origins of the American Suburb, 1820–1939* (New Haven: Yale University Press, 1988), p. 1.
2. See, generally, Kenneth T. Jackson, *Crabgrass Frontier: The Suburbanization of the United States* (New York: Oxford University Press, 1985), and especially Chapter 1 and Chapter 2.
3. Peter S. Nivola, *Laws of the Landscape: How Policies Shape Cities in Europe and America* (Washington, D.C.: Brookings Institution, 1999), p. 1.

and Florida where the fierce political battle over control of growth goes back several decades. Now, sprawl is a major controversy in metropolitan areas in the heartland as well, including in cities that are experiencing only modest population growth, such as Chicago, Cleveland, Kansas City, and St. Louis.

Nevertheless, the term "sprawl" is seldom defined with adequate rigor or consistency. Such imprecision is reminiscent of Supreme Court Justice Potter Stewart's famous remark about pornography: "I can't define it, but I know it when I see it." (Indeed, some environmentalists might consider suburban development a form of ecological pornography.) To most people, "sprawl" simply refers to the low-density residential development beyond a city's limits. Density is measured by the number of residents per square mile. The highest density found in American cities is, not surprisingly, on Manhattan Island, with nearly 50,000 people per square mile. The median density for all U.S. cities with populations of 100,000 or more is 3,200 people per square mile.[4] A specific density threshold to distinguish between sprawl and non-sprawl, however, is seldom offered. In fact, at about 3,800 people per square mile, the population density of Portland, Oregon, the model for crusaders against sprawl discussed in Chapter 9, is half that of the Los Angeles–Long Beach area (about 7,500 people per square mile), which is considered the archetype of sprawling metropolis to be avoided. (Three of the 10 most densely populated cities in the United States are located in the Los Angeles basin: Santa Ana, El Monte, and Inglewood.)

> The term "sprawl" is seldom defined with adequate rigor or consistency.

The irony is that a metropolitan area such as Los Angeles, which virtually defines sprawl in the public mind, has a density on the order of what anti-sprawl advocates are now seeking. It indicates that density alone is not the sole or even the most important determinant of sprawl. The most up-to-date definitions of sprawl emphasize development with several other characteristics: development that is "auto-dependent," that rigidly segregates types of land use, that "leapfrogs" over open space near the existing urban fringe or proceeds ribbon-like along arterial roads deep into the rural countryside, and that encourages retail/commercial units such as strip malls that are auto-dependent and have no central focus, compared with more traditional main streets.

But even these factors do not begin to exhaust the ever broadening circle of issues that are now part of the sprawl debate. Some critics claim that suburban development is the chief cause of the decline of central cities and older historic neighborhoods.[5] The discussion invariably spreads to such hot button issues as the quality of the public schools and the crime rate. Middle-class people flee the central city because the public schools are poor and the crime rate is, on average, four times higher than in the suburbs. A vicious cycle has begun as more middle-class people leave, the central city schools and crime rate worsen, and more people leave. Declining schools and increasing crime rates are called "push" factors because they push the mobile middle class out to the suburbs. Minority groups have been quick to join the rumpus, suggesting that sprawl is a civil rights issue—disregarding the fact that many of

## Notes:

4.  Author's calculations from U.S. Census Bureau data, 1998.
5.  See David Rusk, *Cities Without Suburbs* (Washington, D.C.: Woodrow Wilson Center, 1993); David Rusk, *Inside Game, Outside Game: Winning Strategies for Saving Urban America* (Washington, D.C.: Brookings Institution, 1999); Myron Orfield, *Metropolitics: A Regional Agenda for Community and Stability* (Washington, D.C.: Brookings Institution, 1997); Bruce Katz and Jennifer Bradley, "Divided We Sprawl," *The Atlantic Monthly*, December 1999, pp. 26–42.

those fleeing the older central cities are African-Americans seeking a better life in the suburbs as have other ethnic groups before them.

Another key issue is the cost of sprawl. Sprawl is said to be subsidized by all levels of government, starting with such federal policies as the home mortgage interest deduction and the interstate highway system, and descending down to the local government's provision of roads, water, sewerage, and other services at below their marginal costs. And no discussion of metropolitan growth and land use can avoid grappling with the problems of affordable housing and traffic congestion.

Before long, it is evident that the controversy over growth has itself "sprawled" across the public policy landscape and includes so many factors that discussing it is akin to solving Rubik's Cube—it is very hard to address all of the facets of the issue simultaneously. Nothing is more common than to hear someone say, "You can't solve the sprawl problem until you solve the problem of (schools, or traffic, or urban crime, or downtown revitalization)." Hence, borrowing a favorite term from the lexicon of sprawl, the public discourse over the issue of sprawl quickly reaches *gridlock*.

Yet it is the elasticity of the issue that explains why it has become such a national concern. Sprawl is now the all-purpose scapegoat for our urban discontents. Sprawl has even been blamed for the rise is obesity (Americans drive instead of walk) and as a contributing factor in the Columbine High School shootings (the disconnected auto-dependent housing tracts and impersonal suburban malls generate violent "alienation" among youth).[6] If sprawl can be implicated as a primary cause in these matters, there is very little that can *not* be attached to it. Today, "sprawl" seems to have

> Sprawl is now the all-purpose scapegoat for our urban discontents.

become a substitute for "society" as the general cause of all bad things.

Although controversy over sprawl is not new, what *is* new is the emergence of a national movement with aggressive prescriptions for changing the face of America's metropolitan areas. In a shrewd act of rhetorical labeling, this movement calls itself "smart growth." Maryland Governor Parris Glendening is among the first to make "smart growth" part of his policy agenda. It has caught on like wildfire; half of the nation's governors, from both parties, have embraced "smart growth" or a closely equivalent term. The "smart growth" label puts potential critics on the defensive. Who, except for a cloddish developer, could possibly be for "dumb" growth?

Indeed, even the National Association of Home Builders, whose members will bear the brunt of any new "smart growth" regulations, has publicly endorsed "smart growth" and is merely laboring to refine the meaning of the term.

## PRECEPTS OF "SMART GROWTH" PLANS

Smart growth supporters push a few core concepts that are worth summarizing:

- Infrastructure projects (public works, such as roads, sewers, water mains, and schools) should be more carefully "targeted" so that they will be more "efficient." In practice, this means *less* infrastructure.

- New development should be more "transit oriented," with provision for light rail lines or bus routes.

- Development should be more "compact," or built to higher densities than is typical of suburban development today, partly to accommodate the proposed transit.

**Notes:**

6.  Neal R. Pierce, "Littleton's Legacy: Our Suburban Dream Shattered," *The Washington Post*, June 6, 1999.

- Urban growth boundaries—a defined circumference around existing urban areas beyond which no development is allowed—could be employed (there is no unanimity on this point).

All of these features require "better planning" or "comprehensive planning," which some smart growth advocates say can be accomplished only with a powerful regional government. But even without a regional government, an important component of smart growth known as "the new urbanism" stands ready to supply the "better planning."

New urbanists emphasize a "neo-traditional" community design that evokes the neighborliness of older communities through such features as front porches, shorter setbacks from the street and between houses, narrower streets, and mixed-use development. These features aim to recapture the sense of community that was thought to typify neighborhoods three or four generations ago, as well as achieve higher urban density. New urbanists can point to a number of such communities: Kentlands in Gaithersburg, Maryland; Disney's Celebration, Florida; and Laguna West, California.[7]

One of the surprising and encouraging aspects of smart growth is that its appeal cuts across ideological lines, as the aforementioned embrace by governors of both parties indicates. Although liberals and environmentalists have taken the lead in promoting smart growth, many conservatives agree with much of its critique of urban planning and suburban life. No one loves a strip mall, even though they are so convenient. Indeed, many conservatives have embraced the neo-traditional community design concepts of the new urbanism. In 1996,

for example, the entire November/December issue of *The American Enterprise* magazine was devoted to this topic, and a preponderance of its articles warmly endorsed these concepts.

The most salient point of agreement is that neo-traditional designs usually run into zoning and planning regulations that bar them. Smart growth advocates often criticize rigid zoning and planning codes that prohibit mixed use neighborhoods and stifle any spontaneity in city design. One of the most eloquent new urbanist critics of modern planning, James Howard Kunstler, wrote in "Home From Nowhere" that:

> Almost everywhere in the United States laws prohibit building the kinds of places that Americans themselves consider authentic and traditional. Laws prevent the building of places that human beings can feel good in and can afford to live in. Laws forbid us to build places that are worth caring about.

> Is Main Street your idea of a nice business district? Sorry, your zoning laws won't let you build it, or even extend it where it already exists. Is Elm Street your idea of a nice place to live—you know, houses with front porches on a tree-lined street? Sorry, Elm Street cannot be assembled under the rules of large-lot zoning and modern traffic engineering.[8]

To the extent that the smart growth advocates recognize the ill effects of too much regulation and overzealous planning, it is vindication of Jane Jacobs' great 1961 analysis,

## Notes:

7. For more on the new urbanism, see William Fulton, *The New Urbanism: Hope or Hype for American Communities?* (Cambridge: Lincoln Institute of Land Policy, 1996); Peter Calthorpe, *The Next American Metropolis: Ecology, Community, and the American Dream* (New York: Princeton Architectural Press, 1993); Philip Langdon, *A Better Place to Live: Reshaping the American Suburb* (Amherst: University of Massachusetts Press, 1994); Andrew Ross, *The Celebration Chronicles: Life, Liberty and the Pursuit of Property Value in Disney's New Town* (New York: Ballantine Books, 1999).

8. James Howard Kunstler, "Home From Nowhere," *The Atlantic Monthly*, September 1996, at *http://www.theatlantic.com/issues/96sep/kunstler/kunstler.htm*.

*The Death and Life of Great American Cities.*[9] Jacobs, the preeminent critic of modern urban planning, could see that the centralized planning at the core of the new and fashionable policy to spark "urban renewal" would lead to disaster. This approach taught that human activity needed to be isolated into zones (residential, industrial, commercial, and even recreational). Jacobs argued that cities and neighborhoods were in themselves a spontaneous order, which excessive planning and regulation would only disrupt for the worse.

At the time, Jacobs' book was very controversial among planners and urban politicians, who mostly brushed her aside as a gadfly. One of her early fans, however, was William F. Buckley, Jr., who included a chapter from *The Death and Life* in the first edition of the anthology, *American Conservative Thought in the Twentieth Century,* in 1970.[10] And before Jacobs, conservatives from as far back as the 1950s have criticized the interstate highway system for the effects it would have on life in rural towns that are bypassed by vehicle traffic, as well as the effect interstate highways and urban expressways would have big city neighborhoods.

While conservatives agree with some criticisms of sprawl, back in the 1960s some liberals actually worried that America was not sprawling enough. In 1967, *U.S. News & World Report* covered an interagency task force of the Johnson Administration that sought to stave off over-urbanization, or higher population density in the cities.[11] The time has come, Agriculture Secretary Orville Freeman declared, "to take issue with the urbanist school that believes the megalopolis is the wave of the future, with the countryside being preserved as a kind of huge national park where urbanites rest their nerves

before plunging once again into the maelstrom of the city." We needed *more* "exurban" and rural development, they thought. If nothing was done, the Johnson Administration warned, by the year 2000, 208 million people would be "jammed" into cities on 3 percent of the U.S. land area[12]—in fact, just about where we are today. For liberals in the mid-1960s, this would be too much density; ironically, for the smart growth movement of today, this is not enough density.

Yet conservatives and libertarians find it hard to be card-carrying members of the smart growth movement. Although the smart growth critique offers sensible sound bites about reducing planning and zoning regulations and allowing the market to work, in practice the smart growth agenda is highly prescriptive. With its emphasis on such techniques as "targeting" infrastructure, drawing urban growth boundaries, and creating regional governments, smart growth policy would require more centralized power and a planning prowess that greatly exceeds the scope of existing urban planning. The humility that one might naturally expect after recognizing the planning errors of the past is absent from most smart growth enthusiasts.

One can see this in the fact that many smart growth advocates now champion Jane Jacobs as a hero and leading light for their cause. In the words of one of Portland's regional planners, "A lot of us got tired of protesting the Vietnam War, read Jane Jacobs, and decided to take over Portland."[13] However, such planners have read Jacobs either selectively or uncomprehendingly, for her central point was that well-functioning cities evolve spontaneously, beyond the reach of planners. Indeed, what might be called the latter-day "Jacobins" of smart growth

## Notes:

9. Jane Jacobs, *The Death and Life of Great American Cities* (New York: Random House, 1961). *Death and Life* is in its 14th printing.
10. William F. Buckley, Jr., ed., *American Conservative Thought in the Twentieth Century* (New York: Bobbs-Merrill, 1970).
11. "Open Spaces Get Wider, Cities Grow Denser," *U.S. News & World Report,* December 18, 1967, p. 47.
12. *Ibid.*
13. For a splendid account of the smart growth misappropriation of Jacobs, see Jesse Walker, "Jacobean Tragedy," *Reason,* July 1998, available at *http://www.reason.com/9807/col.walker.html.*

have more in common with the 18th century variety than they do with Jane. And Jacobs herself explicitly warned against trying to apply her urban insights to suburban settings:

> I hope no reader will try to transfer my observations into guides as to what goes on in towns, or little cities, or in suburbs which still are suburban. Towns, suburbs and even little cities are totally different organisms from great cities. We are in enough trouble already from trying to understand big cities in terms of the behavior, and imagined behavior, of towns. To try to understand towns in terms of big cities will only compound confusion.[14]

Kunstler offers a maddening illustration of the contradictory nature of the premises of the smart growth critique of planning and zoning. First, he writes "if you want to make your community better, begin at once by throwing out your zoning laws. Don't revise them—get rid of them. Set them on fire if possible and make a public ceremony of it. . . .While you're at it, throw out your 'master plan' too. It's invariably just as bad." Most conservatives could stand up and cheer at this, but Kunstler's next sentence undoes much of the good of the preceding passage. He continues: "Replace these things with a traditional town-planning ordinance that prescribes a more desirable everyday environment."[15] Note that troublesome word "prescribe."

Even more worrisome is a condescension toward suburbs and suburbanites that suggests many smart growth advocates do not simply want to improve the practical functioning of cities and suburbs; they wish to transform them wholesale. This attitude toward the suburbs is not new. It was perhaps best captured by Herbert Gans in his well-known 1967 book *The Levittowners*.[16] Gans set out to study life in the new post–World War II suburbs of tract homes because, in his words, elite opinion regarded suburbanites as

> an uneducated, gullible, petty "mass" which rejects the culture that would make it fully human, the "good government" that would create the better community, and the proper planning that would do away with the landscape-despoiling little "boxes" in which they live.[17]

That attitude reflects the views of the smart growth elite today. In an overheated speech to the Congress for the New Urbanism in June 1999, Kunstler unleashed his anti-suburban rhetoric:

> It is the dwelling place of untruth. We call it suburbia. A cartoon of rural life, with none of the qualities of it. I believe we in the CNU [Congress for the New Urbanism] recognize its profound culturally toxic nature. . . .The common complaint about these brand-new mega-suburbs is that "everything looks the same." This is only the most superficial symptom of their evil nature
>
> . . . .
>
> Its present is a dangerously provisional collective hallucination, nourished by a sado-masochistic idiot pop culture, which can fall apart at the slightest provocation. We have a name for this collective hallucination, by the way: The American Dream, a sort of mega-lie stating that this sort of ghastly provisional collective hallucination

## Notes:

14. Jacobs, *The Death and Life of Great American Cities*, p. 16.
15. Kunstler, "Home from Nowhere."
16. Herbert Gans, *The Levittowners: Ways of Life and Politics in a New Suburban Community* (New York: Alfred A. Knopf, 1967.)
17. *Ibid.*, p. vi.

is the ultimate state of being worth aspiring to.[18]

In a speech to the National League of Historic Theaters in 1999, Kunstler calls the suburbs "the national car slum," and derides the view that suburbs represent the outcome of the free choice of families as "arguments so dumb they're not worth debating."[19]

Nor is Kunstler an extreme or unusual example. Richard Moe of the National Trust for Historic Preservation calls sprawl, among other things, "socially irresponsible."[20] David Rusk conceived a fable in which sprawl was the evil means by which a foreign enemy went about destroying America's cities.[21] Andres Duany, one of the leading neotraditional planners, wrote that "suburban sprawl is a cancerous growth rather than healthy growth. . . .The suburb is the last word in privatization, perhaps even its lethal consummation, and it spells the end of authentic civic life."[22] Seldom is there even a grudging acknowledgment that most big cities in America have been governed abominably in the postwar decades, or that they have an obligation to get their own houses in order before they start telling others how to order their houses.[23] The same kind of thinking that initiated "urban renewal" 30 years ago now wants to bring about "suburban renewal."

Kunstler says matter-of-factly that "*useless* front lawns are often eliminated" in new urbanist planning schemes.[24] But useless to whom? And who should decide whether they are useless? His statement would not grate if the modifier "useless" had been left out. Yet the urge to describe typical suburban traits in pejorative terms is irresistible and pervasive in smart growth and new urbanist writings.

> The tendency of smart growth policy to approach social engineering is seen most explicitly in discussions of transportation.

The tendency of smart growth policy to approach social engineering is seen most explicitly in discussions of transportation. A few smart growth advocates have warmed to the idea of congestion pricing (i.e., directly charging variable prices for road use depending on the time of day),[25] but most are enthralled with the idea of mass transit—especially rail transit, though it is the least cost-effective mode. The passion for mass transit betrays confused thinking and a misunderstanding of the facts. And if this passion becomes the basis of urban transportation policy, it will result in a significant increase, not decrease, in auto congestion. At the root of their passion is the attitude that cars are evil—

## Notes:

18. James Howard Kunstler, "Reflections on the Columbine School Massacre," speech to the Congress for the New Urbanism, Milwaukee, June 6, 1999.
19. James Howard Kunstler, 1999 remarks to the National League of Historic Theaters at the Allegro Hotel, Chicago, on file with author.
20. Richard Moe, speech to San Joaquin Valley Town Hall, Fresno, California, November 20, 1996.
21. Rusk, *Inside Game, Outside Game*, pp. 82–86.
22. Cited in William Schneider, "The Suburban Century Begins," *Atlantic Monthly*, July 1992, p. 37.
23. See Steven Hayward, "Liberalism's Urban Legacy," *Policy Review*, January–February 1998.
24. Kunstler, "Home From Nowhere." Emphasis added.
25. See Chapter 4 of this volume. Other general treatments of the subject include Erin Schiller, *The Road Ahead: The Economic and Environmental Benefits of Congestion Pricing* (San Francisco: Pacific Research Institute, February 1998).

akin to a rolling cigarette—and that building roads is enabling Americans' dependence on this bad habit.

Rail transit boosters and sprawl critics point to data showing that over the past 25 years the number of vehicle miles traveled has been increasing about twice as fast as population growth. From this it is deduced that people must be driving further to their work or shopping destinations because they are too spread out. In fact, however, the average commuter is traveling no further to work than he or she did 20 years ago. The increase in miles traveled primarily reflects the large numbers of women entering the workforce (thus, more commuters) and the rising number of lower-income workers attaining middle-class incomes and acquiring cars for the first time. It has very little to do with geographic patterns or population density.

In addition, there are more non-work destinations for American families today, including soccer matches, health clubs, sports facilities, and specialty food and retail outlets. In other words, increased driving is a measure of increased affluence.

Another way of arousing alarm about cars is to point out that between 1983 and 1987, the number of cars in the United States increased by 20 million, while population increased by only 9.2 million.[26] But since no one drives more than one car at a time, this must mean that many people who previously did not own cars now do. It is hard to see this as a bad thing.

For ill-tempered critics of automobiles, the link between affluence and driving is just another example of America's "enslavement" to the automobile. Jane Holtz Kay's attack on the auto, *Asphalt Nation*, offers a feminist twist to this argument, saying that women suffer from "vehicular bondage," and that the independent mobility of modern women is "a false form of consciousness that fails to assess woman's enslavement to the motor vehicle in the auto-dependent households and society it has helped install."[27] The director of Maryland's smart growth program, Ron Young, includes in his standard presentation the claim that the average American woman spends as much time in her car as a housewife in the former Soviet Union used to spend standing in line to buy basic necessities,[28] as though these two circumstances were commensurate.

Confronted with such attitudes, it is difficult to have a rational discussion about transportation policy. It becomes apparent that transportation is not the main goal of rail transit projects. Rail transit is viewed increasingly as a means of reshaping and increasing the density of suburban areas. Rail transit stops are presumed to be "magnets" that will attract higher density development—a form of "Field of Dreams" transit planning. If we build rail transit, the density will come.

So far, the evidence for this densifying effect is mixed.[29] Yet smart growth advocates vehemently oppose new roads or even the modest expansion of existing roads—based on the dogmatic view that roads are "growth-inducing."

## Notes:

26. "Indicators of Urban Sprawl," Oregon Department of Land Conservation and Development, May 1992, p. 1.
27. Jane Holtz Kay, *Asphalt Nation: How the Automobile Took Over America and How We Can Take It Back* (New York: Crown Books, 1997), p. 24. For a general survey of anti-auto attitudes, see James Q. Wilson, "Cars and Their Enemies," *Commentary*, July 1997, pp. 17–23; James A. Dunn, Jr., *Driving Forces: The Automobile, Its Enemies, and the Politics of Mobility* (Washington: Brookings Institution, 1998).
28. Ron Young, oral presentation to Growth Management Strategies Symposium, Phoenix, Arizona, May 4, 1999.
29. Several studies have found no densifying effect from rail transit. See, for example, Christopher R. Boolinger and Keith R. Ihlanfelt, "The Impact of Rapid Rail Transit on Economic Development: The Case of Atlanta's MARTA," *Journal of Urban Economics*, No. 42 (1997), pp. 179–204; John Landis and Robert Cervero, "BART and Urban Development," *Access*, No. 14 (Spring 1999), pp. 2–15.

Their logic makes transportation discourse frustrating. Conservatives and libertarians attempt to talk about enhancing mobility through congestion pricing, private toll roads, and transit deregulation, but they face smart growth advocates who care less about mobility than physically reshaping our cities.

## BASIC FACTS ABOUT SPRAWL

Sound thinking about urban policy requires putting the main aspects of sprawl in their proper proportion. The most basic clichés are that sprawl portends the "paving of America" and that we are in danger of "running out of farmland." In fact, all development, including roads, highways, and military bases as well as urban and suburban housing and commercial buildings (in other words, the human "footprint") consumes less than 5 percent of the total land area of the continental United States. (And this figure may be an overstatement, since federal data categorize land in 10-acre chunks, meaning it is possible for 10 acres to be considered "developed" even if only one or two acres actually are developed).

The rate at which land is being used each year is hard to nail down precisely because up-to-date and comprehensive national data are not available. Since the end of World War II, the annual rate of land development has been over 1 million acres a year. In 1979, the National Agricultural Land Survey (NALS) concluded that the rate of land development had tripled during the 1970s to more than 3 million acres. But by the mid-1980s, the U.S. Department of Agriculture admitted that this estimate was grossly in error, and the U.S. Geological Survey confirmed that the amount of land developed each year still was approximately 1.3 million acres—close to the historic post–World War II average.[30] Of the nearly 1.8 billion acres in the continental United States, this amounts to almost 0.07 percent per year.[31] At this rate, it takes nearly 15 years to develop just 1 percent of the nation's land area.

But recently, the preliminary figures from the 1997 National Resources Inventory (NRI) have revived the 3 million acres a year figure. Like the NALS numbers 20 years ago, these numbers are likely to be proven incorrect.[32] First of all, it is rare to experience such a sharp change in basic trends as a *tripling* of land consumption in a five-year period. Second, some of the obvious anomalies in the numbers suggest the margin of error may be huge. For example, the NRI finds that Nevada, the fastest growing state in the nation, developed only 36,000 acres over the last five years, which is about a third of the amount that critics of sprawl have claimed it has used. Meanwhile, next door, Arizona—with one-third the population growth of Nevada—is supposed to have developed four times as much land as Nevada. Table 1.1 shows a simple comparison of population growth and the

**Notes**:

30. Gregg Easterbrook, "Vanishing Land Reappears," *The Atlantic Monthly*, July 1986, pp. 17–18.
31. Interestingly, this number has demonstrated to the author how little the smart growth movement is interested in facts. In several previous articles, I stated the *decimal* fraction of land developed each year according to USGS figures (.00068) as .00068 percent, mistakenly neglecting to move the decimal point over two places to generate the correct *percentage* fraction of .068 percent. Admittedly, this is the kind of mistake that causes many children to fail their math tests. This figure was cited by others, and not once was it questioned. I only discovered the error in doing fresh calculations and took steps to correct it publicly, including in *Newsweek*, which made great play out of my "stupid math mistake." I took small consolation when I heard the Vice President made a similar egregious error in a September 1998 speech in Portland, Oregon, claiming that "40 percent of Portland commuters take light rail to work." Analysts and policymakers must carefully consider the impact of over- and underestimating such figures.
32. Ascertaining the amount of developed land is a secondary purpose of the NRI. Its primary purpose is to determine the amount and condition of various rural land resource categories, especially farmland. Most of its nearly 800,000 "sample points" are in farming and rural areas. The discrepancies and anomalies in the summary data suggest that more needs to be known before the findings of the 1997 NRI for developed land can be taken at face value.

Table 1.1

# In the U.S., Land Developed per Person Varies Widely

|  | Population Increase 1992–1997 | Land Urbanized 1992–1997 in Acres | Acres Developed Per New Person |
|---|---|---|---|
| Nevada | 344,000 | 36,600 | 0.11 |
| California | 1,376,000 | 685,300 | 0.50 |
| Oregon | 268,000 | 141,600 | 0.53 |
| Texas | 1,609,000 | 1,145,700 | 0.71 |
| Maryland | 190,000 | 218,700 | 1.15 |
| New Jersey | 229,000 | 282,300 | 1.23 |
| Arizona | 129,000 | 181,000 | 1.40 |
| Georgia | 725,000 | 1,050,500 | 1.45 |
| Ohio | 186,000 | 519,300 | 2.79 |
| New York | 57,000 | 484,500 | 8.50 |
| Pennsylvania | 39,000 | 1,102,700 | 28.27 |

Source: National Resources Inventory, 1997.

amount of land that the 1997 NRI stated was developed. The wide range of land used per new person casts doubt on the accuracy of the NRI numbers. (Another striking anomaly: If the NRI numbers are correct, then California and Nevada used land more "efficiently" than smart-growth Oregon.) Because only the preliminary data from the 1997 NRI have been released as of this writing, it will be some time before a thorough review and analysis can be made to find and correct the errors.

Arguments over the NRI numbers are likely to last for years. Meanwhile, there is another way of looking at land use numbers that is thought to illustrate Americans' profligate use of land—comparing population growth rates with land use rates, which is sometimes called "the sprawl index."[33] Comparisons of population growth and the growth of developed land area can often sound stark and ominous, however. Smart growth advocates like to cite examples such as the Chicago metropolitan area, whose population grew by just 4 percent

between 1970 and 1990, while the developed land area grew by 55 percent. St. Louis appears even more dramatic; regional population has grown by 17 percent since 1960, but the developed land area has grown by 125 percent.

But these are superficial statistics, because they tacitly assume that significant changes in density should not be expected as household sizes fall and affluence rises. Density in the central cities has been gradually falling and expanding in the suburbs for more than a century. In the 19th century, it was not atypical for U.S. cities to have densities of up to 100,000 people per square mile.[34] Urban reformers of the time thought that cities were overcrowded, and that dispersing people to the suburbs was an improvement. Ironically, the technology for lowering the density of crowded cities was the same technology that supposedly will raise density today: rail transit.

Philadelphia is a good example. At the start of the Civil War, Philadelphia's population density was about 56,000 people per square

## Notes:

33. For example, between 1970 and 1992, the nation's population grew by 26 percent and the number of developed acres grew by 90 percent, yielding a "sprawl index" of 3.46.
34. Jackson, *Crabgrass Frontier*, p. 11.

mile.[35] Commuter rail lines intensified the dispersal of Philadelphians and the rise of the city's suburbs beginning in the late 19th century. Today, Philadelphia's density is only about 11,000 people per square mile (11th in the nation). It is unrealistic to suppose that urban densities would remain constant as the middle class grew more numerous and prosperous, or, for example, that Chicago's new suburbs would develop at the same current density as the central city itself (12,000 people per square mile). As Gregg Easterbrook, senior editor of *The New Republic*, bluntly puts it, "Sprawl is caused by affluence and population growth, and which of these, exactly, do we propose to prohibit?"[36]

The point is that land consumption has been occurring at a rate faster than population growth for more than a century in this country. To have a sprawl index of 1.0—where population growth and land consumption are moving at the same rate—would mean that Americans would have to live at yesterday's central-city density levels, which are incredibly high by today's standards. But even the central cities have been growing less dense. As a practical matter, therefore, smart growth will require telling people that they may not live as they prefer to live, even if they can afford it.

One of the glaring gaps in smart growth is that its advocates never say what density, or range of densities, they consider to be appropriate or optimal. They tend to raise the alarm with superficial statistics such as the "sprawl

> Smart growth will require telling people that they may not live as they prefer to live, even if they can afford it.

index," call for "higher density," but leave it at that. Although modest increases in suburban density may be possible (and in fact are already occurring in many metropolitan areas as land prices increase), smart growth advocates need to be more specific about what range of suburban densities they think are realistic, and how they are to be achieved.

The question about optimal density is often evaded by deploying the argument that the suburbs are massively subsidized. Because suburban homes do not pay their way, the argument goes, they are not entitled to exist at the preferred low densities we currently experience. The range of alleged subsidies includes the home mortgage interest deduction, the interstate highway system and other radial and concentric metropolitan expressways, down to the claim that new housing pays less than the marginal cost for basic public works such as water, sewer, surface streets, new schools, police and fire stations, and so forth. (Some smart growth advocates even claim the defense budget is a suburban subsidy,[37] and that the U.S. military presence in the Middle East exists to protect artificially cheap gasoline prices.) The final variable in this argument is that the lower the density, the more subsidies required.

Innumerable case studies are offered to prove the proposition that the marginal tax revenues that new housing generates are less than the marginal costs of public services it requires.[38] There is a growing cottage industry of consultants with finely honed methodologies

**Notes:**

35. *Ibid.*, p. 23.
36. Gregg Easterbrook, "Suburban Myths," *The New Republic*, March 15, 1999, p. 20.
37. Peter Miller and John Moffat, *The Price of Mobility: Uncovering the Hidden Costs of Transportation* (New York: Natural Resources Defense Council, 1993). This study estimates the subsidy to automobiles to be $1.2 trillion to $1.6 trillion.
38. A thorough survey of the scholarly and technical literature on this issue can be found in National Research Council, Transportation Research Board, *The Costs of Sprawl—Revisited* (Washington, D.C.: National Academy Press, 1998), pp. 45–60.

to prove that new housing development does not pay its way. Such consulting efforts typically are procured by local governments, which then use the results to impose impact fees (essentially an excise tax) on new housing. Although these exercises in forensic fiscal analysis sometimes convincingly establish cost-revenue imbalances on particular subdivisions, this does not prove the general claim that suburban communities depend on massive subsidies.

Consider, first: If suburban growth does *not* pay for itself, exactly when did it *stop* paying for itself? How did all of the suburbs get built in the 1940s, 1950s, 1960s, and 1970s if they were not paying for themselves? It seems unlikely that pervasive cost-revenue imbalances could have persisted over many decades without obvious serious breakdowns in the fiscal structures of local governments.

Duke University's Professor Helen Ladd conducted a major study of the correlation between population growth and fiscal structure in 285 counties in the United States. She found that real (inflation-adjusted) per capita government spending grew more rapidly in fast-growing counties than in slow-growing counties.[39] If suburban growth were not paying for its own cost, one would expect to see per capita spending decline. The key to solving this puzzle is the phenomenon of cross-subsidization of commercial and retail development. Commercial development typically trails new housing growth, but it generates tax revenues far in excess of its cost to the public sector.

It would appear that this cross-subsidy to new homes is now considered illegitimate. Yet civic leaders do not look askance at providing subsidies for sports stadia and convention centers, which do not even come close to paying for themselves. When the issue is framed this way, the complaint about a subsidy for suburban homes is revealed as mere anti-suburban bias.

The plot thickens when the closely related smart growth claims about the efficiency of higher density suburban development are examined. A 1974 study entitled *The Cost of Sprawl* and similar studies often are cited to show that low-density development is one-third to one-half more costly than higher density development.[40] But *The Cost of Sprawl* mixes apples and oranges when comparing costs of development. Nearly all of the savings the report finds for compact (i.e., higher density) development would come from *private* costs borne by the builder and home buyer. These include lower construction costs due to smaller housing units and smaller lot sizes and the public works that builders typically provide, such as local roads, water and sewer hook ups, and open space that builders typically provide, not reductions in the *public* cost of infrastructure.[41] If private individuals are willing to bear the higher cost of low-density housing, why should public policy forcibly prevent them from doing so? Individuals and families could save money by driving Yugos, too, but many prefer larger vehicles such as minivans and sport utility vehicles.

> One of the glaring gaps in smart growth is that its advocates never say what density, or range of densities, they consider to be appropriate or optimal.

## Notes:

39. Helen F. Ladd, "Effects of Population Growth on Local Spending and Taxes" (Cambridge: Lincoln Institute for Land Policy, 1990).

40. *The Cost of Sprawl: Detailed Cost Analysis* (Washington, D.C.: Real Estate Research Corporation, 1974).

41. Duane Windsor, "A Critique of the Cost of Sprawl," *Journal of the American Planning Association*, Vol. 45 (1979), pp. 279–292.

Moreover, the premise that higher density development reduces public sector costs is probably wrong. In fact, urban economists have long believed that the density–cost curve is U-shaped, i.e., public sector costs will increase with density after a point. Ladd concluded:

> [T]he higher density associated with a larger population is likely to *increase* the cost of public services and therefore spending. Higher density represents a harsher environment for providing public services which requires more public sector inputs to provide a given level of service.[42]

A 1993 Brookings Institution study similarly concluded: "Variations in urban form (such as sprawl or jobs-housing imbalance), moreover, appear to have modest effects on infrastructure costs," a statement that contradicts what Brookings scholars say today.[43] And the Urban Land Institute's Douglas Porter warned in 1989 that "the evidence to support the concept of costly sprawl is less than adequate to support its widespread applications in development policies for countless communities across the nation."[44]

If it can be clearly established that new development is paying less than the marginal cost of public services, the fiscal policy should be to charge the full cost, either through tax reform, impact fees, or user fees. But given the difficulties of determining whether new developments are paying their "fair share," a much simpler answer is to privatize more infrastructure and public services. Private companies (telecommunications, for example) are not in the habit of subsidizing new development, and they often have good reasons for uniform or zone pricing (cable television, for example). Privatization is completely missing from the mix of smart growth policy alternatives, most probably because it runs directly counter to the main current of smart growth thought that wishes to impose more, not less, political control.

Finally, any scheme to transform the shape and mode of suburban cities must confront a set of facts about how modern Americans organize their work and leisure activities. First, Americans seem in love with bigger and better. The average size of a new home today is one-third larger than in 1970, even though the average household size continues to fall. This increase in home size is mostly in response to consumer demand. Baby-boomers especially are seeking a roomier "relaxed fit" type of house that is as comfortable as their relaxed-fit blue jeans. New homes today have larger kitchens, bedrooms, garages, playrooms, and, of course, more space for the home offices that are becoming almost a necessity in today's information-based economy. Environmentalists especially deplore the new "monster houses" (or "McMansions," as they are sometimes called) as a moral failing of Americans, but until they can persuade more Americans to join the followers of E. F. Schumacher, the author of *Small Is Beautiful*,[45] trying to coerce people into smaller homes through smart growth land use regulation is going to make housing more expensive for working and middle-class Americans.

Second, Americans, especially those who work in the service professions and who keep complicated schedules, are increasingly geared toward speed and efficiency in their work lives. The popularity of "fast pay" pumps at gas stations is a good example, but so too are ATMs, cell phones, E-Z tags on the interstates, and

## Notes:

42. Helen F. Ladd, "Population Growth, Density and the Costs of Providing Public Services," *Urban Studies*, Vol. 29, No. 2 (1992), pp. 292–293. (Emphasis added.)

43. Alan A. Altschuler and Jose A. Gomez-Ibanez, with Arnold M. Howitt, *Regulation for Revenue: The Political Economy of Land Use Exactions* (Washington, D.C.: The Brookings Institution, 1993), p. 76.

44. James E. Frank, *The Costs of Alternative Development Patterns: A Review of the Literature* (Washington, D.C.: Urban Land Institute, 1989), p. 6.

45. E. F. Schumacher, *Small Is Beautiful* (Point Roberts, Wash.: Hartley & Marks Publishers, 1998).

overnight package delivery. This trend also explains the popularity of strip malls and "big" retailers. They may have a low aesthetic quotient, but they are highly efficient. They enable working people to spend more time with their families. This fact is what makes the nostalgia for rail transit so unrealistic. Even if someone were willing to give up the comfort and four-channel compact disc player of their private car to ride a rail car or bus, he or she does not have the time to do so. The average home-to-work or work-to-home commute trip by rail transit takes twice as long as a car trip, even with heavy traffic.[46]

No amount of pining for the city of the 1920s is going to bring it back. Nor will coercion. The dispersal of economic activity to the suburbs over the past 40 years, a function mostly of falling transportation and communication costs, is likely to accelerate even more in the age of the Internet. The constantly falling prices for the technologies that make low-density suburban living possible are continuing to expand the choices Americans have with regard to how they live and work. A smart growth policy that tries to contravene the expanding realm of personal choice would be a ridiculously ineffective strategy, indeed.

## CONTROVERSY OVER SPRAWL: A MEASURE OF SOCIAL CHANGE

Despite the fact that smart growth can be used to cloak old-fashioned NIMBYism ("not in my back yard"), it is a mistake to think that the agitation about sprawl is phony or elite-driven. For one thing, people do not live by statistics; they live in neighborhoods and communities. It is of little relevance to someone whose town is changing that Wyoming, say, is always going to be 99 percent open space. Families move to the suburbs seeking a sense of permanence and community—generally, conservative values—but find its opposite as traffic congestion increases and open space and farm fields yield

to the bulldozer for another strip mall or development. This has been true for many years. The heightened concern over sprawl is more than simply a by-product of increasing traffic congestion or sentimental regret over the loss of open space. The current controversy over sprawl perhaps signifies that Americans have arrived at a new and unprecedented social moment at the start of the 21st century.

Try the following experiment: Imagine that you are able to bring back some of the architects of the New Deal social policies, the "brain trust" under President Franklin Roosevelt. You show them a photo of a new suburban neighborhood, and explain that new neighborhoods like this are going up all over the country. In addition, you tell them that the homeownership rate in America is approaching 70 percent—a rate few other nations in the world come close to matching—and that minorities are the fastest-growing demographic group of new homeowners.

At this point, our reincarnated New Dealers would swell with pride and say, "By golly, we did it. Our goal of expanding prosperity and extending it to the working class has met with success." But you quickly correct them: "Oh, no, you don't understand," you say, "this is called 'sprawl,' and it is a huge source of controversy and discontent. Lots of people want to stop the spread of suburban housing." I am sure your New Deal friends would be utterly baffled.

How would you explain to them, or even to an early Great Society liberal, the mixed emotions of this achievement? In the 1930s and 1960s, growth of all kinds was the main imperative of policy and the most stubborn challenge of each generation. The answer, I think, can be found in an obscure 1976 book called *Social Limits to Growth* by Fred Hirsch.[47] Hirsch was an economist and journalist who wrote in the aftermath of the infamous Club of Rome report (*The Limits to Growth*[48]) that suggested Western

**Notes**:

46. "Public Transit Takes Longer," *USA Today*, April 14, 1999, p. 2A.
47. Fred Hirsch, *Social Limits to Growth* (Cambridge: Harvard University Press, 1976).

civilization was bumping up against the physical limits of growth because of scarce resources, pollution, the population bomb, and so on. Hirsch, in his book, basically said "nonsense" to this scenario. However, he thought it possible that comfortable middle-class people might come to doubt the value of further economic growth. This, he thought, would represent a fundamental change in the social outlook of modern middle-class democracy.

This change would occur when the nexus between general growth and our personal well-being was broken. All of us naturally want the fruits of growth for ourselves. We all want more income, more education, and other personal amenities. It used to be that this desire led people to be generally pro-growth, which meant that we were all happy to hear the news that a new factory was going up in town. We understood that in a dynamic world, general growth would benefit each of us, even if we were shopkeepers or insurance agents not directly employed at the new factory. But at some point, Hirsch predicted, the nexus between general growth and our personal well-being would be broken.

Growing traffic congestion, Hirsch predicted, would be one of the first causes of this shift. Hirsch wrote: "Once this growth brings mass consumption to the point where it causes problems of congestion in the widest sense—bluntly, where consumption of jobholding by others tends to crowd you out—then the key to personal welfare gain is again the ability to stay ahead of the crowd." Growth not only brings congestion, but also rapid change. As Hirsch put it,

This process of movement will in turn change the characteristics of suburban life, at first to its net benefit but after some point to its detriment. With a declining city on its inner side and another suburb rather than open country on its outer side, the essential character of a suburb will be altered and in part destroyed.

As a result, rather than welcoming new factories and new homes, we would start trying to keep them out.

The Hirsch thesis might be dismissed as merely a highbrow version of NIMBYism. But if Hirsch is right that the large scale and fast pace of change is at the root of the antipathy toward sprawl, then several implications follow. It would mean that even if the smart growth agenda is implemented to its most utopian extent—that is, if Americans live more densely in cities and suburbs—growth still will not be popular with most suburbanites. Projected population growth over the next two decades requires that Americans use up a lot of land on the urban fringe. If, for most citizens, the mere scale of growth, and not its particular form, constitutes sprawl, then even smart growth will mean more sprawl. It is possible that the smart growth movement may wake up one morning 20 years from now to find many urbanites and suburbanites saying that this is not what they had in mind at all.

When people say they want sprawl "controlled" or "managed," they may be engaging in polite euphemisms that mean they want no more of it to take place in any form. The smart growth movement has yet to come to grips

> If, for most citizens, the mere scale of growth, and not its particular form, constitutes sprawl, then even smart growth will mean more sprawl.

**Notes:**

48. Donella Meadows, Dennis L. Meadows, and Jorgen Randers, *The Limits to Growth* (New York: Potomac Associates, 1972).

honestly with the current form of dressed-up NIMBYism that provides it with the bulk of its public support.

On the bright side, it is possible that some of the animus against suburban growth will be mitigated by the intelligent application of smart growth ideas, especially consumer-oriented neo-traditional communities and the revival of main street–style neighborhood centers. Smart growth plans that eschew the impulse of social engineering, and which operate according to individual choice and emphasize deregulation that allows the marketplace to create communities of character, can make a major contribution to America's cities and suburbs. But if smart growth eschews the principles of liberty and choice, then it is easy to predict that this attempt at "suburban renewal" will be a failure as disastrous as that of urban renewal 40 years ago.

# 2

# PLANNING VERSUS MARKET SOLUTIONS

## By Richard L. Stroup

Nearly every American would like to live in a spacious mansion surrounded by lush green lawns, close to many different kinds of stores, parks, and cultural attractions, and within walking distance of work. Few of us, if any, have found such a place. A basic fact of life is that resources such as land and open space are limited, and there just are not enough places around to fulfill every heart's desire.

To a large extent, however, people throughout history have found ways to overcome the scarcity of resources that began, as one economics text put it, with "the fiasco in the Garden of Eden."[1] Just a century ago, for example, people lived in small, cramped homes and primarily walked to their destinations, unless they lived near a trolley or train or had the room and the wealth to own stables and horses. Over time, transactions in the marketplace have spurred changes that provided Americans with more and better options for housing.

As incomes rose, families sought larger houses on larger lots. Cars, roads, and freeways enabled them to travel farther from work to find cheaper land. Improvements in transportation as well as better communication enabled entrepreneurs, too, to locate their businesses farther apart from each other in less expensive surroundings or closer to their customers or raw materials. This increasing mobility and variation in costs spurred the changes in living and commuting patterns to those we find so prevalent today.

Although this mobility has enabled many Americans to fulfill their personal goals, it has also led to frustration; and many of the problems are entangled in what is now known as "urban sprawl." The automobile, which freed so many of us to move away from crowded cities and downtown congestion, also brought congestion and traffic jams to the suburbs. Our move out of the cities gave us green lawns and bigger houses, but made us less connected to our neighbors than our parents and grandpar-

**Notes**:

1. Armen A. Alchian and William R. Allen, *University Economics,* 2nd ed. (Belmont, Cal.: Wadsworth Publishing Co., 1967), p. 3.

ents were in the city. For most Americans, the price we pay for bigger houses and more green space includes being located farther from the central metropolitan areas that still bustle with cultural attractions.

These frustrations, especially concerning traffic, lead many Americans to demand change. The nation is engaged in a contentious debate over the best solutions to the frustrations that follow suburban development.

The most vocal groups believe the best way to solve the problems associated with sprawl is to increase government control with more centrally directed policies. Such anti-sprawl advocates as the Sierra Club unabashedly argue that every level of government—local, state, and federal—should force people to live more closely together so they are less dependent on the automobile. To increase density, they advocate establishing urban growth boundaries—clear lines that define where people will be allowed to build homes. They want to bring back the characteristics of America's traditional urban downtown sector, and they intend to do this by promoting more scientific planning for how land will be used, buttressed of course by strict regulations. They also want the various levels of government, including the federal government, to purchase more land to convert to open space. In short, anti-sprawl advocates want political decisions to override private decisions.

A quieter chorus, which includes many of the authors in this volume, is skeptical of increased governmental control. They argue instead that the government's record in directing urban development has not been impressive, and that voluntary market-based decisions are better able to solve many of today's frustrations. As Donald Leal discusses in Chapter 8, for example, entrepreneurs working in a market setting are identifying the features that people want in their residences and in the design of their communities—such as environmentally sensitive development—and proving that people are will-

> Anti-sprawl advocates want political decisions to override private decisions.

ing to pay for them. Developments like Kentlands outside Washington, D.C., in Maryland and Eagle Rock Reserve in Montana are the result of such market-based approaches. This entrepreneurial response to the market is occurring quietly across the country and operating largely without rancor or animosity.

As the debate over land use develops, it is clear that neither group—those who propose more government control and those who propose less—will win completely. However, the decisions that are made will reflect the deep differences in these two approaches: command-and-control policies carried out by government agencies, on the one hand, and individual decisions responding to the markets, on the other. The purpose of this chapter is to explore these two approaches to achieving the same goal. It will examine the reasons Americans and especially policymakers should favor decreasing government control and enabling market-based decisions. And it will suggest how viable market-led improvements in the process can and will be made if they are allowed to do so.

## COMPETITION FOR SPACE

Although many concerns have been lumped together under the broad term of "sprawl," much of the problem comes down to competition for scarce space. The problem begins (and for some, it ends) with roads and congestion. There does not appear to be room enough on the roads for all those who need to get from their homes to their destinations, making daily traffic slowdowns typical in many metropolitan areas. Second, open space is being replaced by housing and shopping malls as growing populations seek to live and shop in more pleasant areas surrounded by less concrete. Third, many people want to keep outsiders from crowding into their neighborhoods—a form of territorial protection referred to as NIMBYism ("not in my back yard").

These facets of the problem are increasing pressure on government to decide who should win, and who should lose, the competition for control of the available, but limited, space. Surely, say "smart growth" advocates, governments can control where people live, making them less dependent on automobiles and more reliant on mass transit. Through zoning regulations, urban growth boundaries, and carefully contrived plans, governments can shape cities and bring about more efficient and equitable allocations of the scarce space.

Or can they? Economists have long studied how governments operate. They have found that the workings of government, like those of all human arrangements (including markets), are imperfect. Insights from the public choice branch of economics suggest that governmental correction of sprawl-related problems often will be ineffective and quite likely unfair.

Several problems in government decision-making are particularly worrisome.[2] Public choice economists identify these factors as:

1. The rational ignorance of the voter;
2. The special-interest effect;
3. The shortsightedness of the political process;
4. The tyranny of the majority; and
5. The "monkey wrench" effect that can be used when government creates "stakeholders."

All of these elements reduce the ability of government to address sprawl effectively and fairly.

## Voters and Information

Voters are the heart of the political system, yet voters have little incentive to be well-informed about their ballot decisions. Voter ignorance, a concept that is sometimes difficult to accept, is a key insight of public choice economic theory.

Most citizens recognize that their vote is unlikely to determine the outcome of an election. Because a single vote rarely swings an election, a mistaken or poorly informed choice by an individual at election time usually has little consequence. And if the election outcome imposes net costs on the electorate, then the cost is shared among all.

Even in the unlikely case that a voter directly determined the outcome of an election, that voter would have little control over legislative outcomes. Voters must choose among candidates who represent a bundle of positions on issues. The average U.S. Representative may be asked to vote on roughly 9,000 different issues during a two-year term.[3] Voters typically like some decisions of an elected official but not others; yet this subtlety is not captured in elections even in a representative democracy. The voter cannot vote for the tax policies of one candidate and the road construction or crime control policies of another. The voter can only choose the bundle of policies offered by a single candidate.

Because of their limited impact as individuals on elections and subsequent decisions, voters tend to remain ignorant about the details of most issues and of the candidates' positions. In the course of daily living, voters pick up information through television advertisements and campaign literature. They rely on this kind of information when they vote.

Compare the lack of willingness on the part of citizens to study even the most profound public policy issue with their willingness to study much less important but personal ones, such as what automobile to buy. Consider, for example, what car buyers read: There are dozens of specialized magazines containing expert

## Notes:

2. For more on this issue, see James D. Gwartney, Richard L. Stroup, and Russell S. Sobel, *Economics: Private and Public Choice,* Ninth Edition (Fort Worth, Tex.: Dryden Press, 2000), Chapter 6, from which portions of this section were adapted.
3. See "Résumé of Congressional Activity, 105th Congress," Daily Digest, *Congressional Record,* January 19, 1999, p. D29; available at *http://thomas.loc.gov/home/resume/105res.html.*

analyses and opinions on automobile products from almost any point of view. Tens or even hundreds of thousands of readers purchase these magazines each month. From *Consumer Reports* to *Car and Driver,* the consumer has access to scores of publications that provide product evaluations and comparisons of a wide variety of goods.

In contrast, even though public policy magazines such as *The New Republic* and *The Weekly Standard* deal with far more important issues than purchasing a car, their circulation is much smaller. Except for a few magazines mainly for professional lobbyists, the public policy magazines do not report making a profit. There simply is not the same kind of market for their information as there is for consumer information.

A person buying a car knows that a poor decision will have direct personal consequences. It will mean the wrong vehicle is parked in the driveway, paid for personally, not collectively. Each individual has an incentive to avoid costly personal mistakes by taking time to study the choices. Because the buyer is totally in control of each dollar spent on the car, in most cases complete ignorance would be irrational.

In contrast, a mistaken vote by the same individual will have virtually no effect on the election outcome. Because the individual voter cannot control governmental decisions, studying the issues simply does not pay at the personal level. Thus, it is rational for individuals to be relatively ignorant about public issues—even though decisions by many ignorant voters can be costly to society.

This rational ignorance means that political decisions are often conducted without any serious checks by the voter. In the case of zoning regulations and other rules that might affect sprawl, this lack of concern means that much will be done behind closed doors. Indeed, even open meetings are often poorly attended. Without extensive involvement of citizens, there will be little accountability to the public at large; and yet most Americans understandably do not take the time to be informed or involved.

## Special Interests

Unlike the voter, special interests are normally very knowledgeable about their narrow issues. Thus, the second important problem of government control is the role of politically organized special interests. Because the voter only rarely makes a point of monitoring the actions of government, politically active groups who have a strong interest in a particular issue can have a major impact on governmental decisions.

For example, developers who want to change zoning laws so that they can proceed with a project are willing to lobby long and hard and hire politically influential lawyers to help them. Ultimately, they probably will be allowed to do what they want. This is not all bad, since developers are generally trying to provide new customers with features that they want at an attractive cost, and community conditions may have changed significantly since the zoning rules were written. Still, it is naive to believe that regulation occurs in a political vacuum or that regulations will not be modified as a result of lobbying. And, of course, developers are not the only ones who lobby. Firms that build the roads and unions that supply them with labor try to affect government road planning, just as developers affect housing decisions.

Politicians can improve their election prospects by catering to the views of special interests. Because their personal stake is large, members of the interest group (and lobbyists who represent them) have the incentive to be informed and to communicate with legislators. Many will vote for or against candidates strictly on the basis of the candidate's position on their organization's specific goals. In addition, such interest groups are attractive sources for financial contributions, vocal supporters, and campaign workers. In contrast, most other voters will remain largely ignorant, influenced by the costly "image advertising" that special-interest funds support. Thus, politicians tend to support legislation that will provide concentrated benefits to interest groups while spreading the cost widely among unorganized taxpayers.

## Tyranny of the Majority

A different problem can occur when the majority of voters knows what it wants on a specific issue and is able to take it from a minority without compensation. For example, if current residents want to preserve green space without paying for it, they may pressure elected officials to forbid development on open land.

Such controls benefit existing homeowners in two ways. With limits on growth in place, newcomers will bid up the price of existing housing and commercial space, since less new building is allowed. (Reduced supply puts upward pressure on prices.) Second, preserving the open space directly increases the value of housing near open space. Homeowners will benefit because the value of their homes will increase without their having to make any further investment. Renters will not be so lucky; the restrictions will give them green space to enjoy but also will lead to higher rents.

Thus, maintaining open space through regulation (a typical element of anti-sprawl efforts) essentially takes value from a minority—in this case, the owners of undeveloped property and the newcomers looking for land or buildings—to benefit current residents. Those who already own housing or other developed property are rewarded doubly.

The "takings clause" in the Fifth Amendment to the U.S. Constitution was written to reduce such tyranny through government regulation. It states "nor shall private property be taken for public use without just compensation." The underlying idea is that the government can take land for a public purpose, such as creating a park, but the government—representing the people as a whole—must pay for it. In spite of the takings clause, however, courts generally have upheld regulations that reduce the value of property as long as they do not take *all* useful rights and render the land completely without value. Litigation on such issues continues.

## Shortsighted Government

Because of rational ignorance and the complexity of the issues surrounding sprawl, it is difficult for voters to identify the future benefits and costs of government actions. A community may have to decide whether it would be a good investment to build a larger water and sewer system than it needs right now, for example. Or it may face a choice of expanding the city bus system, or building a new light rail system, or deciding whether or not to raise taxes to purchase more park land. These are knotty problems. Few voters will research and analyze the implications of such complex policy alternatives if the impact will be felt primarily in the future.

This situation gives politicians a strong incentive to support policies that generate current benefits at costs that will be paid in the future. It also gives them an incentive to keep those future costs fuzzy and difficult to identify on election day. Economists refer to this bias inherent in the collective decision-making process as the "shortsightedness effect." In other words, there is a bias against actions that involve immediate and easily identifiable costs—such as higher taxes on large numbers of people—in order to produce future benefits, especially benefits that are complex and difficult to identify.

Local governments can help correct this bias by using bonds to finance such investments as a new school. Rather than place heavy taxes on citizens today, governments can issue bonds that will be paid off by a stream of future taxes. If the investment is a good one, these future taxes will be matched by the future stream of benefits flowing from the taxes generated by enhanced property values and higher incomes generated by the new investment. Even here, however, there is a problem: Governments have a temptation to finance their *current* operations (not just capital investments) by issuing bonds, producing benefits now and postponing the tax pain until later.

The shortsightedness problem is made worse by another characteristic of government efforts—the lack of what are called tradeable property rights. For example, compare the town trying to decide how big to make its sewer system with a corporation like General Electric, which is trying to decide how much to invest in manufacturing, what to produce, and where to locate its plants.

General Electric's stockholders elect a board of directors to set policy and select professional management leadership. Like the town, General Electric faces complex choices that are difficult for the individual stockholder to understand and evaluate fully. However, when evaluating the company's decisions, each stockholder has a strong incentive either to be watchful and observant or to join with others who hire someone more knowledgeable to do so.

Any stockholder (or professional stock fund or portfolio manager) who gains information and senses trouble before others do can avoid the potential loss by selling before the price of the stock falls. Similarly, the stockholder (or other observer) who recognizes a good management decision before others do can personally profit by buying stock in the firm before others recognize the potential for added profit. (Just as there are many profitable auto magazines guiding consumers, there are dozens of highly profitable magazines and newsletters for those who follow corporate stocks.)

The choices of informed, decisive stockholders generate benefits that are important beyond the gain to their personal wealth. Their decisions are registered in stock markets almost instantly. Investor decisions to buy or sell stock cause the stock price to rise or fall, signaling whether trouble or a winning program is expected.

No such signaling process exists in governmental decision-making. No one—not the townspeople, the mayor, or the members of the city council—can personally and uniquely benefit by seeking better information about the costs or benefits of community decisions on such things as new sewer systems or parks. Everyone will benefit and pay alike; everyone must live with the decisions that are made. Because the politicians and government officials do not have property rights in the government enterprise, they cannot benefit now from making decisions that will benefit all townspeople in the future. The result is a lack of advance warning about likely mistakes and a lack of advance approval and reward for policy decisions that may be costly now but beneficial in the future. This restricts the planning horizon of elected officials.

> Politicians like to cut ribbons for new buildings but tend to neglect long-term maintenance.

Both the shortsightedness effect and the lack of advance warning help explain why politicians tend to promote programs that provide easily observable benefits before the next election, even when the true cost of these programs outweighs the benefits for citizens as a whole. Politicians like to cut ribbons for new buildings but tend to neglect long-term maintenance.

Frequently, politically appealing short-term initiatives have long-term detrimental impact. For example, rent controls reduce the current price of rental housing—attractive in the short term to renters—but the effects over the long run include housing shortages, black markets, and deterioration in the quality of housing. Similarly, deferred maintenance on government roads, transit systems, and water and sewer systems saves dollars now, but at a large cost to future taxpayers. In contrast, the owner of a private facility will pay the current cost of maintenance but capture the future benefits of such prudent maintenance. There is no bias against the future there. Even if the private facility is sold before the benefits materialize, the potential benefits will boost the price the owner receives.

### "Stakeholders"

Through laws or spending programs, governments can create stakeholders: citizens or groups who have vested interests in those programs. These people have the power to throw "monkey wrenches" into other people's plans without being held accountable legally or financially themselves. For example, individuals who want parks or greenbelts but who do not want to pay for them may be able to push through regulations that give them veto power over the way land will be used. They may be able to keep developers from building on that land even if the developers paid for it.

This "monkey wrench" power is illustrated by the NIMBY syndrome. NIMBY power keeps people from using their own property—to develop it, for example—but those who exercise the power do not have to pay for the cost they impose on the landowners or others, such as customers or renters, who would have benefited as well from its use.

"Monkey wrench" power is different from legitimate denial of actions that could cause harm, such as pollution. In that case, the denial is simply the protection of other people's rights. Relief of that kind always has been available in common law courts. The NIMBY or "monkey wrench" problem occurs when regulation denies the use of land or other property when that use would violate no rights.

The alternative to NIMBYism is a market for the purchase of rights. Today, when a private conservation organization wants to preserve open space, it normally must purchase land. Not only is the initial owner compensated for the land, but the financial cost to the organization (the "opportunity cost" in economic jargon) disciplines the purchaser. The Nature Conservancy cannot simply take property; it must be selective in its use of funds and careful in its choices. Buyers like the Conservancy naturally seek low-cost, cost-effective ways to preserve habitat or keep land in its natural state.

In contrast, regulation can empower some individuals to insist on behaviors that suit them without being held accountable for their effects on others. One result is that negotiation with these "stakeholders" is difficult or impossible. Because they pay little or none of the costs they impose, they often push for everything they can get. And they may get it, because politicians have little incentive to fight the NIMBY syndrome except when organized special interests

oppose it. (In that case, politicians often obtain financial contributions from the special interests.)

A striking illustration of the "monkey wrench" issue is the action of the National Audubon Society in two very different cases—one private and one public. When Audubon owns property, its actions are quite different than when it is a "stakeholder."

The Aubudon Society owns the Rainey Preserve in Louisiana, a wildlife refuge that provides nesting grounds for snowy egrets and other rare birds. Audubon has allowed drilling for natural gas and oil there since the 1940s. Audubon experts and biologists for the oil and gas production companies worked out methods of drilling and production that do not harm the wildlife or the habitat. The companies had to meet the Audubon Society's strict stipulations —they could not drill during nesting season, for example. Audubon gave up substantial income by demanding the stipulations, but by doing so it protected the natural habitat. The cooperation between the National Audubon Society and the production companies benefited both. Over the years, Audubon has received about $25 million in royalties.

Both parties have an incentive to cooperate. Both have something to trade: Audubon owns mineral rights and the companies have exploration and drilling expertise that can benefit Audubon. They operate in a market setting that encourages mutual cooperation for the benefit of all parties.

The story is far different on land when it is owned by the government. The Audubon Society is adamantly opposed to oil drilling in the Alaska National Wildlife Refuge. "A wildlife refuge is no place for an oil rig!" says one of its flyers, vehemently arguing that such drilling would be destructive. Although there may be some problems with drilling on the refuge, Audubon has little incentive to seek mutually beneficial decisions because it will not directly benefit from the drilling there.[4]

## PROBLEMS WITH GOVERNMENT SOLUTIONS

The characteristics of government described above will surface if governmental actions become the major focus for controlling sprawl. Policies will be poorly monitored by the voters and thus will be subject to special interests or populist pressure, will favor short-term over long-term decisions, and will empower some citizens to take advantage of others—in some cases giving the majority the right to take value from the minority without compensation.

One of the tenets of the smart growth movement is that people should travel by mass transit (light rail is the currently fashionable means of transit) rather than by automobile. A number of cities, including Portland and Atlanta,[5] have built rail lines to bring people to the downtown section, just as the New York City subway system did many years ago. However, the history of the New York subway is a sobering one.[6]

The New York subway is the world's oldest and largest system; with its hundreds of miles of track snaking throughout the five boroughs, it is a magnificent engineering achievement. It is owned and operated by the public New York City Transit Authority. Politics has always influenced the subway system. (In fact, the first attempt to build one was blocked by politically powerful horse-car companies.) The first two subway lines, built before 1920, were privately owned. Each company obtained construction funds from the city in return for a promise to keep the subway fare at 5 cents.

As time went on, political pressure to keep the subway fare low increased, with growing interest on the part of the city to take control. This pressure led to the bankruptcy of one line and the takeover of both lines by the city in 1940.

Once publicly owned, the Transit Authority appeased riders by continuing to offer rides at a low price. The subway, consequently, failed to generate sufficient funds to cover its costs. At the same time, transit workers' unions were able (sometimes by dramatic strikes or strike threats) to keep wages relatively high—much higher than the system could afford. Like municipalities and other governments around the world, the city was forced to skimp on maintenance, and the subway deteriorated. Dirt and crime increased because, unlike a private facility, the resulting reduction in willingness of riders to pay did not cut into an owner's profit. Gradually, the subway became unattractive, even with its low fares.

This track record illustrates several of the flaws of government control listed above: poor monitoring by the voter, political pressure for current benefits (low fares) by the majority, actual control of the system by special interests (unions seeking higher wages), and the failure of the government to invest in the future due to the shortsightedness effect.

Smart-growth advocates may argue that this series of events will not happen to the light rail systems that are being proposed around the country. But why should consumers expect government administration of light rail to be different? Indeed, smart-growth advocates should be well aware of the long-term harm that government's decisions can cause. The reason: Governmental regulations from an earlier era already are blocking their agenda.

It is clear by now that the biggest obstacles to the "new urbanist" community designs that reflect the more traditional city blocks are zoning regulations, as Samuel Staley shows in Chapter 5. And prominent smart-growth advocates Henry L. Diamond and Patrick F. Noonan

**Notes:**

4. Pamela Snyder and Jane S. Shaw, "PC Oil Drilling in a Wildlife Refuge," *The Wall Street Journal*, September 7, 1995.

5. The experience of Portland and Atlanta are discussed in more detail in Chapters 9 and 10.

6. See James B. Ramsey, "Selling the New York City Subway: Wild-Eyed Radicalism or the Only Feasible Solution?" in Steve H. Hanke, ed., *Prospects for Privatization,* Proceedings of the Academy of Political Science, New York, Vol. 36. No. 3 (1987), pp. 93–103.

note that, "Ironically, the American system of land use controls has gradually become so complex that it is now prohibitively expensive and cumbersome to develop old and new sites in the image of the traditional American community."[7]

Perhaps the strongest indictment of a reliance on government to achieve a better community is the growing menace of traffic congestion. This is the worst element of sprawl in the minds of most people (see, for example, Wendell Cox's discussion in Chapter 4).

Traffic congestion is not a sign of market failure. There is no market. If there were, demand for space on the roads would push the price of road space at peak times higher ("congestion pricing"). The higher price would moderate highway use but also provide funds to implement technological solutions such as better traffic control to allow traffic to flow more smoothly. Traffic congestion is an illustration of the effects of government control (or, more accurately, government's inability to control).

With a few exceptions, virtually all roads in the United States are governmental responsibility. And urban and suburban areas are plagued by the results of poor government decisions—not building roads when they are needed, letting innovations in road and traffic control pass by, and neglecting proven improvements, such as peak-hour pricing to modulate demand and fund improvements.

Governments handle roads so poorly because they have little incentive to do otherwise. The inability of voters to monitor government decisions effectively and the tendency of governments to focus on the near term explain most of the failure.[8] In addition, conflicts among jurisdictions over who will pay for any road (which usually would be funded by a combination of state, local, and federal dollars) often delays construction for years. This is a far cry from the reaction of businesses in the private sector to anticipated demand.

There is one other important reason to question government control. So far, we have considered whether government control would achieve the objectives that the "smart growthers" want. Equally relevant is whether it *should* try to achieve their objectives; that is, are these objectives sought by most Americans? Backers of increased density and traditional town designs may be out of touch with the preferences of average Americans. The fact that people who receive *Sierra* magazine (primarily the members of the Sierra Club) have incomes nearly twice that of average Americans[9] explains their willingness and ability to pay for high-cost, amenity-driven policies. However, it does not justify their imposition of those policies on others.

New urbanist policies are costly. As John Charles points out in Chapter 9, the urban growth boundary and related policies in Portland have substantially increased housing costs. When high-income people use markets to purchase the amenities they desire, the results are both more efficient and more equitable than when these amenities are obtained through pol-

**The strongest indictment of a reliance on government to achieve a better community is the growing menace of traffic congestion.**

## Notes:

7. Henry L. Diamond and Patrick F. Noonan, *Land Use in America* (Washington, D.C.: Island Press, 1996), p. 64.
8. One exception can be seen in cities, notably Chicago, and states where the highway construction special interests are big donors to politicians; in those cases, special interest lobbying may have a favorable impact.
9. *MRI Reader Survey* (San Francisco: Sierra Club, 1992), p. 1.

icies that force all citizens to pay for the preferences of a few.

## THE ROLE OF MARKETS

Although many people are clamoring for more government control to curtail sprawl, there is, in fact, another alternative. Markets can address these issues effectively. Indeed, markets address such issues daily.

To understand how markets could solve the problems of sprawl, it is important to understand what we mean by "markets." A market is more than a place; it is a process. In his book, *The Making of Economic Society,* Robert Heilbroner quotes a hypothetical adviser as saying, "Oh, nobody runs the market....It runs itself. In fact there really isn't any such *thing* as 'the market.' It's just a word we use to describe the way people behave."[10] Another economist, Friedrich von Hayek, described the market as a spontaneously evolved order that comes about as people make decisions. To a large extent, Hayek explained, they are responding to changing prices. As prices go up or down, people make different choices about what to buy and what to offer in the market.[11] The point of these descriptions is that people—acting voluntarily, making numerous decisions on their own initiative daily—are what we mean by the market. It is diverse and dynamic and under the control of no single person or entity.

Although we sometimes think of cities as being designed by urban "planners," the mar-ket is a major force in guiding development in and around American cities. Consider how the market addresses an important planning question of interest to many residents: How many restaurants should there be in the city, what size should they be, and what sort of food should they serve?

This question is not answered by a governmental planning agency, but by the market. Buyers communicate their desires by what they buy. Suppliers respond by meeting those consumer demands. Competition among suppliers forces them to offer the best food and service they can, in places and times when people want them, and at prices the consumer-buyers can afford.

> Although we sometimes think of cities as being designed by urban "planners," the market is a major force in guiding development.

Unlike the atmosphere at zoning meetings, which involve lobbying, extended arguments, high-priced attorneys, and public input from "stakeholders"—just to determine the location of one or two developments—there are few arguments and little public bickering over what should be offered in the myriad of restaurants in any town or city. Market responses settle the questions. There is, of course, "planning" in a market, but it is quite different from government planning. In effect, it is conducted first by investors, who create developments offering space for businesses, shopping, and residences. Investments in better designs and better locations are rewarded as buyers and renters drive up prices, competing for them. Other investors emulate the best of these, while owners of less attractive properties cut their losses by converting their properties to more desired uses. Ultimately, through this pro-

**Notes**:

10. Robert L. Heilbroner, *The Making of Economic Society* (Englewood Cliffs, N.J.: Prentice-Hall, Inc., 1962), p. 16.

11. See, for example, Friedrich A. Hayek, "The Use of Knowledge in Society," *American Economic Review,* September 1945, pp. 519–530.

cess, development in a market is guided by individual consumers, whose responses are communicated through their decisions over what to buy or not to buy.

The same process occurs as hundreds of kinds of goods and services are purchased in a city, from hardware and clothing to hotel rooms. Competition is constant, but it seldom generates heated debate. Passion may be evoked, but it tends to be passion for reducing costs and expanding the production and sale of the goods or services offered, rather than the passionate hatred of plans proposed by others that is so typical of public decision-making today.

## MITIGATING SPRAWL

Just such a market process is currently addressing the concerns about sprawl throughout the country. Not only are entrepreneurs redesigning subdivisions to please customers (see Chapter 8), but people are making daily decisions that mitigate the unpleasant effects of sprawl, such as traffic congestion. Because no one, not even the millionaires among us, can have all the amenities they want, people must make choices. As we will see in Chapter 4, over the past decade or so commuters have increased their travel times only slightly, but the average speed at which they travel has increased. It appears that commuters prefer faster routes, not being caught in stop-and-go traffic; and they have adjusted their commutes accordingly.

Thus, individuals acting on their own initiative are doing what they can to correct the misallocation of transportation funding. Similarly, employers are offering more flexible hours and revising work patterns to allow workers to shorten their commutes, and changing requirements so that more of their employees can telecommute and not drive to work at all.

These do not represent an ideal or even best possible solution to the problem of traffic congestion. But until government decisions become less bureaucratic, less politicized, and more responsive to motorists in the design and construction of America's roads, these alternatives may be the best that we will achieve. Fortunately, the other problems that are covered by the term "sprawl"—low-density and spread-out developments, for example—involve the private sector more directly. To address those problems in ways that produce the best possible results for individuals of widely varying incomes and tastes, we should look where Americans have always looked—to the market.

# NATURE IN THE SUBURBS

3

*By Jane S. Shaw*

Environmentalists criticize urban sprawl on many grounds. One of the most emotionally charged criticisms is that sprawl eats up land that otherwise would provide habitat for wildlife or, at the very least, serve as productive farmland.

"Sprawl, by definition, fragments landscapes—and fragmented landscapes are the biggest threat to America's wildlife heritage," writes Carl Pope, executive director of the Sierra Club.[1] As he explains, such landscapes are "very good for the most adaptable and common creatures—raccoons, deer, sparrows, starlings, and sea gulls," but "devastating for wildlife that is more dependent upon privacy, seclusion, and protection from such predators as dogs and cats."

Other commentators are even more disparaging of the wild animals that survive in the suburbs. They call them "weedy species." The term usually refers to exotic, non-native species like the kudzu vine that invade new areas and

then are hard to get rid of, but the name also has been applied to a larger number of species that are not necessarily invaders. Nature writer David Quammen defines weedy species as animals and plants that "reproduce quickly, disperse widely when given a chance, tolerate a fairly broad range of habitat conditions, take hold in strange places, succeed especially in disturbed ecosystems, and resist eradication once they're established." They are found in "human-dominated terrain because in crucial ways they resemble *Homo sapiens*: aggressive, versatile, prolific, and ready to travel."[2]

Although it is true that animals like grizzly bears and elk are not likely to be found in the suburbs, humans may be more compatible with wildlife than most people think. This chapter will explore the evidence. To begin with, the impression that nothing is left but weedy species deserves careful scrutiny. Yes, such animals may be "common" and "adaptable" (they are "common" almost by definition), but this does not mean that nobody wants them—quite the

**Notes**:

1. Carl Pope, "Americans Are Saying No to Sprawl," *PERC Reports*, February 1999, p. 6.
2. David Quammen, "Planet of Weeds," *Harper's,* October 1998, p. 67.

contrary, in fact. Nor is it evident that growing suburbs necessarily push out large animals. In some cases, there were few before the suburbs arose because the land was being cultivated intensively. In other cases, large animals still lurk nearby.

In fact, one observer of sprawl sees the new suburbs as abounding in wildlife—at least in comparison to the urban areas in which most Americans grew up. In his book *Edge City*, journalist Joel Garreau discusses the newest suburbs, the towns on the edge of metropolitan areas to which people increasingly gravitate. Garreau says that this distant suburban growth has put people back in touch with nature.

In these new cities, "more humans are getting closer to other high-order species than at any time in the past century," he contends. Garreau claims that for the first time since the industrial revolution, "the majority of the American people—whether they know it or not or like it or not—may soon be sharing their territory with fairly large wild animals."[3]

Change is occurring in America's growing metropolitan areas and, as every ecologist knows, all change helps some species and hurts others. "The 'normal' state of nature is not one of balance and repose," says science writer Stephen Budiansky; "the 'normal' state is to be recovering from the last disaster. In most ecosystems the interval between disturbances—fire, frost, flood, windstorm—is almost always less than the life span of an individual member of the dominant species. So much for balance."[4]

When people move onto what once was rural land, they provide a new form of disturbance.

> Humans may be more compatible with wildlife than most people think.

They modify the landscape by building more streets, more parking lots, and more buildings. Wetlands may be drained, hayfields may disappear, trees may be cut down, and pets may proliferate. At the same time, however, the new residents will build ponds, establish gardens, plant trees, and set up bird nesting-boxes. Ornamental nurseries and truck farms may replace cropland, and parks may replace hedgerows. The new ecology is different, but not necessarily worse.

When land is taken out of agriculture for residences, it is not clear that the habitat for wildlife is impoverished. Farmland provides open space because it has few buildings, but it has been occupied and cultivated by humans, often for generations. It may not have been the home of large mammals in recent times.

Indeed, in other contexts environmentalists frequently criticize agricultural land as a monoculture with little biodiversity. The environmental essayist Donald Worster says that traditional agriculture was "highly diversified," but that changed dramatically: "[T]he trend over the past two hundred years or so has been toward the establishment of monocultures on every continent."[5]

The broader concern about the loss of farmland, and thus agricultural production, is readily resolved. As Samuel Staley of the Reason Public Policy Institute explained in a recent report, the amount of land devoted to agriculture is declining, but it declined fastest in the 1960s and the loss has moderated since then. Using statistics from the National Agricultural Statistics Service, Staley calculated that during the 1990s, the nation lost about 2.6 million

**Notes**:

3.  Joel Garreau, *Edge City: Life on the New Frontier* (New York: Random House, 1991), p. 56.
4.  Stephen Budiansky, *Nature's Keepers: The New Science of Nature Management* (New York: Free Press, 1995, p. 71.
5.  Donald Worster, *The Wealth of Nature: Environmental History and the Ecological Imagination* (New York: Oxford University Press, 1993), p. 59.

acres of farmland per year, compared with an average of 7.3 million in the 1960s. Much of this "lost" farmland was converted to pasture, grazing land, forest, and recreational uses. Only 26 percent (676,000 acres) appears to be "lost" due to urban or suburban growth. And since agricultural production is at all-time highs, there is little reason to be concerned about raising food.[6]

## HISTORICALLY CHANGING ENVIRONMENTS

Perhaps the most objective way to look at the impact of suburban growth on nature is to recognize that each area has a unique past and its own changes. Although some changes may impoverish wildlife, others may lead to a more ecologically diverse setting.

One example of the positive impact of growth is the rebound of the endangered Key deer, a small white-tailed deer found only in Florida and named for the Florida Keys. According to *Audubon* magazine, the Key deer is experiencing a "remarkable recovery."[7] The news report continues: "Paradoxically, part of the reason for the deer's comeback may lie in the increasing development of the area." Paraphrasing the remarks of Roel Lopez, the researcher at Texas A&M University who quantified the deer population, the reporter says that human development "tends to open up overgrown forested areas and provide vegetation at deer level—the same factors fueling deer population booms in suburbs all over the country."

James R. Dunn, a geologist who has pieced together some of the wildlife history around Albany, New York, has a similar analysis to explain what he views as a proliferation of wildlife in suburban areas.[8] He describes several important land-use changes that occurred during the past few hundred years in that region. The first occurred when colonial settlers farmed the area, probably after extensively logging the forest. Later, during the 19th century, as farming shifted westward to the more fertile fields of the Midwest, many New York farms were abandoned. The forest began to grow back.

During the second half of the 20th century, the gradual growth of population led suburbs to develop around Albany. As they moved out, people began to settle this land again. Some of it had reforested; some was still meadow, and some was still agricultural. "During my years as a geologist in this area," writes Dunn, "I discovered that many roads on old topographic maps are no longer used. These roads serviced a checkerboard of farms, orchards, and grazing lands during the 1800s and until about 1920. The roads were abandoned when agricultural lands were no longer needed."[9]

Dunn sees this process as creating today's "suburban" mixture of forest, field, home, and street. In his view, the result is an enriched habitat, not a diminished one. His backyard, he claims, has more than 50 bird species.

Dunn goes further. He contends that when it comes to deer, suburban habitat is more productive than the forests of New York, such as those of the Adirondack Mountains.[10] Dunn cites statistics on the harvest of buck deer reported by the New York State government to argue his point. He observes that since 1970 the deer population multiplied 7.1 times in suburban areas (an increase of 610 percent) and only 3.4 times (an increase of 240 percent) in the state overall. (See Chart 3.1.)

**Notes:**

6. Samuel R. Staley, *The "Vanishing Farmland Myth" and the Smart-Growth Agenda* (Los Angeles: Reason Public Policy Institute, 1999), p. 4.
7. Nancy Klingener, "Doe, Re, Key Deer," *Audubon,* January-February 2000, p. 17.
8. James R. Dunn, "Wildlife in the Suburbs," *PERC Reports*, September 1999, pp. 3–5. See also James R. Dunn and John E. Kinney, *Conservative Environmentalism: Reassessing the Means, Redefining the Ends* (Westport, Conn.: Quorum Books, 1996).
9. Dunn, "Wildlife in the Suburbs," p. 4.
10. The Iroquois word for "Adirondack" means "bark-eater," suggesting that the area may never have been rich with food.

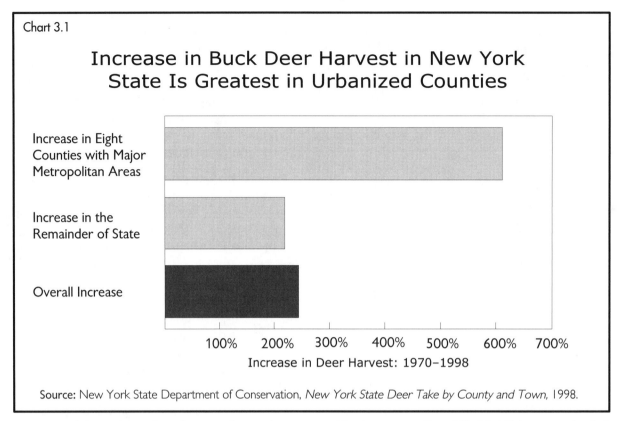

Chart 3.1

## Increase in Buck Deer Harvest in New York State Is Greatest in Urbanized Counties

Increase in Eight Counties with Major Metropolitan Areas

Increase in the Remainder of State

Overall Increase

100%  200%  300%  400%  500%  600%  700%

Increase in Deer Harvest: 1970–1998

**Source:** New York State Department of Conservation, *New York State Deer Take by County and Town,* 1998.

He explains that the forests have been allowed to regrow without logging or burning, so that today they lack the "edge" that allows sunlight in and fosters vegetation suitable for deer. That is why the counties with big cities (and therefore with suburbs) have seen a greater increase in deer populations than have the isolated, forested rural counties.

Certainly, the regrowth of Eastern forests is a dramatic occurrence that unfolded throughout most of the 20th century. In 1991, a research organization in Washington, D.C., Resources for the Future, estimated that the percent of land forested in New Hampshire had increased from 50 percent in the 1880s to 86 percent 100 years later. Forested land in Connecticut, Massachusetts, and Rhode Island increased from 35 percent to 59 percent over that same period.[11]

Environmentalist Bill McKibben exulted in this "unintentional and mostly unnoticed renewal of the rural and mountainous East" in a 1995 *Atlantic Monthly* article. Calling the change "the great environmental story of the United States, and in some ways of the whole world," he added, "Here, where 'suburb' and 'megalopolis' were added to the world's vocabulary, an explosion of green is under way."[12] Along with the reforestation come the animals; McKibben cites a moose "ten miles from Boston," as well as an eastern United States full of black bears, deer, alligators, and perhaps even mountain lions. Unlike Dunn, McKibben does not differentiate among the kinds of land—full forest or fragmented forest—but he paints a dramatic picture of new, emergent wilderness.

## Notes:

11. Roger A. Sedjo, "Forest Resources," in Kenneth D. Frederick and Roger A. Sedjo, eds., *America's Renewable Resources: Historical Trends and Current Challenges* (Washington, D.C.: Resources for the Future), p. 109.
12. Bill McKibben, "An Explosion of Green," *Atlantic Monthly*, April 1995, p. 64.

## Abundance of Deer

These days, deer are the most prominent species proliferating in the suburbs. The increase in the number of deer in the United States is so great that many people, especially wildlife professionals, are trying to figure out what to do about them. In 1997, the Wildlife Society, a professional association of wildlife biologists, devoted a special 600-page issue of its *Bulletin* to the subject of "Deer Overabundance." The lead article noted, "We hear more each year about the high costs of crop and tree-seedling damage, deer-vehicle collisions, and nuisance deer in suburban locales."[13] Insurance companies are worried about the increase in damage that results when automobiles and deer (and similar-sized animals) collide. And there are fears that the increase in deer in populated areas means that the deer tick could be causing the rise in reported cases of Lyme disease.

Yes, the proliferation of deer poses problems, as does the restoration of geese, whose flocks can foul ponds and lawns, and of beaver, which can cut down groves of trees. Yet these problems are manageable, and their very existence undercuts claims that suburban growth destroys wildlife. The proliferation of deer is a wildlife success story ("one of the premier examples of successful wildlife management," says Robert J. Warren, editor of the *Wildlife Society Bulletin*[14]). Noting that today's deer population in the United States may be as high as 25 million, Richard Nelson, writing in *Sports Afield,* says:

**The proliferation of deer is a wildlife success story.**

Just a few decades ago, if anyone had predicted that deer would join robins and gray squirrels as denizens of the suburbs. . . that sage would likely have been shrugged off as a lunatic. But in many parts of the country, deer have become so abundant that they're causing serious problems on the roadways and in our neighborhoods, natural preserves and farmlands.[15]

Not surprisingly, people have mixed feelings about the deer. In the *Wildlife Society Bulletin,* Dale R. McCullough and his colleagues reported on a survey of households in El Cerrito and Kensington, two communities near Berkeley, California. Of those who respon-ded to the survey, 50 percent reported seeing deer "frequently" and 25 percent "occasionally." Twenty-eight percent reported severe damage to vegetation by the deer, and 25 percent reported moderate damage. Forty-two percent liked having the deer around, while 35 percent disliked them and 24 percent were indifferent. The authors summarized the findings by saying: "As expected, some residents loved deer, whereas others considered them 'hoofed rats.'"[16]

This mixture of attitudes is not merely a California phenomenon. Two members of the Missouri Department of Conservation report "a management dilemma" in urban areas where deer are proliferating and hunting is not allowed.[17] Yet, in spite of problems such as auto accidents and destruction of gardens and native vegetation, "surveys of Missouri urban-

**Notes:**

13. Donald M. Waller and William S. Alverson, "The White-Tailed Deer: A Keystone Herbivore," *Wildlife Society Bulletin.* Vol. 25, No. 2 (Summer 1997), p. 217.

14. Robert J. Warren, "The Challenge of Deer Overabundance in the 21st Century," *Wildlife Society Bulletin* 1997, Vol. 25, No. 2 (Summer 1997), p. 213.

15. Richard Nelson, "Deer Nation," *Sports Afield*, September 1998, p. 40.

16. Dale R. McCullough, Kathleen W. Jennings, Natalie B. Gates, Bruce G. Elliott, and Joseph E. DiDonato, "Overabundant Deer Populations in California," *Wildlife Society Bulletin,* Vol. 25, No. 2 (1997), p. 481.

17. Lonnie Hansen and Jeff Beringer, "Managed Hunts to Control White-Tailed Deer Populations on Urban Public Areas in Missouri," *Wildlife Society Bulletin*, Vol. 25, No. 2 (Summer 1997), p. 484.

ites indicate white-tailed deer are highly popular." In fact, they report that the deer was voted "the wild animal that urban Missourians most enjoyed viewing."[18]

## Other Proliferating Species

Of course, deer are not the only wild animals willing to live around growing urban areas. Joel Garreau cites black bears, red-tailed hawks, peregrine falcons, and beaver in his list of animals that find niches in the new, distant suburbs. Garreau still considers these suburbs a "far less diverse ecology than what was there before." However, "if you measure it by the standard of city, it is a far more diverse ecology than anything humans have built in centuries, if not millennia,"[19] he writes.

James Dunn lists the species that inhabit the suburbs in his region in addition to deer: birds such as robins, woodpeckers, chickadees, grouse, finches, hawks, crows, and nuthatches, as well as squirrels, chipmunks, opossums, raccoons, foxes, and rabbits.[20] Deer attract coyotes, too. According to a 1999 article in *Audubon*, biologists estimate that the coyote population (observed in all states except Hawaii) is about double what it was in 1850.[21]

Although deer and coyotes can be described as common, adaptable, and perhaps even "weedy species," a more accurate term is the one coined by University of Florida biologist Larry Harris, "meso-mammals," or mammals of medium size.[22] They do not need broad territory for roaming to find food, as moose and grizzly bears do. They can find places to feed, nest, and thrive in the suburbs, especially those where gardens flourish.

Not all the wild animals who turn up near home sites and commercial areas are small. In fast-growing Orange County, California, deer serve as prey for mountain lions, according to studies by Paul Beier, a professor at the University of California at Berkeley.[23] In 1994, two people in the area were killed by mountain lions. Although mountain lions had been recognized as present in the nearby Mount Hamilton region, by 1997 "the number of reports has increased considerably, and it seems likely that resident animals are present."[24]

An article in a Montana newspaper, also citing Paul Beier's work, reported that mountain lion encounters are increasing around the country. The article noted that according to "conventional wisdom," the encounters occur because more people are moving into the lions' habitat; however, the author says that the reverse is true also. Lions "are spending more time in what has long been considered human habitat, our cities and towns and subdivisions."[25] Even in the East, mountain lions may be coming back. Bill McKibben reported in 1995 that the Eastern Puma Research Network had been told of 1,800 puma (a mountain lion) sightings during the previous 10 years. The National Wildlife Federation reports a resurgence of cougars (another mountain lion) in California, where they are endangering bighorn sheep in the Sierra Nevadas.[26]

Although black bears are smaller than the relatively rare and dangerous grizzlies, they can be sizable, and they appear to be moving into urban areas, too. Writing in *The New York Times*, reporter Robert Hanley noted that a 175-pound black bear was discovered in "the heart of the

## Notes:

18. *Ibid.*, citing a 1990 Missouri Conservation Department study.
19. Garreau, *Edge City,* p. 57.
20. Dunn, "Wildlife in the Suburbs," p. 3.
21. Mike Finkel, "The Ultimate Survivor," *Audubon,* May-June 1999, p. 58.
22. Larry D. Harris, in e-mail communication with the author, January 16, 2000.
23. McCullough *et al.,* "Overabundant Deer Populations in California," p. 479.
24. *Ibid.*
25. Scott McMillion, "Cat Power," *Bozeman Daily Chronicle,* November 28, 1999, pp. 33ff.
26. Martin Fortenzer, "Clawing Its Way to the Top," *National Wildlife,* February-March 2000, at *http://www.nwf.org/natlwild/2000/mtlionfm.html.*

business district" of West Haven, Connecticut. "The world of wildlife is far different from what it was a generation ago," Hanley noted, "as more housing eats into once distant wilderness. All sorts of species no longer stay secluded in deep woods." He specifically cited "moose on the developing outer fringes of suburbia; coyotes, fox, deer and the ubiquitous Canada geese in older suburban towns; bears and turkeys in cities."[27]

Even elk have been infiltrating subdivisions in Jefferson County, Colorado. According to the *Rocky Mountain News*, state wildlife officials estimate that 2,500 elk live in the area between Denver and the Continental Divide. "The increase has occurred entirely in residential subdivisions such as Evergreen Meadows, not in the area's vast expanses of national forests, according to state wildlife biologist Janet George,"[28] the article stated.

The renewal of wildlife is not limited to the United States. A news report in the *Sunday Times* of London recently reported that seals are again swimming up the Thames River and entering London.[29]

## Wild Backyards

Some environmental groups acknowledge the richness, or potential richness, of the suburban environment. A project of the National Wildlife Federation is called "Backyard Wildlife Habitat." It is both an informational program and one that certifies backyards as attractive for wildlife.

For example, one Colorado backyard habitat certified by the National Wildlife Federation started with a pond, berry bushes, and spruces.

Today the owner finds mallard and wood ducks, herons, hawks, kingfishers and other large birds, snakes, foxes, and skunks on her property. She has chickadees in a nest box and finches in a thistle feeder. "Before" and "after" photos on the National Wildlife Web site are impressive.[30]

Through its Web site, the National Wildlife Federation offers advice to amateur naturalists on how to develop certifiable wildlife-friendly yards. Would-be habitat builders are led through the "basics" of improving their backyards. Other advice is more complex. In "Learn How to Build a Simple Pond," Doug Inkley, a senior scientist for the Federation, describes how to design a pond to include fish and frogs.[31]

The average person's fascination with—and easy access to—wildlife explains the success of Keeping Track, a Vermont organization that teaches volunteers how to monitor signs of wildlife. Susan Morse, founder and program director, says: "We offer the average citizen something physical they can do for wildlife in the community to stop the damage they see happening."[32] Founded in 1994, the organization has approximately 600 members and 55 groups, primarily in New England. The goal is to identify wildlife so that local planning commissions will make wiser decisions. "We urgently need to make a planned attempt to create buffer-lands around wilderness areas and protect the rural working landscapes," Morse told the *Amicus Journal*, a publication of the Natural Resources Defense Council.[33]

A Keeping Track group in New Hampshire documented the presence of bobcats at one site. Their records led to a decision to relocate a

## Notes:

27. Robert Hanley, "Coyotes, Turkeys and Bears, Oh My!" *The New York Times*, June 18, 1999, p. B1.
28. Berny Morson, "Worn-Out Welcome," *Rocky Mountain News*, August 24, 1997.
29. Jonathan Leake, "First Seals in the Thames for 150 Years," *The Sunday Times* (London), December 19, 1999.
30. See *http://www.nwf.org/habitats/backyard/certifysample.cfm* (February 9, 2000).
31. See *http://www.nwf.org/habitats/backyard/beyondbasics/hints/frogpond.cfm* (February 9, 2000).
32. Steve Lerner, "A Walk on the Wild Side," *Amicus Journal*, Summer 1999, at *http://www.nrdc.org/nrdc/eamicus*. Ironically, this issue of the *Amicus Journal* also included an article entitled, "The New Suburbanites," which lamented the supposedly detrimental effect of sprawl on wild animals.
33. *Ibid.*

proposed electric utility transfer station and to defeat plans for a snowmobile trail. Bobcats? In suburbia? No, but close to it. The group was the Piscataquog Watershed Association based in Weare, New Hampshire, a town in the growing southern part of the state.

Meanwhile, studies are beginning to show that even urban areas are richer in wildlife than most people assume. *Science* magazine recently reported on a six-year, $4.4 million study of animal species in Phoenix, Arizona. Researchers identified "over 75 species of bees, 200 species of birds, and hundreds of insect species within metropolitan Phoenix," reported freelance writer Keith Kloor. "True, some heavyweights are absent," the author notes. Bighorn sheep and "other animals that need room to roam aren't going to make it in Phoenix," he says. However, he quotes Charles Redman, an anthropologist at Arizona State University who helped oversee the study: "The simple notion that a city diminishes biodiversity is wrong."[34]

## APPARENT COMPATIBILITY

What Americans are seeing is an apparent compatibility—albeit perhaps an uneasy one—of animals and humans in growing metropolitan areas. This should not really surprise us. Suburbs have grown in large measure because people have the wealth and the mobility to move into less-dense environments. Economic studies show that as income rises, people begin to take better care of their surroundings and show greater interest in protecting their environment. Although they may rely on shopping malls and drive on highways, they also like open space, gardens, and trees—all characteristics that are likely to attract or nurture wild animals.

Studies show the connection between increasing wealth and environmental protection in a variety of settings, from controlling air pollution[35] to passing laws that protect open space.[36] The connection is even illustrated by the fact that environmentalists tend to have significantly higher incomes than other Americans. A typical reader of *Sierra*, the magazine of the Sierra Club, earns nearly twice the average income of Americans.[37] It is intuitively clear that for many people one reason to move to the suburbs, including the distant suburbs, is to be closer to nature.

Some entrepreneurs, responding to this interest in nature, are making deliberate efforts to maintain the natural environment when they develop home sites. In the West, entrepreneurs are integrating homes with habitat for wildlife, including such large animals as elk and bears. Lee Poole is developing Moonlight Basin, a mountainside community that combines homes with easy access to ski lifts and large areas of wildlife habitat near Big Sky, Montana. William Ogden is doing something similar on a smaller scale with nearby Eagle Rock Reserve. Other "eco-developments" include Farmview in Pennsylvania and Wildcat Ranch near Aspen, Colorado (see Chapter 8). There are even "eco-sensitive" golf courses. An

> What Americans are seeing is an apparent compatibility—albeit perhaps an uneasy one—of animals and humans in growing metropolitan areas.

**Notes**:

34. Keith Kloor, "A Surprising Tale of Life in the City," *Science*, Vol. 286, No. 22 (October 1999), p. 663.

35. Gene M. Grossman and Alan B. Krueger, "Economic Growth and the Environment," *Quarterly Journal of Economics,* Vol. 110, No. 2 (1995), pp. 353–377.

36. Don Coursey, *The Demand for Environmental Quality* (St. Louis, Mo.: John M. Olin School of Business, Washington University, December 1992).

37. The Sierra Club, "MRI Reader Survey," San Francisco, 1992, p. 1.

international certification program evaluates golf courses on the basis of their preservation of natural habitat, their conservation of water, and other environmental features.

One of the most intriguing ways to combine nature and residences is by restoring native plants. Ron Bowen, president of Prairie Restorations, Inc., is a pioneer in this endeavor. On his "farm" in southern Minnesota, Bowen raises plants like wild rye and thimbleweed, vegetation native to the prairies and savannahs of the Midwest. Until recently, residents routinely replaced such plants on their lawns with imported vegetation, such as Kentucky blue grass. But some years ago, Bowen dreamed of bringing back native vegetation by designing landscapes that resembled the traditional fields of southern Minnesota. Today, his restorations can be found on the lawns of corporate headquarters and private homeowners.(Bowen sells a "plant-it-yourself" package of seeds for the less affluent client).[38]

Similar efforts are being made by entrepreneurs and nonprofit organizations around the country. Yet the phenomenon of privately restored mini-prairies cannot occur without the open space that suburbs make possible. Maintaining "native prairie" means setting fires periodically—as American Indians did—to rejuvenate the vegetation. Bowen's efforts would be severely restricted in a dense urban setting. And while it is possible for governments and non-profit organizations to create prairie preserves in large areas, only low-density suburbs can bring the experience of prairie life to individuals on a day-to-day basis.

In addition to such entrepreneurial efforts, citizens in jurisdictions throughout the country are taking political action in an attempt to set aside more open space—another sign that increasingly affluent Americans are willing to spend money to maintain natural habitat where they live. In 1998, voters in many states passed ballot measures to provide funds for additional open space set-asides. In his 1991 book, Joel Garreau remarked that the New Jersey state plan (a growth-management strategy) urged company headquarters to become "refuges for wildlife" and new residential developments to be "clustered and adjoin protected natural streams and wooded areas."[39] The opportunity for intimacy with nature is one that many people welcome, and one to which developers and corporate executives are responding.

## SHARING OUR TURF

Whatever happens to resolve the issue of sprawl, a major concern in the coming years certainly will be how to live harmoniously with a reviving natural world of wildlife. Indeed, unless most people are willing to give up their broad lawns and single-family homes, the issue of integrating wildlife with day-to-day human life may well turn out to be more compelling, and perhaps more divisive, than today's controversy over sprawl.

If wealth continues to grow in the next decades, this new century is likely to be an environmental one, with the many positives and some negatives this term implies. On a broad scale, if less land is needed for farming, there likely will be a continual proliferation of forest land, and with it the resurgence of large mammals, from grizzlies to cougars. More locally, we are likely to see an increasing array of efforts to create parks and preserve open space in growing metropolitan areas. This will mean more of the birds and meso-mammals we now see in the suburbs.

Most significantly, it also will mean that we will see more organizations and entrepreneurs devoting their resources to figuring out ways to integrate nature into the human landscape. The magnitude of endeavors along these lines, from the National Wildlife Federation's "backyard habitats" to the emerging business of native

**Notes**:

38. Linda E. Platts, "Enviro-Capitalists: Who Are They?" *PERC Reports* (Bozeman, Mont.: Political Economy Research Center), December 1998, pp. 7–11.
39. Garreau, *Edge City*, p. 57.

plant restoration, may well dwarf the actions of politicians and bureaucrats. Sprawl may become a side issue as the process of protecting and enhancing the relationship of human beings with nature takes center stage.

# 4

# COPING WITH TRAFFIC CONGESTION

## By Wendell Cox

Americans, who are used to coming and going as they please, are upset about traffic. In a recent survey, 79 percent of respondents identified traffic congestion as one of the most unfavorable aspects of urban and suburban growth. Crime, at 47 percent, came in second. And traffic congestion is increasing in urban areas. According to the Federal Highway Administration, traffic congestion grew 26 percent from 1982 to 1996. In 1996, a study found that the volume of traffic exceeded roadway capacity in 39 out of the 70 urban areas surveyed; in 1982, only 10 of the areas exceeded capacity.[1]

New urbanists, who favor policies that would restrict suburban growth, point to the frustration that suburbanites experience because of traffic congestion and propose a number of strategies to improve the situation. They argue that the use of automobiles[2] must be limited and that people must begin to rely on alternative forms of transport, such as transit, bicycles, and walking, for a significant percentage of their travel. To accomplish these goals, they suggest:

- Commercial and residential development that creates higher population densities to encourage more walking and the use of public transit to reduce travel by automobile.

- New transit systems, especially light rail, as alternatives to the automobile.

- Less new highway development (if not stopping it completely), because they believe highways cause significantly higher amounts of driving. (Smart growth advocates often reason that "you can't build your way out of congestion.")

- Higher fees for highway users to discourage automobile use.

Not every advocate of these strategies is convinced that they will reduce traffic congestion.

**Notes:**

1. Texas Transportation Institute, *Roadway Congestion Index*, Texas A&M University, 1996.
2. The term "automobile" is used to connote personal vehicles, including light trucks and sport utility vehicles.

But virtually all supporters expect them to improve access to destinations throughout the urban areas. Some even hope that most people will react to their frustration over traffic congestion by abandoning their automobiles altogether and using transit.

The leading urban model for new urbanists is Portland, Oregon, as John Charles discusses in Chapter 9. Portland has delineated an "urban growth boundary" beyond which development is largely forbidden, and within which the city has been encouraging and subsidizing pedestrian and transit-oriented commercial and residential development. It is expanding its light rail system, and as a matter of policy will minimize investment in new highways.

In spite of the desires of the smart growth proponents and new urbanists to counter growth, the evidence from Portland makes clear that the policies they are proposing will do just the opposite—they will increase traffic congestion, increase travel times, and even increase air pollution.

As this chapter will show, there are several factors that render these policies and proposals unrealistic. Despite heavy investment in efforts to control growth, in urban areas around the country:[3]

- Higher population density *increases* traffic congestion.

- Higher population densities *increase* air pollution.

- Travel times *increase* where there are higher densities.

- Access is *retarded* by higher densities because travel times increase.

- Demand for personal mobility (and automobiles) cannot be transferred to public transit, bicycles, or walking.

- Building sufficient highway capacity to accommodate traffic growth is possible.

- Higher highway user taxes are not likely to materially reduce urban automobile use.

Before any state, regional, or local government decides to invest heavily in transit to solve the problem of traffic congestion, it would be wise to consider the fact that new transit systems have not resulted in any material reduction in traffic congestion in the United States.

## EFFECTS OF POPULATION DENSITY ON TRAFFIC

Increasing population density is fast becoming the mantra of the smart growth movement. Yet, data on traffic in the United States and anecdotal information from around the world indicate clearly that traffic congestion is worse where population densities are higher. Traffic congestion in America tends to get worse as established urbanized areas increase in population.

One accurate measure of traffic congestion is the Roadway Congestion Index (RCI) developed by the Texas Transportation Institute for the Federal Highway Administration.[4] The Index compares an urban area's roadway capacity with its traffic demand. An RCI score of more than 1.00 indicates that an urban area's roadway capacity is insufficient for its traffic

**Notes:**

3. See Texas Transportation Institute, *Roadway Congestion Index,* 1996. Portland is already suffering the consequences of its new urbanist policies. Traffic congestion has increased at a much faster rate than the national average. Among urban areas of similar or smaller size, only the San Bernardino–Riverside area of Los Angeles and the fast-growing area around Las Vegas had higher Roadway Congestion Index scores in 1996.

4. *Ibid.* The Roadway Congestion Index is computed by dividing total traffic volume (number of vehicles) per roadway lane in an urbanized area by the capacity of the lane. Where demand exceeds supply, a number above 1.00 is obtained. Where there is an excess of roadway capacity, a number below 1.00 is obtained.

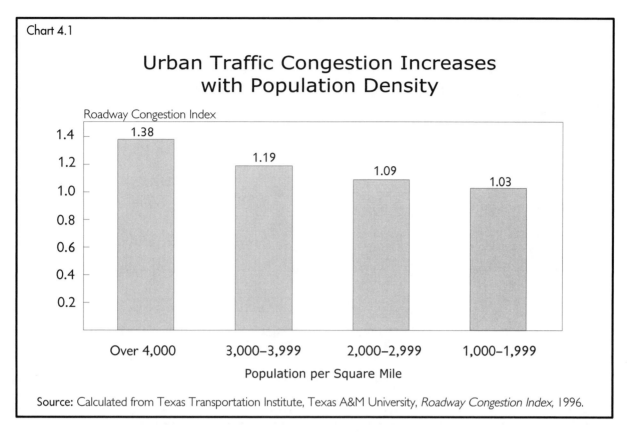

Chart 4.1

## Urban Traffic Congestion Increases with Population Density

Roadway Congestion Index

Population per Square Mile

**Source:** Calculated from Texas Transportation Institute, Texas A&M University, *Roadway Congestion Index*, 1996.

demand, and thus traffic is excessive; an index score of less than 1.00, on the other hand, would mean that there is more roadway capacity than traffic demand—which is a desirable situation. In 1996, urbanized areas with low population densities—less than 2,000 residents per square mile—had an average RCI score of 1.03. Although this is not ideal, it is considerably lower than the 1.38 of urbanized areas with more than 4,000 residents per square mile, such as New York and Los Angeles.[5]

As Chart 4.1 illustrates, the congestion index tends to increase exponentially as population density increases. The difference in RCI score between the 1,000 to 1,999 category and the 2,000 to 2,999 category is approximately 5 per-

cent. Between 2,000 to 2,999 and 3,000 to 3,999, the difference in score rises to 9 percent; and between 3,000 to 3,999 and 4,000 and above, it escalates to more than 15 percent.[6]

As urban area density increases, so do vehicle miles traveled per square mile (see Chart 4.2). In urban areas with population densities greater than 4,000 per square mile (such as Chicago, Los Angeles, Miami, New York, San Francisco, and San Jose), vehicle miles traveled per square mile is more than double that of urban areas with population densities of 1,000 to 1,999 per square mile.

Although comparable data on international traffic congestion are not available, it appears that traffic congestion is considerably greater in

## Notes:

5. An urbanized area is a developed area that includes a central city of at least 50,000 and has an overall population density of 1,000 per square mile or more. In this chapter, the term "city" will be used only to refer to a legal jurisdiction, such as the city of Los Angeles or the city of Pasadena (a relatively small part of the Los Angeles urbanized area).

6. A similar conclusion was reached by David T. Hartgen and Daniel O. Curley, *Beltways: Boon, Bane or Blip: Factors Influencing Changes in Urbanized Area Traffic, 1990–1997* (Charlotte, N.C.: University of North Carolina–Charlotte, Center for Interdisciplinary Transportation Studies, August 1, 1999).

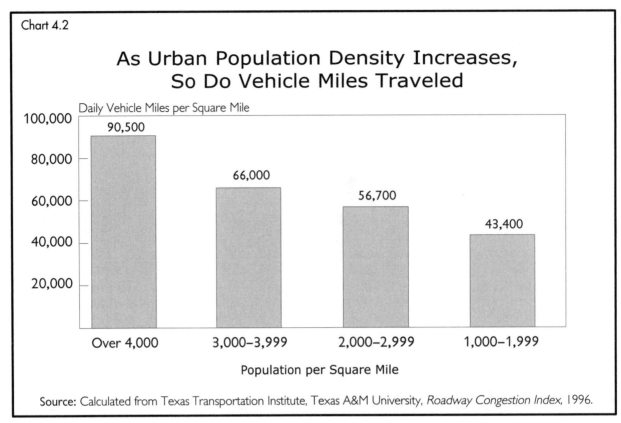

Chart 4.2

## As Urban Population Density Increases, So Do Vehicle Miles Traveled

Daily Vehicle Miles per Square Mile

Population per Square Mile

**Source:** Calculated from Texas Transportation Institute, Texas A&M University, *Roadway Congestion Index,* 1996.

foreign urban areas that have higher densities, such as Hong Kong, London, Paris, and Tokyo, than it is in U.S. urban areas, which tend to be less dense. Tourists can certainly attest to the greater traffic congestion in these foreign metropolitan areas compared with those in America.

### Density and Automobile Travel Time

As the above observations show, because smart growth or new urbanist proposals would increase traffic congestion, travel time will only increase if those policies are adopted. And for the average motorist, these policies will make the current problem more severe. Even if residents in denser urban areas realize slightly shorter average miles per trip, their time spent in the automobile will increase.

People tend to perceive travel in terms of time more than distance. They are more likely to be frustrated by the stop-and-go traffic that is typical of dense urban centers than by the free traffic flows that occur in urban areas with greater roadway capacity. Shortening the distance traveled while maintaining or even increasing travel time will not be perceived by travelers (and voters) as progress.

Evidence of this is the fact that average work-trip commute times have changed only modestly since the early 1980s. In 1983, the average work trip was 18.2 minutes, compared with 20.7 minutes in 1995. Over the same period of time, the average travel speed for work trips rose 20 percent, from 28 to 33.6 miles per hour.[7] People are going slightly longer distances but driving faster. As traffic congestion increases, people respond by moving farther away from congested areas. This is rational behavior: As traffic gets worse, people make choices that make their automobile commutes easier.

### Notes:

7. U.S. Department of Transportation, *Our Nation's Travel: 1995 NPTS [Nationwide Personal Transportation Study] Early Results Report,* 1997.

## Density and Access to Destinations

Even if a new urbanist policy did not reduce congestion, could it improve people's ability to reach their desired destinations conveniently, whether they be places of employment, shopping malls, or other locations? New urbanist policies are expected to improve access by shortening travel distances; homes, shopping destinations, and employment would be located closer together. Some trips might involve walking or bicycling.

Yet it is difficult to imagine that walking and bicycling will replace automobile trips to any great extent in the United States. The distances and travel times of trips are generally too long, and weather conditions can be unsatisfactorily cold, humid, or rainy. Nor is it plausible to expect that Americans will develop the high-density, apartment-based urban areas that are necessary to make walking and cycling feasible for any but a small number of trips.

The fact is that new urbanist policies will not improve access for two key reasons:

*First,* they will increase traffic congestion, and thereby increase travel time.

*Second,* those who switch to public transit generally will find that they have to walk farther at each end of their trip to reach their destinations. Moreover, commuters will find that their work trip—the journey that transit is most effective in providing—requires nearly twice as much time as it would if they drove.

- According to the U.S. Department of Transportation's 1995 *Nationwide Personal Transportation Study,* average automobile (personal vehicle) work-trip travel time was 22.9 minutes, while average public transit work-trip travel time was 41.6 minutes.[8] Even in Paris's urban area—which has more than double the population density of any U.S. urban area and perhaps the West's most comprehensive public transit system—transit times are more than twice that of automobile travel times.[9]

New urbanist policies are incapable of improving access for the overwhelming percentage of Americans.

## Density, Traffic Speed, and Air Pollution

America has been reducing air pollution from mobile sources (street and highway traffic) significantly. Increasing the density of urban areas will stop that progress.

Chart 4.3 shows that, as vehicle miles traveled have increased, air pollution has gone down. From 1970 to 1997, carbon monoxide emissions dropped 43 percent, volatile organic compound emissions fell by 60 percent, and nitrogen oxide ($NO_x$) emissions were reduced 5 percent.[10] At the same time, total vehicle miles traveled increased more than 130 percent.[11] Even in Los Angeles, which has had the worst air pollution in the nation, significant progress has been made. From 1976 to 1998, the number of days per year on which federal ozone standards were violated fell by nearly 70 percent,[12] despite a more than 75 percent increase in traffic volumes.[13]

Moreover, revolutionary automobile technologies are on the horizon that are likely to reduce air pollution further. Honda and Toyota are now marketing hybrid gasoline-electric vehicles that substantially increase gasoline mileage and reduce air pollution. A number of manufacturers are working on fuel cell propulsion technol-

## Notes:

8. U.S. Department of Transportation, *Nationwide Personal Transportation Study,* 1995.
9. Christian Gerondeau, *Transport in Europe* (Boston: Artech House, 1997), p. 226.
10. Calculated from data from the Environmental Protection Agency, *National Air Pollutant Emission Trends Update: 1970-1997,* March 1999.
11. U.S. Department of Transportation, *National Transportation Statistics 1998* and *Highway Statistics 1997.*
12. Southern California Air Quality Management District, "Historic Ozone Air Quality Trends," at *http://www.aqmd.gov/smog/o3trend.html.*
13. Estimated from Federal Highway Administration data.

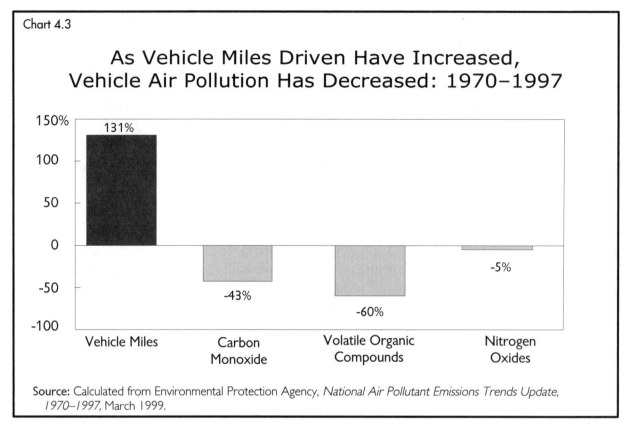

Chart 4.3

## As Vehicle Miles Driven Have Increased, Vehicle Air Pollution Has Decreased: 1970–1997

**Source:** Calculated from Environmental Protection Agency, *National Air Pollutant Emissions Trends Update, 1970–1997,* March 1999.

ogy that would be non-polluting. Honda has announced that it will market fuel cell automobiles in California by 2003.[14]

Nonetheless, it will take at least two decades for the nation's vehicle fleet to be converted; hence, mobile source pollution will continue to be a concern. Moreover, increasing population densities will only make pollution worse for two reasons:

1. **Higher densities lead to more vehicle miles traveled per square mile and to more severe air pollution.** As Chart 4.4 indicates, urban areas with the lowest air pollution have population densities under 1,750 per square mile. Urban areas that have "extreme" air pollution have average population densities about

double that of the urbanized areas with no air quality problems.

2. **As traffic congestion reduces average speed, air pollution increases.** For carbon monoxide and volatile organic compounds, two of the three primary mobile source pollutants, the optimal average operating speed is approximately 55 miles per hour.[15] As average speed goes down, pollution increases. Nitrogen oxides are different: The optimum speed is 20 miles per hour, although little additional pollution is produced at speeds up to 45 miles per hour.[16] Thus, with respect to air pollution, the optimum operating speed for nitrogen oxides is approximately 45 miles per hour. Nationally, average work trip speeds are

## Notes:

14. "It's Official: Honda and Volkswagen Join California Fuel Cell Partnership," *Hydrogen and Fuel Cell Letter,* November 1999, at *http://www.hfcletter.com.*

15. Calculated from Environmental Protection Agency, Office of Mobile Sources, "AP42, Air Pollutant Emission Factors," at *http://www.epa.gov.*

16. Above 45 miles per hour, nitrogen oxide pollution increases more rapidly.

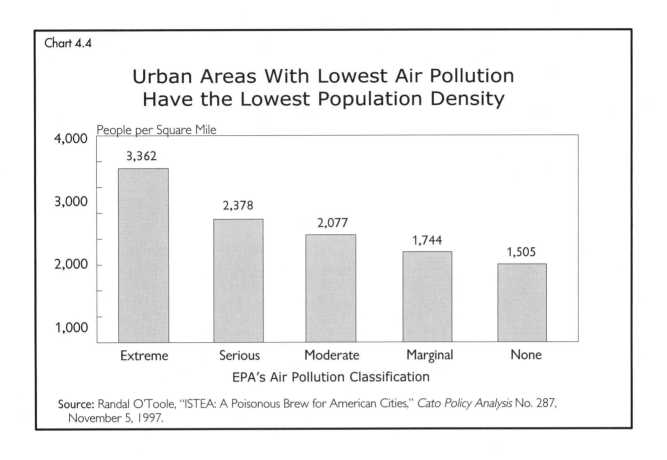

Chart 4.4

## Urban Areas With Lowest Air Pollution Have the Lowest Population Density

People per Square Mile

EPA's Air Pollution Classification

**Source:** Randal O'Toole, "ISTEA: A Poisonous Brew for American Cities," *Cato Policy Analysis* No. 287, November 5, 1997.

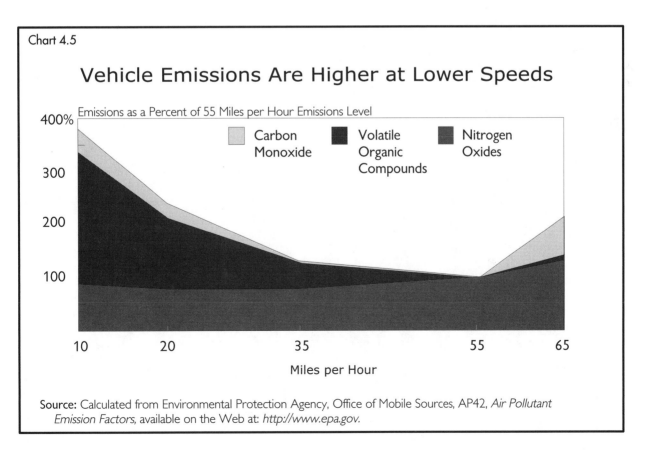

Chart 4.5

## Vehicle Emissions Are Higher at Lower Speeds

Emissions as a Percent of 55 Miles per Hour Emissions Level

Carbon Monoxide   Volatile Organic Compounds   Nitrogen Oxides

Miles per Hour

**Source:** Calculated from Environmental Protection Agency, Office of Mobile Sources, AP42, *Air Pollutant Emission Factors,* available on the Web at: *http://www.epa.gov.*

less than 34 miles per hour,[17] indicating that air pollution generally could be improved by increasing average automobile operating speeds. (See Chart 4.5.)

## IS TRANSIT THE SOLUTION?

Smart growth strategists presume that transit-oriented commercial and residential development, along with higher densities, will reduce reliance on automobiles significantly. The data suggest otherwise.

A favored strategy is the use of surface[18] light rail or trolleys. Light rail is a new adaptation of the electric trolley technology that most cities had abandoned by the 1960s. The theory is that light rail will get people out of cars; indeed, it is sometimes claimed that light rail can carry the equivalent of six or more lanes of freeway traffic.

A number of U.S. urban areas have opened new trolley systems in the past two decades. None of the new trolley systems carries more than 35 percent of the traffic volume of the typical freeway lane; the average is 20 percent.[19] Even during peak hours, the impact is slight. In Portland, which is often cited as a major light rail success, the trolley carries barely 40 percent of the volume of each adjacent freeway lane.[20]

The comparatively small ridership on transit has had even less of an impact than the numbers suggest. Studies generally show that one-half or more of transit ridership simply transferred from riding the bus.[21] A number of systems offer free rides within downtown areas, but these do virtually nothing to reduce traffic congestion during peak hours. And many new riders are former passengers in car pools. The actual number of passengers that were former automobile drivers tends to be approximately 22 percent.[22]

As a result, the new trolley systems have had virtually no impact on traffic congestion on adjacent freeways. For example, traffic volumes on Interstate 84, adjacent to Portland's eastside trolley line, have increased 70 percent since the light rail opened—more than any other radially oriented freeway in the Portland area.

Finally, light rail is very expensive. With respect to virtually all new systems, it would have been less expensive to lease each new commuter a car in perpetuity—in some cases, a luxury car, such as a Jaguar XJ8 or a BMW 740i.[23]

Light rail has failed to reduce traffic congestion for two fundamental reasons:

1. **Light rail is slow.** New systems average less than 18 miles per hour.[24] Even dur-

## Notes:

17. U.S. Department of Transportation, *Nationwide Personal Transportation Study,* 1995.
18. Generally, "surface" refers to non-grade separated rights-of-way, though the system often operates in exclusive rights-of-way.
19. "New Light Rail Volumes Compared to Freeway and Arterial Lanes," *The Urban Transport Fact Book*, at *http://www.publicpurpose.com/ut-fwy&lrt.htm* (December 1998).
20. "Peak Light Rail Volumes Less Than Freeway Lane: Portland and St. Louis," *The Urban Transport Fact Book*, at *http://www.publicpurpose.com/ut-lrt-pk.htm* (March 1999).
21. *Ibid.*
22. Calculated from data in Metropolitan Washington Council of Governments, *The First Four Years of Metrorail: Travel Changes*, September 1981, and San Diego Association of Governments, *The San Diego Trolley: The First Three Years*, November 1984; and Jonathan E. D. Richmond, *New Rail Transit Investments—A Review* (Cambridge: John F. Kennedy School of Government, Harvard University, 1998). Even the 22 percent overstates light rail's contribution to traffic congestion, since not all diverted automobile trips are during peak congestion periods. Further, many people who have switched from driving still use their cars to reach the light rail lines. For these, light rail has not eliminated an auto trip; it has merely made time in the car shorter.
23. "Comparison of Light Rail Cost per New Trip and the Cost of Leasing or Buying a New Car," *The Urban Transport Fact Book*, at *http:// www.publicpurpose.com/ut-newcar.htm* (April 1999).

ing congested peak hours, it takes 50 percent to 100 percent longer to complete work trips by rail than by automobile. Other forms of transit, such as subways and express buses, are faster than trolleys but still generally are slower than automobiles.

2. **Light rail provides auto-competitive trips to only a small part of an urban area.** This is a disadvantage shared with other forms of transit, even the far more expensive and rapid heavy rail systems ("subways" or "metros"). The frequent, no-transfer (express) service that is capable of attracting automobile-commuting workers goes only into historic downtown areas (that is, downtown areas established before 1930). This is because only the historic downtown areas have sufficient employment densities to allow large numbers of people to walk to work from transit stops. It is true that transit accounts for a significant market share in some historic downtown areas—nearly 75 percent in Manhattan, 60 percent in Chicago, and more than 25 percent in Boston, Brooklyn, Philadelphia, Pittsburgh, San Francisco, Seattle, and Washington, D.C.[25] However, historic downtowns are no longer the dominant regional employment centers. On average, barely 10 percent of employment in major metropolitan areas is in downtown

areas. Even the world's largest central business district, in New York City, accounts for less than 20 percent of metropolitan employment.[26]

Transit represents a much smaller share of work trips to employment centers located outside the downtown area. Commuters traveling to other locations, such as edge cities or secondary business centers, invariably find that using transit service means time-consuming transfers, often in uncomfortable weather conditions, and slow, non-express operation.

> Light rail is very expensive. It would have been less expensive to lease each new commuter a car in perpetuity.

As a result of these factors, transit commuters other than those commuting to and from a downtown area usually are those who have no access to automobiles because of low income. Transit riders commuting to locations other than downtown typically have incomes 40 percent below average.[27]

This is not to suggest that grade-separated urban rail[28] (rail that has no at-grade road, rail, or pedestrian crossings) cannot make a material contribution in some applications. Where population densities are extremely high, such as in Hong Kong (250,000 per square mile), or where central business districts are exceptionally large, such as in New York, London, Paris, and Tokyo (with approximately 1 million to 2 million people employed), rail can make a significant difference in traffic congestion. Ridership is so high in London and Tokyo that these systems earn an operating profit (in London's case, this is

**Notes:**

24. Calculations using data from Federal Transit Administration, "National Transit Database," 1996.
25. Data from the U.S. Census, 1990.
26. "Employment: Major US Central Business Districts," *Demographic Briefs*, available at *http://www.demographia.com/dm-uscbd.htm* (December 1999).
27. The Public Purpose, "Average Income of Commuters: Public Transport & Single Occupant Auto: Metropolitan Areas with the 25 Largest Central Business Districts (Downtowns)," *The Urban Transport Fact Book*, at *http://www.publicpurpose.com/ut-25cbd$.htm* (October 1998).
28. This excludes light rail, except where largely grade-separated because of slow operating speeds.

before depreciation). Even so, traffic conditions in these urban centers are far worse than in most U.S. urbanized areas. By comparison, U.S. urbanized areas have population densities of less than 6,000, and the largest central business districts outside New York have less than one-fifth its employment level.

The futility of trying to reduce traffic congestion with new rail strategies is illustrated in Atlanta. Over the past 20 years, Atlanta has opened the nation's fastest operating metro (subway or heavy rail)[29] system, which extends more than 45 miles, has 36 stations, and cost approximately $3 billion. Yet only downtown Atlanta has direct, no-transfer service from throughout the area, and less than 1 percent of the urban area is within walking distance of a rail station.[30] Meanwhile, traffic volumes have more than doubled over the same period, and Atlanta receives considerable publicity for having some of the worst traffic congestion nationally. (See Chapter 10.)

The mode of public transit responsible for virtually all of transit's modest ridership increase since 1980[31] is commuter rail—conventional inter-city rail service that primarily serves distant suburbs from a single downtown station. Ironically, commuter rail encourages

> **Transit is not a substitute for urban automobile travel because it is structurally incapable of taking enough people where they want to go.**

longer commutes downtown and, as a consequence, has been an agent of urban de-concentration, rather than urban concentration.

Despite the new rail systems, more than 99 percent of new travel in major U.S. metropolitan areas during the 1990s was by automobile. The urban areas most successful in encouraging transit travel have been New York (where less than 5 percent of new travel is by transit) and Boston (3 percent transit). Transit in Portland and St. Louis, which have been widely promoted as light-rail success stories, accounts for less than 2.5 percent and 1 percent of new travel, respectively. Similar trends have been occurring in Europe and Japan, where automobile market shares have been rising strongly since the early 1970s.[32] Transit is not a substitute for urban automobile travel because it is structurally incapable of taking enough people where they want to go in a time that competes with automobile travel.

### Transit as Urban Development Strategy

Light rail is often promoted as a mechanism of urban development. The theory is that light rail should concentrate real estate development in the urban areas, thereby reshaping a city into spatial patterns that reduce automobile depen-

**Notes:**

29. Metro systems tend to operate at somewhat higher speeds than light rail, which makes them more attractive to automobile users for the small percentage of potential trips for which they are competitive. Average heavy rail operating speed is 21 miles per hour, compared with an average speed of 17 miles per hour for the new light rail systems (calculated from the National Transit Database information).
30. The area within walking distance (one-quarter mile) of a rail station is approximately 7 square miles, out of an urbanized area of 1,785 square miles.
31. From 1980 to 1997, travel by commuter rail increased from 6.5 billion to 8.4 billion passenger miles. Travel on all other modes of public transit combined decreased from 33.4 billion to 32.9 billion passenger miles over the same period. Commuter rail uses rail cars similar to conventional intercity (Amtrak) rail coaches and typically operates to a single downtown station, with suburban stations spaced at longer intervals than light rail or metro systems.
32. "Passenger Travel By Mode: European Union, Japan and the United States: 1994," *The Urban Transport Fact Book*, at *htpp://www.publicpurpose.com/ut-eujus.htm* (August 1997).

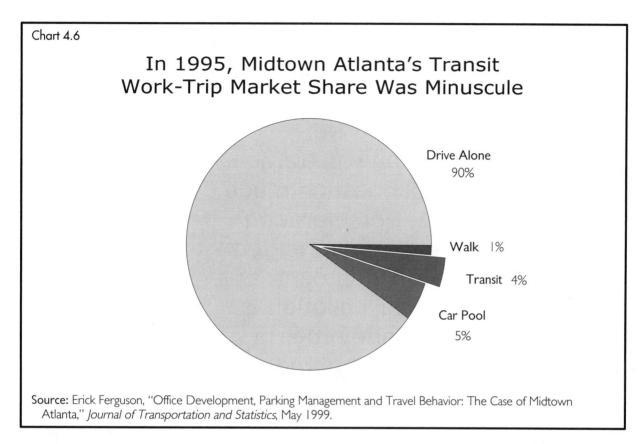

Chart 4.6

## In 1995, Midtown Atlanta's Transit Work-Trip Market Share Was Minuscule

Drive Alone
90%

Walk 1%

Transit 4%

Car Pool
5%

**Source:** Erick Ferguson, "Office Development, Parking Management and Travel Behavior: The Case of Midtown Atlanta," *Journal of Transportation and Statistics*, May 1999.

dency, while generating more favorable traffic levels and improving access. Portland's planners, for example, predicted that light rail would result in a "reurbanization" of the light rail corridor. Density would increase along the corridor, growth would slow outside the corridor, and automobile use and ownership would decline.[33] In fact, nothing of the sort has occurred. But as Chapter 9 shows, automobile usage has continued to increase at a far greater rate than has transit use, and light rail development has been heavily subsidized. Growth continues to be concentrated in outlying areas, not along the light rail corridor.

Light rail has not reshaped the cities because it has not generated significant transit-related real estate development. The majority of development cited by light rail promoters has taken place through government projects or tax-subsidized projects. Portland and St. Louis built publicly financed stadiums and convention centers (as have cities without light rail, such as Charlotte, Detroit, Minneapolis, and Seattle). Portland's transit-oriented residential developments received tax subsidies and tax abatements. The city of Portland now grants 10 years of property tax abatement for developments within walking distance of light rail stations. Tax and subsidy policy, not light rail, is the engine behind such real estate development.

Light rail–oriented development will make traffic and air pollution worse, not better, because the overwhelming majority of trips to new developments will continue to be taken by automobile. Atlanta's Midtown is served by the Metropolitan Area Rapid Transit Association

## Notes:

33. S. M. Edner, G. B. Arrington, Jr., *Urban Decision Making for Transportation Investment: Portland's Light Rail Transit Line* (Washington, D.C.: U.S. Department of Transportation, 1985), in Peter Newman and Jeffrey Kenworthy, *Cities and Automobile Dependence: An International Sourcebook* (Aldershot, U.K.: Gower Technical, 1991).

(MARTA) metro system. It can be classified as transit-oriented commercial development, yet more than 95 percent of those who commute to this growing employment center do so by automobile, not transit (see Chart 4.6).[34]

Virtually the same problem exists with respect to transit-oriented residential development. For example, the transit-oriented development around the Ballston, Virginia, subway station (near Washington, D.C.) is five times as dense as in neighboring communities and generates four times as many vehicle trips per acre.[35] Not only is traffic congestion made worse around transit-oriented development, but air pollution is one order of magnitude worse, because of the inevitably slower average speed of vehicles commuting in the area.

> Not only is traffic congestion made worse around transit-oriented development, but air pollution is one order of magnitude worse.

If transit were able to "reshape" cities, then it would already be working in Washington, D.C., and in Atlanta, where a total of nearly $15 billion has been spent to build expensive heavy rail systems radiating out from downtown. Because of their higher operating speeds and the number of lines that have been built, they have encouraged far greater development than could be expected from the slower and more limited light rail systems. And indeed, at a few suburban stations, office and residential construction has occurred. But transit's share of work trips at these locations is far lower than in the downtown historic areas. The overwhelming percentage of commuting to the new jobs has been by automobile. As a result, traffic congestion throughout the Washington and Atlanta urbanized areas is among the worst in the nation.[36]

## HIGHWAYS AND CONGESTION

In contrast to transit's failure to deliver on its promises, highways and roads still offer the most convenient, timely, and cost-effective mode of surface transportation for most Americans. Yet opposition to building more highways is a fundamental tenet of the smart growth and new urbanist strategies. These proponents argue that building new roads is futile because they simply fill up; in other words, they induce more demand. Two studies are often cited to demonstrate that accommodating traffic by building more roadways is pointless:

- The first study, published in *Transportation Research A*, concluded that the mere provision of additional capacity causes people to drive more than they would otherwise.[37] Specifically, the researchers found that if the number and length of freeway lanes are increased by a specific percentage, freeway traffic increases by almost as much. This pattern is referred to as "induced demand." This study and others cause some to believe that it is impossible to "build our way out of congestion," that is, to deal with traffic congestion by building more roads.

- A report by the Surface Transportation Policy Project (STPP)[38] analyzed 70 urbanized areas (those studied in the 1996 Texas Transportation Institute Roadway Congestion Index survey). Dividing the urban areas

### Notes:

34. Erick Ferguson, "Office Development, Parking Management and Travel Behavior: The Case of Midtown Atlanta," *Journal of Transportation and Statistics*, May 1999.
35. "Transit Oriented Development (TOD): Vision and Reality," *Innovation Briefs*, May–June 1999.
36. In 1996, Washington had the second highest Roadway Congestion Index and Atlanta had the seventh highest.
37. Mark Hansen and Yuanlin Huang, "Road Supply and Traffic in California Urban Areas," *Transportation Research A*, Vol. 31 (1997).

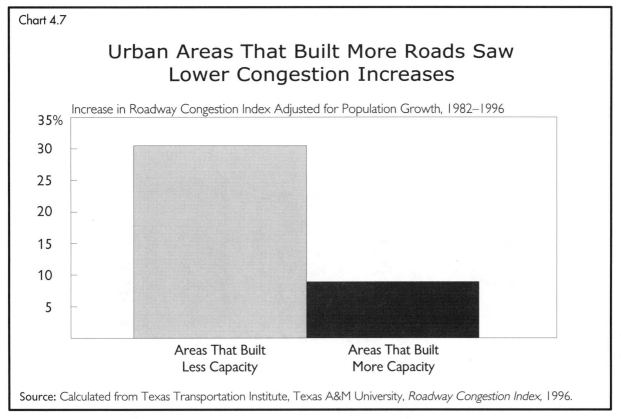

Chart 4.7

## Urban Areas That Built More Roads Saw Lower Congestion Increases

Increase in Roadway Congestion Index Adjusted for Population Growth, 1982–1996

Areas That Built Less Capacity

Areas That Built More Capacity

**Source:** Calculated from Texas Transportation Institute, Texas A&M University, *Roadway Congestion Index,* 1996.

into two groups (those that built more roads and those that built fewer between 1982 and 1996), the STPP found that the one-half of the urbanized areas that had built fewer new roadway miles had approximately the same congestion index as those that had built more.

However, both of these studies are flawed, and other evidence suggests that additional roadways are necessary to reduce traffic congestion. The *Transportation Research A* study was limited to freeways and did not quantify the impact of freeway expansion on adjacent arterials and other surface streets. When freeways are opened, drivers are likely to switch to them from slower routes. It is likely that a large percentage of the "induced demand" found by the researchers was simply travel that transferred to the new routes from other roadways.[39]

The STPP report failed to note that, while the congestion index scores for the two sets of cities were approximately the same, in fact the congestion index in urbanized areas that built fewer roads had increased by one-third more than it had in those that built more roads. Moreover, the STPP failed to account for differences in population growth—the areas that built more roadway had increased in population by 15 percent more than the areas that built less roadway (see Chart 4.7).

If merely providing more highways generated additional traffic, then per capita street and highway travel should have increased signifi-

## Notes:

38. Surface Transportation Policy Project, *An Analysis of the Relationship Between Highway Expansion and Congestion in Metropolitan Areas: Lessons from the 15-Year Texas Transportation Institute Study,* Washington, D.C., November 1998.

39. One advantage of building freeways is improved safety. In 1994, fatalities per 100 million passenger miles were 60 percent lower on freeways than on the rest of the roadway system (calculated from data from the Federal Highway Administration).

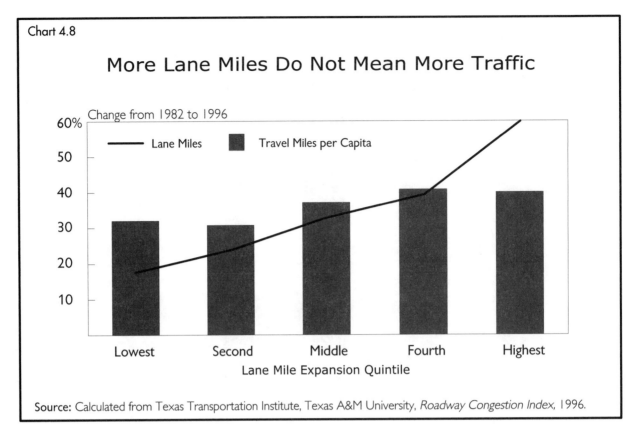

Chart 4.8

## More Lane Miles Do Not Mean More Traffic

Change from 1982 to 1996

— Lane Miles   ■ Travel Miles per Capita

Lane Mile Expansion Quintile: Lowest, Second, Middle, Fourth, Highest

Source: Calculated from Texas Transportation Institute, Texas A&M University, *Roadway Congestion Index,* 1996.

cantly more in the urbanized areas that had expanded their highway systems faster. This, however, is not the case.[40] As Chart 4.8 shows, urban areas that expanded their roadway lane miles the most saw only modestly higher per-capita increases in the amount of street and highway travel. The quintile that expanded the lane miles the most saw 24 percent more travel than did the lowest quintile. This is barely one-tenth the rate of roadway expansion (240 percent).

A similar conclusion was reached recently by a University of North Carolina–Charlotte study, which found that the building of beltways around urban areas was not a material factor in increasing traffic volume. Doing so may con-tribute to lower overall traffic levels because they provide additional roadway capac-ity.[41] There is a rather weak and insignificant relationship between roadway expansion and the increase in per capita vehicle miles trav-eled.[42] It is possible to build sufficient highway capacity to accommodate demand.

This is not to suggest that there may not be a small increase in miles traveled as a result of new roadways. Faster roadways make it possi-ble for people to gain access to more distant locations without increasing their travel time. This may encourage longer trips, but the actual time traveling is not likely to increase—as illus-trated by the fact that the time of the average journey to work has changed little in recent

### Notes:

40. Analysis of Texas Transportation Institute, *Roadway Congestion Index* data, 1982 to 1996, for urban areas of more than 1 million population.
41. Hartgen and Curley, *Beltways: Boon, Bane or Blip.*
42. Lane miles per capita is used to factor out the traffic volume–increasing impact of a larger population. A regression analysis found the relationship between lane miles added and the change in vehicle miles per capita to be not statistically significant in urban areas of more than 1 million people ($r^2$ of 0.009, number of cases = 40).

years. As traffic congestion worsens, people make adjustments so that their travel times do not materially increase.

Other circumstantial evidence supports the view that building roads is a reasonable way to deal with traffic congestion. Planned freeways were canceled in a number of communities, such as Chicago, Los Angeles, and Washington, D.C., in the 1960s and 1970s. Today, these three urbanized areas have the greatest traffic congestion. Such cancellations were often conscious decisions made in a policy environment that did not anticipate that traffic congestion would become much worse as a consequence. The intervening quarter-century has proven just that.

Thus, while it may not be popular to say so, *the fundamental cause of traffic congestion in U.S. urbanized areas is insufficient road space.* Generally, the most congested urbanized areas have lower ratios of lane-miles to population. For example, Kansas City is one city that has ample lane miles in relation to population (with a Roadway Congestion Index of 0.81). If all urbanized areas with congestion indexes greater than 1.00 had the same ratio of lane miles to population as has Kansas City, then all but one would have a congestion index lower than 1. This would be true even of Los Angeles (see Table 4.1).

These figures indicate that additional roadway capacity could be built to accommodate virtually any reasonably anticipated increase in traffic. Many cities that have failed to add capacity have experienced increasing traffic congestion as a result.

America's urban freeway system was largely designed for a time and traffic volume that has long since passed. The interstate highway system, which comprises most of the urban freeway mileage, was designed in the middle 1950s to accommodate traffic volumes anticipated in 1975. Few new urban roads have been added to that system and a number have been canceled.

Further, there is more to the problem than the need for new roads to accommodate an increase in demand. The nature of the demand has changed. Many elements of the 1975 system in place are simply not sufficient to deal with the changing travel patterns and higher traffic volumes. For example, in many cities interstate highways become narrower in the downtown areas, reflecting the 1950s assumption that a significant amount of the traffic would exit to access downtown employment. It seemed that lesser capacity was required *through* downtown areas. Yet, downtown areas now have a relatively small portion of metropolitan employment, and much of the traffic in downtown-oriented corridors travels through, not to, downtown.

> While it may not be popular to say so, the fundamental cause of traffic congestion in U.S. urbanized areas is insufficient road space.

Similarly, the 1975 system was designed to radiate out from the downtown area, again on the assumption that downtown was the primary focus of automobile traffic. This is no longer the case. In fact, in some suburban areas, comparatively little non-radial freeway capacity has been built, but arterial systems that could ease congestion are often disconnected and have low traffic-volume capacities.

## Higher Highway User Fees

It is popular to ascribe to the automobile a whole host of "social" costs that are not paid by users. These range from the medical costs of air pollution to uninsured accident losses, estimated excess costs of time spent in traffic, and even the value of the time spent shopping for cars.[43] Some new urbanists propose charging some or all of these social costs to motorists through highway user fees.

Most attempts to quantify the social costs of the automobile are comparatively silent about

Table 4.1

## 1996 Roadway Congestion Index if Selected Urbanized Areas Had the Same Lane Miles per Capita as Kansas City

| | Actual Roadway Congestion Index for 1996 | Index Value if Area Had Same Lane Miles per Capita as Kansas City |
|---|---|---|
| Los Angeles CA | 1.57 | 0.85 |
| Washington DC-MD-VA | 1.43 | 0.72 |
| Chicago IL-Northwestern IN | 1.34 | 0.51 |
| Miami-Hialeah FL | 1.34 | 0.67 |
| San Francisco-Oakland CA | 1.33 | 0.74 |
| Seattle-Everett WA | 1.27 | 0.79 |
| Detroit MI | 1.24 | 0.75 |
| Atlanta GA | 1.24 | 0.96 |
| San Diego CA | 1.23 | 0.75 |
| San Bernardino-Riverside CA | 1.22 | 1.04 |
| Las Vegas NV | 1.20 | 0.40 |
| New York NY-Northeastern NJ | 1.18 | 0.41 |
| Portland-Vancouver OR-WA | 1.16 | 0.56 |
| Phoenix AZ | 1.14 | 0.67 |
| Minneapolis-St. Paul MN | 1.12 | 0.65 |
| Denver CO | 1.12 | 0.72 |
| San Jose CA | 1.11 | 0.81 |
| Houston TX | 1.11 | 0.76 |
| Dallas TX | 1.11 | 0.81 |
| Baltimore MD | 1.09 | 0.69 |
| Boston MA | 1.09 | 0.62 |
| New Orleans LA | 1.09 | 0.45 |
| Cincinnati OH-KY | 1.07 | 0.71 |
| Sacramento CA | 1.07 | 0.73 |
| Philadelphia PA-NJ | 1.07 | 0.39 |
| St. Louis MO-IL | 1.05 | 0.86 |
| Milwaukee WI | 1.03 | 0.58 |
| Ft. Lauderdale-Hollywood-Pompano Beach FL | 1.03 | 0.56 |
| Cleveland OH | 1.02 | 0.59 |
| Fort Worth TX | 1.01 | 0.79 |
| Columbus OH | 1.01 | 0.71 |
| Indianapolis IN | 1.00 | 0.82 |

Note: Table includes urbanized areas with Roadway Congestion Indexes of 1.00 or higher in 1996. Calculation uses freeway equivalent lane miles. Arterial lanes are weighted at their capacity of 0.386 freeway lane miles.

Source: Calculated from Texas Transportation Institute, Texas A&M University, *Roadway Congestion Index*, 1996.

its social benefits, which may well be far greater than the social costs. Because they assume that the automobile is costly to society, new urbanists want to increase the cost of operating automobiles substantially. They believe that this will encourage people to use more socially beneficial modes of transport, such as transit, walking, and bicycling. The new urbanists assume that because petroleum is underpriced in the United States, auto use is being subsidized. Although petroleum currently costs less in the United States than it does in Europe and Japan, virtually all of the difference between higher foreign petroleum prices and the U.S. prices is taxation. Taxes represent 85 percent or more of the retail price in Europe. Even in the United States, a significant portion of the retail price of gasoline is highway user fees or taxation. And, despite assertions to the contrary, highway user fees are approximately equal to what is spent building, maintaining, and administering the nation's streets and highways.[44]

Raising the price of gasoline is not likely to reduce driving by a significant amount. Europe proves the point. Due to heavy taxation, gasoline prices in Europe are up to five times higher than they are in the United States. European cities are far more compact and have far more comprehensive public transit systems than does the United States. Destinations are more concentrated in European cities. Automobiles are significantly more expensive. Yet 78 percent of travel in Europe is by automobile, a figure not far behind the 85 percent figure in the United States. In Japan, which has more concentrated cities with higher densities than does Europe, high gasoline prices, even more comprehensive public transit systems, and very expensive tollways between cities, automobile use is expanding at a rapid rate.[45]

> It would be as accurate to characterize Americans as having a love affair with the refrigerator or the air conditioner as it is to suggest their love affair with the automobile.

## Persistent Demand for Auto Travel

It is often suggested that Americans have a "love affair" with the automobile. But Americans have no choice. The dispersed land-use patterns of U.S. urban areas and dispersed trip patterns render transit incapable of competing for all but a small portion of trips. Walking and bicycling are even less competitive because of the long travel distances in U.S. urban areas. The automobile is a prerequisite in all but a few enclaves of the United States[46] and a large portion of western Europe.[47] It is a modern convenience that enhances the quality of life. It would be as accurate to characterize Americans as having a love affair with the refrigerator or the air conditioner as it is to suggest their love affair with the automobile. Like people around the world, Americans continually seek a better quality of life. In that equation, the automobile plays an important part.

**Notes:**

43. Mark Delucci, *Annualized Cost of Motor Vehicle Use in the United States*, Institute of Transportation Studies, University of California, Davis, 1996–1997.
44. Public Purpose, *The Highway and Motorway Fact Book*, at *http://www.publicpurpose.com/hwy-us$93&c.htm*.
45. See *http://www.publicpurpose.com/ut-eujus.htm*.
46. Examples are Manhattan and Chicago's "Gold Coast."
47. Which includes dense central cities such as Paris. Europeans in the suburbs rely heavily on automobiles, just as they do in American suburbs, because transit is incapable of providing sufficient access to the desired destinations.

The new urbanists' preoccupation with attracting people away from automobiles into transit has failed. Between 1975, the first year of federal transit operating subsidies, and 1997, annual passenger miles in automobiles have increased by more than 1 trillion. Transit passenger miles have increased 1/500th of this amount, despite spending more in subsidies than was required to build the interstate highway system.[48] During the 1990s, transit passenger miles declined slightly, while automobile passenger miles continued to increase.

The continued growth in automobile travel is driven by a number of factors, including population growth, a disproportionate increase in the number of licensed drivers, and increasing use of automobiles by women (as automobile travel rates by women converge on those of men).[49] Further, automobile availability is spreading to lower-income citizens (disproportionately minorities, such as African–Americans and Hispanics) and could result in a "democratization" of mobility and access.[50]

Nonetheless, the unparalleled mobility and access provided by the automobile cannot be made available to all. Some disabled people and low-income people remain without access to automobiles. For the disabled who are not able to operate automobiles, public transit's paratransit services (dial-a-ride) represents an effective, though comparatively expensive, option. Since World War II, transit service has increasingly served this social function, which could emerge over the long run as the dominant function of transit in the American urban area.

## Consumer Resilience

Consumer surveys confirm that traffic congestion is the biggest problem for most people in the suburbs. In today's city, only the automobile can meet the needs of the nation's urban dwellers. Public transit service is competitive only in a narrow range of niche markets, such as downtown employment trips and trips to major sporting events. Walking and bicycling are not credible alternatives for most people. The dispersed nature of origin–destination patterns in the modern city makes the automobile the only mode of transport capable of meeting the mobility and access needs of U.S. urban dwellers.

New urbanist policies that create higher population densities and higher development densities will increase both traffic congestion and air pollution. They will increase travel time while making the driving experience more frustrating. For the overwhelming percentage of the population, transportation access will be retarded and the quality of life worsened. Maintaining the quality of life in the more dense communities will require building considerably more intense roadway systems.

Drivers have proven to be resilient with respect to traffic congestion, adjusting their travel patterns to minimize the impact of congestion (as, for example, finding longer but faster routes). They will continue to be resilient. Moreover, many employers are responding with flexibility in scheduling and telecommuting. Ironically, the less convenient driving environment that new urbanist policies would create could provide yet another artificial impetus to suburbanization, as people move farther into rural areas and smaller urban areas. Fifty years ago, Phoenix and Las Vegas were not among the nation's 50 largest urban areas. Fifty years from now, if present urban areas reject growth, urban areas now unknown to most Americans could be among the largest in the nation.

### Notes:

48. "US Public Transport Subsidies from 1960," *The Urban Transport Fact Book*, at *http://www.publicpurpose.com/ut-ussby.htm*

49. Don Pickrell and Paul Schimek, "Growth in Motor Vehicle Ownership and Use: Evidence from the Nationwide Personal Transportation Survey," *Journal of Transportation and Statistics*, May 1999.

50. Alan E. Pisarski, *Cars, Women and Minorities: The Democratization of Mobility in America* (Washington, D.C.: Competitive Enterprise Institute, 1999).

## LESSONS LEARNED

The choice for planners, then, is between two fundamentally different policies:

1. Not to accommodate the inevitable increase in demand for automobile travel and hope that people can be attracted to (or herded into) alternative modes of travel, such as transit, bicycles, and walking (such wishful thinking will result in more intense traffic congestion and air pollution and retard the quality of life), or

2. To accommodate the inevitable increase in automobile demand, which will reduce traffic congestion and air pollution while improving the quality of life. This seems the better choice for the driving and voting public.

The evidence indicates clearly that there is only one option if Americans hope to improve the quality of urban and suburban life—and that is to accommodate the inevitable increase in demand for personal vehicle travel. The solution is to provide additional roadway capacity, and to use roadways more efficiently.

Successful implementation of these two strategies can reduce the time that people spend in automobiles by increasing average operating speeds. It will improve air quality by increasing average speeds toward the optimum 45 miles per hour. Each strategy will be aided by the demographic and telecommunications trends of the future. However, there is a need for additional research to better quantify the extent to which road infrastructure is required to support the various patterns of urban and suburban development likely to occur.

### Expanding Roadways

The first order of business should be to expand roadways where appropriate. The following steps should be considered:

- **New Roadways**. Both freeways and arterial roads should be built to serve growing suburban areas where most of the population increases are occurring. It is particularly important to provide cross-suburban capacity to augment the often substantial radial (downtown-oriented) capacity. Because these areas are the least dense and are still developing, new roadways are less likely to intrude upon residential and commercial development.

- **Expansion of Existing Roadways**. In many corridors, there is sufficient space to add lanes to existing freeways with little need to acquire right-of-way. In some cases, urban freeway systems are considerably under-built with four- or six-lane roadways. In a number of areas, states are using funding from the Transportation Equity Act for the 21st Century (TEA–21) to rebuild urban freeways. This opportunity should be taken where capacity is insufficient. Somewhat more intrusive roadway expansions are possible, including double-decker freeways as in Austin and San Antonio or building two-deck freeways above major surface arterials, such as Tokyo and Osaka have done.

- **Elimination of Traffic Bottlenecks**. Expanding capacity at the nation's 18 most congested freeway interchanges would save commuters an average of nearly 40 minutes per day while reducing local mobile source air pollution significantly.[51]

  Moreover, there is a need to provide controlled access interchanges between toll roads and other limited-access highways. For example, travelers in the northern Philadelphia suburbs on Interstate 95 and the Pennsylvania Turnpike, two high-volume highways, are required to use surface roadways to go from one to another. Similarly, no direct access is provided between the

### Notes:

51. Cambridge Systematics, Inc., *Unclogging America's Arteries: Prescriptions for Healthier Highways*, (Washington: American Highway Users Alliance), November 1999.

Santa Ana Freeway in Orange County, California, and a new toll road.

- **Limited-Access Commercial Bypasses.** As new retail and employment centers are built in developing areas, the surface arterials on which they are located become congested. Traffic congestion could be relieved by building new bypass roadways that may or may not be grade-separated but on which entrance and egress is controlled. These arterials would be similar to the New Jersey surface expressways described below.

- **High Occupancy Toll Lanes.** High occupancy toll (HOT) lanes allow faster trips for people willing to pay a toll for access to a less crowded lane (or to carpool). The benefits extend to the entire freeway. Southern California's Route 91 HOT lane improved operating speeds on the adjacent freeway lanes as well, reducing peak period congestion by one hour in each direction each day.[52]

- **High Occupancy Vehicle (HOV) lanes** can be effective in high-volume radial (downtown-oriented) corridors. They are considerably less costly than urban rail systems but they carry higher volumes of travelers.

- **Metroroute Tunnels.** A minimally intrusive mechanism for expanding roadway capacity is the Metroroute, a single tunnel carrying two decks of automobile traffic. Limiting access would allow the tunnel to have a smaller diameter, which would make it considerably less costly. Paris, with the Western world's most intensely developed urban rail system, is planning to build 60 miles of under-city tunnels to alleviate traffic congestion.[53] Despite exceedingly high costs, city leaders recognize that additional capacity must be provided for increasing travel demand. As in Paris, the high cost of construction could be financed by tolls.

- **Truck Freeways.** Exclusive roadways can be built in congested corridors for commercial, largely truck, traffic. Such a system has been proposed for the Los Angeles area to be financed by tolls.

## Improving Roadway Efficiency

**Traffic Management.** In addition to adding roads, a number of strategies are available to facilitate more efficient use of roadway systems—that is, to increase a system's speed and capacity without requiring physical expansion. For example, improving traffic management would increase roadway capacity. This can be accomplished through:

- **More Turn Lanes.** Right- and left-turn lanes and protected left-turn movements at busy intersections would speed the movement of traffic through intersections and reduce congestion.

- **Metering Freeway Entrance Ramps.** Metering of freeway approaches (on ramps) from surface arterials can smooth and optimize the flow of traffic.

- **Creating Surface Expressways.** Surface arterials can be converted into "surface expressways" by limiting at-grade crossings to intersections that have signals and by forcing drivers on access roads who want to turn left to go off the road at the right. New Jersey pioneered this strategy decades ago on surface roadways such as US 1 and US 22. Las Vegas has considered a similar concept called "super streets."

**Intelligent Transportation Systems.** Another approach involves investing in intelligent transportation systems. These systems, which use emerging information and telecommunications technology to improve traffic movement, include:

- **Computerized Traffic Signal Controls** to optimize traffic flow through busy intersections.

## Notes:

52. "Express Lanes Hit Break Even," *Public Works Financing*, Vol. 120 (July/August 1998).
53. Gerondeau, *Transport in Europe.*

- **Computerized Navigation Systems**, already available in some cars, can guide drivers to alternate routes to avoid traffic congestion.

- **Improved Accident Reporting and Response Systems** to minimize traffic disruption. Accidents and other incidents cause 10 percent more freeway traffic delays than insufficient freeway capacity.[54]

- **Collision Avoidance Systems.** On-board safety systems that provide collision warnings to drivers or even prevent collisions are likely to be available in the near future.

- **Vehicle Guidance Systems.** Technology to increase the "throughput" capacity of congested roadways includes "automated highway" systems, which would assume control of automobiles in congested freeway corridors. In effect, the automated highway system would operate as interactive speed control (cruise control), which would make it possible to reduce distances between cars while still maintaining safety. This could more than double traffic capacities where applied. Implementation of such systems is at least a decade away.

- **Automated Tolls.** Automated tolling systems are eliminating traffic congestion caused by toll booths. Toronto's outer beltway (Route 407), for example, uses a system that allows electronic collection of tolls while vehicles pass at full speed.

- **Electronic Road Pricing,** which would replace or supplement today's system of funding roads by gasoline tax with charges based on miles driven or peak-period use. Higher user charges during peak travel periods would divert some vehicle travel to less congested times of the day. This technology is in use in Singapore.

In addition, further research is needed in roadway system and capacity design. It would be useful for roadway capacity guidelines to be developed to accommodate the variable travel demands of different urban and suburban densities and land-use configurations. These guidelines could be used by growing communities to ensure that sufficient roadway capacity is available as population increases, especially in suburban areas where the more limited system of non-radial freeways and arterials is often inadequate.

The U.S. Department of Transportation has a large research budget, and funds are also available from the states. Transportation-related institutes at universities and research organizations should direct their attention to quantifying methods for accommodating the inevitable increase in travel demand. Local officials, who face the frustration of the voters most directly, should encourage the research community to undertake these programs.

## Competitive Provision of Roadway Systems

Because of advances in automated tolling and electronic road pricing, it is possible for communities to franchise their roadway systems. This would de-politicize the provision of roads while improving their efficiency. A community could specify standards, such as average speeds, service levels, safety considerations, and capacities, and then open the roadways to competitive bidding. An important consideration will be to make the conversion to competitive road franchising "revenue neutral," so that users do not pay both road user fees and fuel taxes.

At the same time, roadway authorities should develop plans to improve road systems to accommodate the growing demand for travel. This is not without difficulty. In congested suburban areas, it will be necessary to build and expand roadways through developed areas. However, the mistakes of the 1960s and 1970s—such as the failure of government to tell the public the consequences of canceling planned freeways—should not be repeated. The public deserves to be made aware of the possi-

**Notes:**

54. Calculated from Texas Transportation Institute, *Roadway Congestion Index* data, 1996.

ble choices. If there is insufficient political will to take the actions necessary in such areas, at least a choice will have been made based upon complete and reliable data. In developing areas, it will be easier to accommodate the traffic volumes. But forward-looking officials and developers should take the initiative in this effort.

### Emerging Trends

While all these steps should be explored and further research conducted, there are indications that the worst traffic congestion may be over. Future traffic growth may be considerably lower than in the past. At least three trends support this conclusion:

- Demographic trends that have been driving the rapid expansion of traffic largely have passed. Women now drive nearly as much as men, the ratio of vehicles to drivers has reached saturation levels, and the overwhelming majority of adults hold driver's licenses.[55]

- Drivers are accommodating their travel patterns to traffic congestion. People will continue to choose their residential and employment locations in ways that minimize inconvenience.

- Internet commerce and telecommuting are increasing their market shares, which is likely to reduce the demand for shopping and employment travel.

### THE FUTURE OF TRANSPORTATION

Traffic congestion is not the product of sprawl. On the contrary, traffic congestion is a cause of sprawl as people move to more sparsely populated areas to escape excessive traffic. The problem is that all too often in these more remote suburbs, roadway systems designed for rural volumes have not been upgraded to accommodate a growing population.

Without an aggressive strategy for adding sufficient roadway capacity, policies that increase the density of population and development will be counterproductive. Whatever decisions are made about density, public officials need to develop plans for the reality of life in the future, rather than for idealized notions that will require behavioral and developmental changes. Experience demonstrates that such changes are simply not going to materialize.

### Notes:

55. Pisarski, *Cars, Women, and Minorities.*

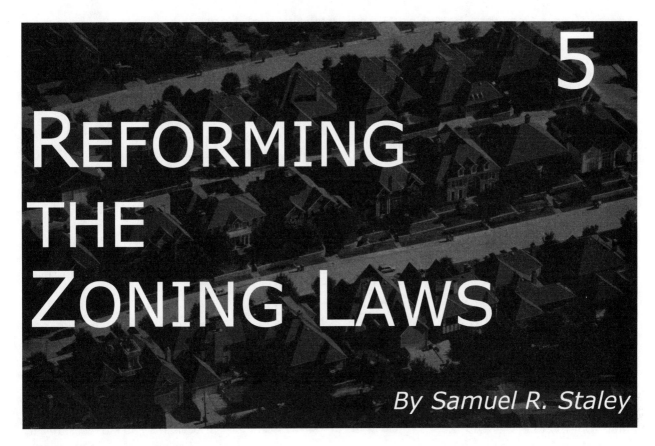

# 5

# REFORMING THE ZONING LAWS

*By Samuel R. Staley*

The United States has entered a new political era: For the first time, land use and growth management have emerged as key national policy issues. Although little action on these issues has occurred at the federal level, state and local governments across the nation are grappling with problems of growth and the political hornet's nest these issues have created.

The new infusion of planning has increased pressure to use land more "efficiently," which usually means using less land, increasing residential and commercial densities, allowing for mixed uses in the same sections, and relying more heavily on public transportation. When actual implementation is tried, however, this planning approach known as "smart growth" is encountering rough water. Even Berkeley, California, often considered the bulwark of progressive politics, has rejected higher densities because they threaten the community's character and quality of life.

It is important to clarify the shortcomings of today's planning and zoning policies and the flaws in today's smart growth planning alternative, and then to identify a more market-ori-

ented, consumer-choice approach. Such an approach would allow local officials to employ changing land uses as a building block for community development.

The current system based on land regulation, planning, and zoning contributes to so-called suburban sprawl by encouraging or requiring large lots, low density, wide roads, and single-use concentrations. Current planning suffers from two other major flaws:

*First,* the current system attempts to use the planning process to achieve an "ideal" vision of the community 20 or 30 years into the future. As a practical matter, this is impossible, given the dynamic nature of the American economy. Already, telecommuting accounts for the equivalent of 50 billion passenger miles of travel annually, 25 percent more than all mass transit in the United States.[1] The explosion of e-commerce (online Internet purchases, trading, and marketing) is ushering in a revolution in retailing and dramatically changing the role geography plays in consumer buying patterns.[2]

*Second,* current planning imposes high costs on property owners who want to respond to changing social and market realities. Under

61

most development regulations—whether they are zoning ordinances or subdivision regulations—virtually every major project is subjected to the vagaries of rezoning and the uncertainties associated with discretionary review by a planning commission and, ultimately, a city council. The planning process creates unnecessary costs and delays and inhibits valuable investments in land as communities evolve and grow over time. At the same time, the present planning and zoning process often fails to protect those who live adjacent to new developments—even though this was one of the original goals of zoning.

Modern planning tools often rely on master plans that are rarely updated. Columbus, Ohio, for example, adopted its first zoning code in 1923, but did not update it comprehensively until the 1950s, and did not update that re-write until 1992. In other cases, cities try to plan for growth and land-use changes that may be impossible to predict. Cary, North Carolina, for example, had a population of just 43,858 in 1990 but almost doubled its size to 82,700 by 1997 and is expected to grow to 209,308 by 2010.

These master plans unrealistically presume that local and regional governments can predict and control future land-use patterns. This presumption limits the ability of communities to adapt spontaneously and efficiently to changing needs and preferences. Once land uses are established by ordinance in the zoning map, and deviations from the zoning map must be

> Master plans unrealistically presume that local and regional governments can predict and control future land-use patterns.

reviewed and approved by planning commissions and city councils, innovation becomes an uphill battle.

Ironically, these characteristics of modern zoning practices are impeding many of the smart growth prescriptions, which require deviations from traditional zoning in response to changing consumer tastes. However, the danger is that smart growth advocates, whose ideas are popular in intellectual circles, will succeed in simply replacing the current rigidity with new equally rigid rules. This would be unfortunate, since many smart growth prescriptions diverge from family housing preferences, according to recent data. Neither the rigid planning of the past nor the prescriptions of the smart-growth advocates necessarily fit the changing patterns of today's consumers.

Surveys of home buyers and consumers consistently find that Americans prefer homes in larger lots (a quarter-acre or more) in low-density neighborhoods. When the National Association of Home Builders recently surveyed 2,000 households nationwide, 83 percent said that they would prefer buying a single-family detached home in an outlying suburban area rather than a townhouse of the same price in an urban setting.[3] The same survey also found that 54 percent would oppose building townhouses in their neighborhood and 78 percent would oppose building multifamily housing.[4] Forty percent would strongly oppose higher-density residen-

## Notes:

1.  The Buckeye Institute for Public Policy Solutions, *If You Build It, Will They Ride? The Potential for Rail Transit in Ohio's Major Cities*, Columbus, Ohio, October 1999, p. 27.
2.  Joel Kotkin, "The Future of the Center: The Core City in the New Economy," Reason Public Policy Institute *Policy Study* No. 264, November 1999, pp. 30–38.
3.  National Association of Home Builders, *Smart Growth: Building Better Places to Live, Work and Play*, Washington, D.C., 1999, p. 16.
4.  *Ibid.*

tial development of single-family homes, while 37 percent said they would simply oppose multifamily housing.[5]

At the same time, however, Americans are living in slightly higher densities than they did in the recent past. The average lot size has fallen from 10,000 square feet in 1990 to 9,100 square feet in 1996, almost a 10 percent decline.[6] The size of new homes increased over eight years from 2,000 square feet in 1990 to almost 2,200 square feet in 1998.[7] Buyers prefer larger homes, but will accept smaller lots. A trend toward higher density is also evident in the increasing demand for cluster-home developments, where houses are placed on smaller lots to preserve larger tracts of publicly or privately maintained open space such as parks or farmland.[8] (See Chapter 8.) Only flexible and open-ended planning can respond adequately to the changing desires on the part of consumers.

## TO PLAN OR NOT TO PLAN?

Today, planning has taken on an increasingly prominent role, partly because planners have extended their influence from the local to the regional and state levels. More than 19 states have adopted some form of statewide growth-management law or addressed the issues of farmland preservation and development through state-level task forces.[9] Oregon and Florida, in particular, are lauded as examples of effective statewide planning because they fea-

> Only flexible and open-ended planning can respond adequately to the changing desires on the part of consumers.

ture strong centralized control over land development and enforcement of state planning goals. Under most state plans, cities, villages, and townships are empowered to create master plans (usually with 10- to 20-year time horizons) that are consistent with the planning goals and objectives established by the state.[10]

A typical master plan usually encompasses all types of land uses (e.g., residential, commercial, industrial, and open space). It does the following:

- **Segregates** uses into separate zones even when demand exists for mixing them;

- **Specifies** very precisely the types of uses allowed, leaving little up to spontaneous evolution of the market or community;

- **Adopts** a long time horizon, often 20 or more years;

- **Prohibits** market adjustments to land-use trends and demand; and

- **Presumes** political decisions over future development of the community are superior to economic decisions.

In essence, modern planning often attempts to convert "open" systems, where property markets adjust spontaneously to changes in demand, to "closed" systems, where changes must be approved by a local planning agency and conform to a master plan. The view is that

**Notes**:

5.  *Ibid.*

6.  National Association of Home Builders, at *http://www.nahb.org.*

7.  *Ibid.*

8.  See Samuel R. Staley, "The Sprawling of America: In Defense of the Dynamic City," Reason Public Policy Institute *Policy Study* No. 251, January 1999.

9.  *Ibid.*

10. John DeGrove and Patricia Metzger, "Growth Management and Integrated Roles of State, Regional, and Local Governments," in Jay M. Stein, ed., *Growth Management: The Planning Challenge of the 1990s* (Newbury Park, Cal.: Sage Publications, 1993), p. 6.

if cities, communities, and neighborhoods can be "designed" or engineered in the right way, they will function properly.

Initially, zoning ordinances were justified on the premise that proper planning could mitigate the impacts of nuisance from industrial and commercial development, although zoning was often used as a defensive strategy in many cities to preserve the status quo.[11] Theoretically, by separating land uses, zoning could alleviate nuisances from industrial and commercial development by preventing incompatible land uses (e.g., a factory and a home) from locating near each other, diminishing property values, and reducing the overall quality of life.

The pervasiveness of zoning—almost all major cities have zoning and comprehensive plans in place—can be attributed to three factors. One is genuine concern over nuisances; the others are the ability to target benefits to special-interest groups (e.g., developers or anti-growth activists) through the rezoning process,[12] and the widespread belief that central planning can solve urban problems by regulating land use and urban design.

While the goals of conventional zoning and planning are lofty, the reality of plan implementation diverges significantly from the ideal. One indicator is the cost of implementing plans. Surveys of the impact of zoning and other land-use controls suggest that local regulations add 20 percent to 30 percent to the cost of housing.[13] Moreover, planners are absorbed by the "business of planning"—the implementation and enforcement of the master plan—and rarely have time to focus on larger strategic issues such as how public facilities and services affect land-use patterns. A survey of 178 California cities, for example, found that land-use permit processing and rezoning accounted for almost 60 percent of planners' time.[14] Planners surveyed spent less than 10 percent of their time in general-plan preparation—that is, broad planning that guides the overall development of a town. Because zoning codes and comprehensive plans are not updated to reflect contemporary trends and realities, unobtrusive uses can be frozen out of development simply because they differ modestly from uses 20 years ago.

Modern planning also has spawned an unbounded politicization of decision-making regarding land use. Builders and developers must face detailed scrutiny of projects, down to the colors on outside walls, signage, and materials used, often for purely aesthetic reasons. Public hearings allow significant delays as organized interest groups bog down project approval. The mere expression of a concern can prompt delays and costly studies and investigations financed by a prospective builder or developer. This is because zoning confers development rights on property irrespective of actual, tangible impacts (see Chapter 2).[15]

## Notes:

11. See, for example, the overview in John M. Levy, *Contemporary Urban Planning*, 2nd ed. (Englewood Cliffs, N.J.: Prentice-Hall, 1991), pp. 41–43.

12. James Clingermayer, "Distributive Politics, Ward Representation, and the Spread of Zoning," *Public Choice,* Vol. 77, No. 4 (1993), pp. 725–738.

13. Anne B. Shlay and Peter H. Rossi, "Putting Politics into Urban Ecology: Estimating Net Effects of Zoning," in Terry Nichols Clark, ed., *Urban Policy Analysis: Directions for Future Research* (Beverly Hills, Cal.: Sage Publications, 1981), pp. 257–286; Norman Karlin, "Zoning and Other Land Use Controls," in M. Bruce Johnson, ed., *Resolving the Housing Crisis: Government Policy, Decontrol, and the Public Interest* (San Francisco: Pacific Institute for Public Policy Research, 1982), pp. 35–55; Lawrence Katz and Kenneth Rosen, "The Interjurisdictional Effects of Growth Controls on Housing Prices," *Journal of Law and Economics,* Vol. 30, No. 1 (April 1987), pp. 149–160; Farhad Atash, "Local Land Use Regulations in the USA: A Study of their Impacts on Housing Cost," *Land Use Policy,* Vol. 7, No. 3 (1990), pp. 231–242; Jane H. Lillydahl and Larry D. Singell, "The Effects of Growth Management on the Housing Market: A Review of the Theoretical and Empirical Evidence," *Journal of Urban Affairs,* Vol. 9, No. 1 (1987), pp. 63–77.

14. Linda C. Dalton, "The Limits of Regulation: Evidence from Local Plan Implementation in California," *Journal of the American Planning Association,* Vol. 53, No. 2 (Spring 1989), p. 156.

Take the following case: A veterinary clinic that would have served small domestic animals on an outpatient basis was not allowed to move into a suburban Midwestern community because local zoning would not accommodate a change in use. The preferred property was a residence on a major road leading into the city's historic downtown. Community growth and evolving land-uses along the corridor had reduced the building's desirability as a home (few families want to locate near busy roads). However, the community's zoning code could not allow the small-scale, unobtrusive commercial use of the property as a veterinary clinic without rezoning that would create legal entitlements to develop the property for more intrusive uses, such as video or convenience stores. Although this particular property probably would not have been suitable for those uses, shortages of land available for those uses (also a byproduct of zoning) encourage the redevelopment of residential buildings for intensive, high-traffic purposes.

As a result, the planning board rejected the rezoning request. The community lost a viable business that would have maintained the residential character of the neighborhood, and the property owner (a retiree) was unable to capitalize on the full market value of his home.

These regulatory obstacles apply to projects larger than small veterinary clinics. New urban architects Andres Duany and Elizabeth Plater-Zyberk found that local planning and zoning codes held back innovative design. "Regulatory

**Modern planning also has spawned an unbounded politicization of decision-making regarding land use.**

codes lie at the heart of Duany and Plater-Zyberk's work," observes architect and author William Lennertz. "Early in their work they realized that existing zoning ordinances—more than economics or planning and design philosophies—were impediments to achieving more urbane communities."[16] "The traditional pattern of walkable, mixed-use neighborhoods has been inadvertently proscribed by these ordinances."[17] An alternative framework, rooted in a market-oriented approach to development regulation, would have examined the proposals based on their impacts on neighbors and potential for generating a nuisance rather than the particular use of the property.

Developers are also given little latitude in determining what kinds of infrastructure may be most appropriate for projects. Often, high-cost infrastructure mandated by local codes exceeds a project's needs. For example,

- Local governments sometimes specify roads with lane-widths appropriate for interstate highways (12 feet). Such lane-widths impose higher costs but are unnecessary for safety or smooth traffic flow on residential streets.

- Local storm drainage regulations require piping large enough to accommodate flows many times greater than any calculated necessary capacity.

- Many communities also require site landscaping according to prescriptive rules

**Notes:**

15. See Robert H. Nelson, "Zoning Myth and Practice—From Euclid into the Future," in Charles M. Harr and Jerola S. Kayden, eds., *Zoning and the American Dream: Promises Still to Keep*, (Chicago: Planners Press, APA, 1989); William Fischel, *The Economics of Zoning Laws: A Property Rights Approach to American Land Use Controls* (Baltimore: Johns Hopkins University Press, 1985).
16. William Lennertz, "Codes," in Alex Krieger and William Lennertz, eds., *Andres Duany and Elizabeth Plater-Zyberk: Towns and Town-Making Principles* (Cambridge, Mass.: Harvard University Graduate School of Design, 1991), p. 96.
17. *Ibid.,* p. 102.

rather than allowing site developers to landscape according to what is prudent and aesthetically attractive to potential buyers and tenants.

- Subdivision regulations in many regions of the country require that roads have concave crowns (that is, roads bow upward) to force stormwater to drain to pipes on both sides of the road. Yet new technology and materials permit lower-cost convex crowns toward the center line where one pipe drains stormwater.

As a result of these and other rigid and costly rules, few communities have the flexibility to accommodate innovative community development ideas. Deregulating the property market in a responsible way can go a long way toward promoting more efficient land use and address the concerns of many opponents of suburbanization and so-called suburban sprawl.

Unfortunately, it appears that neotraditional planning of the sort spurred by smart growth advocates, fails to move toward market-driven development. Architect and urban designer Peter Calthorpe provides 12 guiding principles for new urban or neotraditional planning, but then goes on to provide detailed design specifications for nine core characteristics of communities: ecology and habitat, core commercial areas, residential areas, secondary areas, parks and plazas, streets, pedestrian movement, the transit system, and parking requirements. Calthorpe's design criteria show what buildings should look like, how much space should be

> **Deregulating the property market in a responsible way can promote more efficient land use and address the concerns of many opponents of sprawl.**

allocated to parks and at what scale, and where specific uses should be located in what density, and take consumer support on faith.

Indeed, a crucial tenet of the current smart growth movement is that markets need government guidance to avoid excess and irrational investments in housing and land. Farmland preservation was one of the primary reasons Oregon implemented regional planning and urban growth boundaries in the 1970s.[18] Controlling sprawl was one of the primary reasons Florida adopted its statewide growth management system in the mid-1980s.[19]

## THE MARKET-ORIENTED ALTERNATIVE

The alternative to the present rigid, top-down system is market-oriented planning. Market-oriented planning retools the approval and rezoning process to facilitate market trends while protecting the interests of neighbors and community residents, as conventional zoning is supposed to do but sometimes does poorly.

Markets force developers to respond swiftly to consumer preferences. To see how this process operates, consider this case. A developer proposed building a 26-unit housing development with average home prices in the range of $300,000 to $500,000. After two years, only 10 lots had sold. The houses that had been built were on the market for unexpectedly (and thus, unprofitably) long periods. So, the developer changed the design of the development. He decided to target the new lots and homes toward empty nesters. The market had sent a

**Notes:**

18. Deborah A. Howe, "Growth Management in Oregon," in Stein, *Growth Management*, pp. 61–75.
19. Randall G. Holcombe, "Growth Management in Florida: Lessons for the National Economy," *Cato Journal*, Vol. 10, No. 1 (Spring/Summer 1990), pp. 109–125; Reid Ewing, "Is LA-Type Sprawl Desirable?" *Journal of the American Planning Association*, Vol. 63, No. 1 (Winter 1997), pp. 107–126.

clear message to the developer about what consumers wanted and were willing to pay for.

Later, the developer returned to the local planning board to get approval for his concept on a cul-de-sac design. One of the planning board members noted that an area of the project had been redesigned to include a park where, previously, a small pond had been planned for aesthetic reasons. When asked why the pond was deleted, the developer said that, as he began to sell lots, he noticed that lots closest to the pond were not selling. The developer quickly determined that older couples considered these lots less desirable because the pond was a hazard for small children, particularly grandchildren. Once again, the developer was responding quickly to market signals. He substituted a park in place of a pond.

The developer used information from consumers to redesign his project in very subtle ways to provide a product that people wanted to buy. The market imposed "order" on the desires of the developer (and, in this case, the local planning board) through the profit and loss system of the land market.

Fortunately, in this case the local planning board was open to the desires of the consumer, as interpreted by the developer. The key is to provide a system for regulating land development that also allows for these spontaneous market adjustments while protecting neighbors and other residents from spillover effects and unintended consequences of development.

Market-oriented planning allows buyers and sellers to determine the general outline, pace, and details of development. Rather than make detailed decisions about projects, the planning process provides a general framework for market adjustments and adjudicating disputes when conflicts arise among property owners.

Market-oriented planning would allow a variety of densities, for example. For some homebuyers, higher densities may be attractive. In addition to taking up less space, smaller lots translate into less linear feet of roads, sewers, stormwater drainage pipes, and other infrastructure. Research by Robert W. Burchell and his colleagues at Rutgers University suggests road costs could be reduced by as much as 25 percent and utility costs by as much as 15 percent.[20]

In some cases, homebuyers simply want the larger lots and are willing to accept the extra infrastructure costs to obtain them. Larger lots are a social benefit that would be diminished by smaller-lot mandates. In other cases, however, the large lots are a product of outdated regulations, poor infrastructure pricing, and mandated minimum lot sizes in zoning codes.

Half-acre lot sizes are citywide standards in many Midwestern states. This lot size, however, was often established in the 1950s and 1960s, when homes were serviced by septic systems, and a half-acre was considered the minimal area needed to serve the waste needs of households adequately. Now, most cities are serviced by a citywide sewer system, and the original justification for the minimum lot size has disappeared. But the large lot standard persists. In these cases, local regulations may be imposing higher costs on homebuyers because they would prefer smaller lot sizes but the zoning code does not give them that choice.

Although Portland, Oregon, may be best known for its top-down, centralized approach to planning and development (see Chapter 9), it also provides important evidence of the ways

> **Markets force developers to respond swiftly to consumer preferences.**

## Notes:

20. Robert W. Burchell, Naveed A. Shad, David Listokin, *et al., The Costs of Sprawl—Revisited,* Transit Cooperative Research Program Report No. 39, Transportation Research Board (Washington, D.C.: National Academy Press, 1998), pp. 135–140.

real estate markets react to deregulation. In the early 1990s, pursuing its goal of increasing densities, Metro (the Portland-area planning agency) experimented briefly with freeing up the real estate market. It prevented city zoning codes from prohibiting "granny flats" (rooms in homes that could be rented out) and raising minimum lot sizes. The result was higher-density residential development without mandates. While this trend was encouraged by the regional urban growth boundary, which was becoming binding in the mid-1990s, the experience suggests that real estate markets might well develop at higher densities if they were allowed to operate more freely. Indeed, some economists have argued that densities are artificially low due to the restrictive nature of zoning codes.

A market-oriented approach embraces the open-ended evolutionary concept of the city. Thus, a market-oriented approach (unlike many current smart growth approaches) does not preempt or foreclose future development paths; it does not choose a high or low density, automobile-oriented or transit-oriented, single-use or mixed-use vision. Rather, it accommodates consumers as they respond to opportunities and choices made available through the real estate market.

In addition, rather than using broad-brush approaches to regulating land use and development, a market-oriented approach focuses on the specific issues and consequences of development rather than general concerns about potential impacts.

Several strategies could help public officials to accommodate changes in consumer and citizen wishes while helping prepare their community for the future:

## STRATEGY #1: Facilitate market trends; don't hinder them.

The view that communities can be designed or built according to some static, grand design is outmoded and inconsistent with real-world experience. Technology is radically changing the concept of the city and the role of geography in residential and commercial location. Home offices are occupying third and fourth bedrooms as residential space is transformed to business uses to accommodate family, personal, and professional demands. The pace of change is likely to increase as electronic commerce, the Internet, and innovation continue to alter patterns of buying, working, and living.

Nearly 20 years ago, Lloyd Rodwin, an internationally recognized planner and former chairman of the Department of Urban Studies and Planning at the Massachusetts Institute of Technology, recognized the ability of markets to organize and direct development in a more productive and efficient way. "In short," he wrote in his book *Cities and City Planning*, "it does not take great insight today [in 1981] to see that, however inadequate the market may be, there is no reason to suppose the urban planners will necessarily do a better job, at least in the short or intermediate term. This reality of the inadequacy of planners and their tools offsets the other reality of the inadequacies of the market and price mechanism."[21]

An alternative strategy is to harness the power of the property market to improve communities by allowing them to change over time in ways that allow consumers to achieve their wishes while maintaining long-term community stability. Local officials have a number of market-oriented policy options available to them.

- **"As of right" development.** Property development should be permitted "as of right." Under this doctrine, attempts to change land uses are automatically protected, unless the planning board or local legislative body takes explicit action to hold up approval for further evaluation. Project proposals should be subjected to public hearings only if city staff, council members, planning commission members, or parties directly affected by the project identify tan-

## Notes:

21. Lloyd Rodwin, *Cities and City Planning* (New York: Plenum Press, 1981), p. 230.

gible impacts on the interests of neighbors or the public sector. This can be coupled with maximum time limits for review by staff, planning commissions, or local legislative bodies. Market-oriented planning incorporates market impacts directly into the planning and development process. Developers would be required to notify neighbors and others directly affected by their proposed projects so that any harms or potential spillover effects can be identified and addressed directly.

- **Overlay Zoning Districts.** Several communities have opted to establish zoning "overlays" that provide for expedited review of development proposals if they achieve certain goals. An overlay is a regulation (e.g., a code or zoning district) that supersedes the underlying regulation under specific conditions. Most cites have zoning ordinances that mandate certain densities for residential neighborhoods. An overlay would allow for deviations from that standard under certain circumstances. For example, the city of Barberton, Ohio, developed an overlay district for neotraditional neighborhood development, or new urbanism, that minimizes the uncertainty of case-by-case review.[22] By meeting specific design and architectural review standards, new developments will receive automatic approval without discretionary review. Similar types of performance zoning have cut plan processing times significantly.

Overlays could be created for more conventional suburban site design. For example, an innovative concept called "coving" uses large front yard setbacks, home site location, and winding roads. These create larger public open spaces, enhance the feel of openness in the community, and reduce the costs of infrastructure (e.g., road, sewer, and water) by 10 to 20 percent.[23] The coving concept is more consistent with the traditional desire of suburban residents for open space near where they live but is sensitive to housing affordability and the costs of providing infrastructure. Developed by Minneapolis-based urban designer Rick Harrison, the coving concept is an innovative way to use planning to improve a sense of community in a suburban setting. Most of its features, however, would be prohibited by conventional zoning codes. (For more about coving, see Chapter 8.)

- **Mixed-Use Zoning.** Defining zones broadly to accommodate more than one use will allow communities to change and evolve. Mixed-use districts are an excellent mechanism for promoting diversity within communities. A less ambitious option would be to adopt broadly defined single-use zoning districts that allow for multiple land uses within and among zoning districts and categories. For example, commercial districts could allow a wide range of uses, from retail to professional offices to hospitals, universities, high-density residential or medium-density residential developments. Reducing the number of districts while broadening the number of uses permissible within each district would reduce processing and approval time by minimizing the likelihood a specific project will be subjected to the rezoning process.

- **Market-Determined Densities.** Communities should allow consumers to determine appropriate densities. This could be achieved through "performance zoning," a reform that establishes standards for congestion, landscaping, open space, and other design elements but does not spell out how the standards must be met. These standards are incorporated explicitly into the

### Notes:

22. John L. Gann, Jr., "Creating Modified TND in a Heartland Community," *Land Development,* Winter 2000, pp. 11–14.

23. "Coving Creates New Site Design," *Professional Builder,* March 1999, pp. 24–26; Rick Harrison, "Coving in Residential Subdivision Design," *Urban Land,* August 1998, pp. 41–43; Robert Sharoff, "A New Concept in Subdivision Layouts," *The New York Times,* February 15, 1998, p. Y41.

approval process. Alternatively, communities can avoid codified standards (standards established by ordinance) by adopting a nuisance-based approach to development regulation. Regulations would stop development only if nearby residents showed that they would experience a direct and harmful nuisance as a result and that it could not be mitigated through compensation, modification of the site design, or other adjustment to the project.

## STRATEGY #2: Make nuisance and third-party harm the focus of planning and development review.

Governments are most effective when they protect clear and definable interests. When activities impose costs on third parties—that is, people who are not directly involved in the activity—government or an independent private mediator may be required, if only to mediate between parties. Examples of these impacts include noise, air pollution, or traffic congestion caused by the activity. Also, in theory at least, markets may fail to provide enough of what are called "public goods," such as open space and habitat protection.[24]

As discussed earlier, the original intent of zoning was to protect neighbors against development that could reduce property values by imposing harms.[25] Zoning was upheld by the U.S. Supreme Court as an appropriate use of the "police powers" of government to protect the general welfare. However, before restrictive public intervention occurs, the negative impacts of property development should be demonstrable, and developers should be given the opportunity to correct for these impacts. To a limited degree, the rezoning and plan-approval process accomplishes this goal by vetting plans in public hearings. But the open-ended nature of this review today creates substantial uncertainties and delays, increasing development costs.

Furthermore, the approval process creates a bargaining environment in which developers and property owners must meet *all* concerns raised by elected officials, planners, and local citizens, regardless of their actual impacts. Often, proposed developments are scaled down to inefficient levels or are forced to adopt less innovative or aesthetically pleasing designs because developers must allay citizen opposition based on vaguely defined and unsubstantiated concerns over property values or "community impact."

Getting zoning approval is only one step in the process. The second step is negotiating what the final development will look like (the site-plan review). Thus, while the Santa Barbara coastal commission approved 95 percent of zoning requests, it allowed only 60 percent of the housing units proposed by the project developers.[26] In another case in the Midwest, vocal opposition from a grassroots slow-growth group led the local planning board to require that a new housing development hook up to a nearby city's sewer system, even though using a proposed septic system was both environ-

## Notes:

24. Even in these cases, if amenities are valued by consumers, developers have an incentive to provide them. Often, for example, apartments that face lakes or scenic areas rent for higher prices than apartments that face streets, driveways or other less picturesque scenes. Developers will provide lakes, ponds, open space, and other fields if they believe consumers are willing to pay to enjoy them. Thus, many planned communities represent attempts by developers to provide specific amenities and services through the private sector. See Fred Foldvary, *Public Goods and Private Communities: The Market Provision of Social Services* (Brookfield, Vt.: Edward Elgar, 1994).
25. This does not imply that politics was absent from the adoption of zoning laws. Historically, zoning ordinances were adopted in cities with ward-based election systems, suggesting that politicians adopted zoning to confer benefits on specific, geographically targeted constituencies. See Clingermayer, "Distributive Politics, Ward Representation, and the Spread of Zoning."
26. Bernard H. Siegan, "Land Use Regulations Should Preserve Only Vital and Pressing Government Interests," *Cato Journal*, Vol. 10, No. 1 (Spring/Summer 1990), pp. 127–158.

mentally safe and less expensive.[27] The requirement was added because of unsubstantiated fears, aired in public hearings, that the development would lower water pressure for nearby residents.

- **Nuisance Standards for Approval.** There is a traditional common law principle of nuisance, and this should be the standard for government regulation of private activity. Developers should be expected to modify projects to minimize the negative impacts of their proposed development, but these impacts should be tangible and measurable. Groundwater run-off or traffic congestion, for example, are identifiable and measurable impacts that can be assessed objectively. Developers should be expected to consider the neighborhood and third-party costs imposed by their project on neighbors and the community.

This focus differs from traditional zoning practice, which confers development rights on property owners regardless of the impact on adjacent property owners; therefore, this recommendation strengthens the role of the nearby neighbors.[28] It also differs from modern practice. The "use as of right" notion, embodied in traditional zoning, has become subject to manipulation through the political process, since regulation is not grounded in a common law principle. Today's review process requires modifications to projects even where impacts are trivial or represent purely subjective perspectives of local officials, citizens, and planners.

By contrast, a nuisance standard of the sort traditionally upheld by the courts would give the neighbor standing to insist on mitigation of or compensation for clearly substantiated damages resulting from the redevelopment. This approach requires demonstration of actual "harm" or impact in order to require compensation or "nuisance" mitigation. Thus, this approach enhances the role of planners as mediators within the community while still preserving spheres of autonomy for property owners.

By adopting administrative approval procedures that favor market trends in land development, the arbitrariness of development approval is minimized. By limiting standing in public hearings to directly affected property owners, the impact of special interests in the development control process is also minimized.

- **Limit Objections Based on Aesthetics.** Empirically, the impacts of spillover effects tend to be very localized, affecting close neighbors rather than entire neighborhoods or communities.[29] Thus broad citywide applications of development controls to specific projects should be avoided. Rather, regulatory control should be focused on the impacts of individual development proposals and projects. In general, planning and zoning approval should not control development for aesthetic reasons or concerns over layout and density unless the project is located in a district with a clear purpose, intent, and identity (e.g., historic districts or other special districts). Aesthetic issues are so general and so rarely have tangible impacts that they cannot be handled objectively through the planning process.

- **Preapplication Meetings.** "Preapplication" meetings with staff and planning boards can be effective ways to identify problems before significant resources have been invested in a project. Modifications are more efficiently incorporated at the early stages of the design process. Later changes

## Notes:

27. Samuel R. Staley, *Urban Planning and Economic Development: A Transaction Cost Approach*, Columbus, Ohio, The Ohio State University, doctoral dissertation, 1997, p. 119.

28. Fischel, *The Economics of Zoning Laws.*

29. J. M. Pogodzinski and T.R. Sass, "Measuring the Effects of Municipal Zoning Regulations: A Survey," *Urban Studies,* Vol. 28, No. 4 (1991), pp. 597–621.

can significantly increase costs. Mandatory preapplication meetings before developers make formal commitments can minimize some of these costs and lay the groundwork for a working relationship among developers, planners, and other public officials.

### STRATEGY #3: Adopt administrative rather than legislative reviews of development applications.

By subjecting development projects to legislative review, local governments are forced into a case-by-case review of land development irrespective of its impact on the community or neighborhood. Relatively minor and innocuous changes in use end up being subject to the same approval processes as large, integrated, mixed-use developments. Ultimately, this lengthens the approval process, slows land redevelopment, and subjects projects to an often arbitrary and unpredictable approval process.

Recent trends toward "ballot-box zoning," in which voters determine the fate of everything from rezonings to major projects (e.g., new housing subdivisions or shopping malls), is an unstable, uncertain, and slow approval mechanism. It can also be arbitrary and unfair. In the San Francisco Bay Area, a citizen-based planning group is promoting the concept that any development project that includes more than 10 housing units should be subject to voter approval.

When applied to economic decisions, political processes tend to generate inefficiencies as well as inequities. An analysis of 63 Ohio cities found that cities that use the ballot box on zon-

> **Ballot-box zoning, in which voters determine the fate of everything from rezonings to major projects is an unstable, uncertain, and slow approval mechanism.**

ing issues suffer a "growth penalty": Growth is lower in communities that place zoning decisions on the ballot.[30] In fact, the analysis found that communities with ballot-box referenda experienced lower growth whether the decision favored or opposed the proposed change. Thus, the mere fact that communities subjected land use decisions to the ballot box discouraged investment. Communities run a very real risk of reducing the quality of property development and redevelopment because of the transaction costs implicit in this arrangement.

The case of ballot-box zoning has an important lesson more generally: The discretionary nature of voter approval creates uncertainty, which in turn discourages investment and land development. Reducing uncertainty (without jeopardizing legitimate public concerns) is an important element of improving the development climate for communities.

- **Limit Standing in Public Hearings to Affected Parties.** Public hearings should be used primarily to disclose tangible, measurable spillover impacts so they can be addressed in the project proposal. The current approval system gives standing to anyone within the community to comment, delay, or object to a development proposal, regardless of the project's actual impacts. Intensive development of a property may tangibly affect neighbors who might now be subjected to more traffic congestion, noise pollution, or other tangible impacts. Developers should address these concerns by modifying their projects. Alternatively, if agreement between developers and prop-

### Notes:

30. Samuel R. Staley, "Ballot-box Zoning, Transaction Costs and Land Development," Urban Futures *Working Paper* 98–2 (Los Angeles, California: Reason Public Policy Institute, June 1998), at *http://www.urbanfutures.org*.

erty owners cannot be reached, third parties such as conflict-management teams or local courts can mediate and adjudicate disputes.

- **Administrative Site-Plan Review.** Once land is rezoned, site plans should be reviewed as quickly as possible. In many jurisdictions, site plans are evaluated through legislative review at the local level when issues and questions such as drainage, traffic flow, or landscaping could be handled quickly and efficiently by relying on the technical expertise of planners, engineers, and other professionals. In most cases, an administrative review process can be adopted with clearly defined criteria for what is acceptable by local planning standards. Administrative site-plan approval also can be coupled with performance bonuses to encourage the inclusion of certain characteristics. For example, when Fort Collins, Colorado, experimented with flexible zoning, it allowed higher densities if developers incorporated certain features such as landscaped buffers between roads and buildings into their development plan.[31] The critical element of the Fort Collins model was flexibility, so that developers could make trade-offs based on market conditions and trends.

- **One-Stop Shop for Planning and Permit Approvals.** In a number of cities, different permitting processes and locations exist for zoning certificates and applications, site-plan and engineering approval, and other development permission forms. One-stop permit processing streamlines the permit application and approval process, particularly for small and less-experienced developers. This approach could significantly reduce the transaction costs associated with development permission and approval once projects have been committed to.

- **Supermajority for Overriding Planning Board Decisions.** While local governments should provide an appeal process, city officials should presume that recommendations of planning boards are fair and accurate. A supermajority requirement for city councils to override planning board decisions would build certainty into the planning process and strengthen the ability of planning boards to mediate between affected parties, while providing a local appeal process.

## STRATEGY #4: Align Costs with Property Development.

Property owners and developers should bear the full costs of property development. Local communities should not be expected to subsidize property development by extending sewers, roads, and other infrastructure to the site while failing to charge property owners and developers the full cost of these improvements.

Nor should new residents be expected to subsidize existing residents by paying fees in excess of their true costs. While impact fees—assessments on new projects to cover the fixed costs of extending services and infrastructure—are sometimes used to cover the fixed costs of extending services, these fees are often abused and become another source of general revenues for local governments. In some cases, development agreements using impact fees have helped to provide the site-specific revenues necessary for improvements to sites,[32] but impact fees have also been used to force new residents to subsidize existing residents by funding community-wide services and facilities.

## Notes:

31. William D. Eggers, "Land Use Reform Through Performance Zoning," Reason Foundation *Policy Insight* No. 120, May 1990.
32. See John J. Delaney, "Development Agreements: The Road from Prohibition to 'Let's Make a Deal,'" *The Urban Lawyer*, Vol. 25, No. 1 (Winter 1993), pp. 49–67, and Arthur C. Nelson, James E. Frank, and James C. Nicholas, "Positive Influence of Impact-Fee in Urban Planning and Development," *Journal of Urban Planning and Development,* Vol. 118, No. 2 (June 1992), pp. 59–64.

A study of the suburban Chicago housing market found that impact fees reduced the supply of housing and increased home prices significantly, sometimes more than double the amount of the fee imposed.[33] Moreover, the fees bore little relationship to the costs of the infrastructure provided to the new homes.[34] Another analysis found that more than 22 categories of facilities and activities were legally categorized for impact-fee financing. Most did not support facilities and traditional public goods such as roads, sewers, and public schools, which would serve the needs of the new subdivision or project. Instead, they reflected political goals—public art, low-income housing, mass transit, historical preservation, day-care facilities.[35]

- **Developer Payment for On-Site Infrastructure.** A more appropriate mechanism would simply require private developers to pay the full financial burden of extending sewer lines, roads, and other utilities to their property using materials and technology consistent with the existing infrastructure and their own development needs. Such a developer-pay approach needs to be accompanied by flexible design criteria, so that individual developers can determine what level of infrastructure and what construction standards make sense for the intended users of that infrastructure.

- **Full-Cost Pricing for Infrastructure.** An alternative to both on-site provision of infrastructure and public provision of infrastructure is full-cost pricing. Full-cost pricing requires the public sector to include all costs—operating, maintenance, capital costs, and debt service—in the provision of water, sewer, and other utilities that service

development. Privatization of infrastructure would automatically solve the pricing decision problem, since private companies cannot afford to subsidize customers over the long run.

- **Public Planning for Future Infrastructure.** State and local governments typically make long-term investments in core infrastructure such as roads, sewers, and water systems with little consideration for the impacts on land development and the real-estate market or regional planning. One example is Lancaster County, Pennsylvania, which has implemented regional planning and growth boundaries to direct real estate development. Growth boundaries are politically determined lines beyond which development is either prohibited or discouraged. Land inside the boundary is intended to be developed more quickly.

About half of the land inside Lancaster County's growth boundaries, however, is outside planned sewer-service areas; half of the land inside the sewer-service areas is outside the growth boundaries.[36] In other words, the boundary is at odds with the infrastructure that is already built, and thus the sewer-service areas and growth boundaries are working at cross-purposes. In this case and others, current planning practice regulates private-property development without imposing similar restrictions on the public sector. This is particularly troublesome given the wide range and variety of long-term investments in infrastructure made by state and local governments.

As long as state, local, and regional governments invest in capital-intensive public services

## Notes:

33. Brett M. Baden, Don L. Coursey, and Jeannine M. Kannegiesser, *Effects of Impact Fees on the Suburban Housing Market*, Policy Study No. 93 (Chicago: Heartland Institute, November 1999).
34. *Ibid.*
35. Dennis H. Ross and Scott Ian Thorpe, "Impact Fees: Practical Guide for Calculation and Implementation," *Journal of Urban Planning and Development,* Vol. 18, No. 3 (September 1992), pp. 106–118.
36. Samuel R. Staley, Jefferson G. Edgens, and Gerard C. S. Mildner, *A Line in the Land: Urban-Growth Boundaries, Smart Growth, and Housing Affordability*, Reason Public Policy Institute, *Policy Study* No. 263, October 1999 , p. 26.

with long-term development impacts, they should be required to plan the location of infrastructure and secure the necessary rights of way and easements before development takes place. This does not imply that the public agencies should begin constructing infrastructure immediately. On the contrary, public agencies might lay out clearly where they expect to place key infrastructure such as roads, bridges, interchanges, sewers, and water lines. Actual construction would be triggered by development patterns and private-sector investment thresholds, and tied to specific performance measures. This would provide certainty for private developers but would not obligate the public sector to infrastructure development until land-use patterns were well established through market processes. This also would give flexibility to infrastructure agencies (public or private): They could construct a two-lane road at early stages of development, expand to a center-lane road later in the development phase, and eventually develop the roadway into a four-lane highway.

If public agencies were subject to mandatory planning requirements, and were required to buy rights of way early in the process, many of the objections to traffic congestion and other nuisance effects of development might disappear, reducing the politicized nature of the zoning and planning process.[37]

## INTEGRATING MARKET PRINCIPLES IN PLANNING

The smart growth movement has brought growth management and planning issues to the forefront of public debate on the state, local, and national levels. Unfortunately, most of the proposals to date have tended to opt for top-down solutions that fail to capture the natural efficiencies and broad-based nature of competitive real estate markets. One of the most important tasks confronting citizens and their elected officials is to determine how they will integrate market-oriented thinking into planning practice. Planning should not rely on static prescriptions to direct land-use and property development. Rather, by attempting to work with the dynamic nature of the real estate market, planning can be retooled to ensure more efficient land use, facilitate the adaptation and evolution of local communities, and strengthen their long-term economic viability.

**Notes**:

37. Note that this recommendation is not the same as end-state planning as it is currently practiced. In Portland, an end-state vision of what Portland should look like is used to guide public investment in rail transit, and private investment is directed by the regional plan to fit the plan's vision, not consumer markets.

# 6

# THE RELATIONSHIP OF CITIES AND SUBURBS

*By Ronald D. Utt*

**B**ecause the growth of the suburbs over the past 50 years has paralleled the decline of some central cities, many commentators have concluded that the two are interrelated—suburbanization has contributed to urban decline, and vice versa. In its extreme version, this view also assumes that the suburban populations consist largely of former city residents and those who would live in the city if it were a more attractive environment. If such claims were true, the policy implications would be significant: Efforts to revitalize the deteriorating central cities across America would discourage suburban development, and efforts to deter sprawl through limits on growth and the creation of urban boundaries would encourage people and businesses to stay in the city to help revitalize it.

Certainly, revitalizing America's declining central cities is an important national concern, but achieving that goal will have only a mar-ginal impact on the process of suburbanization that has been underway in metropolitan areas for most of the postwar era. As this chapter will show, *the suburbs did not grow because of the decline of the cities.* Moreover, reversing the decline of the cities, however crucial, will not stop suburban growth.

Indeed, there is evidence that revitalizing a city will benefit its entire metropolitan area and contribute to overall growth affecting both the city and its suburbs. It may well improve the state of the suburbs, too.

## CITIES AND SUBURBS IN PERSPECTIVE

Between 1950 and 1998, America's population grew by 80 percent, or 119 million people, and many of these new Americans had to look beyond the crowded central cities to find a place to live.[1] Most older cities, particularly in the Midwest and East, were already fully devel-

**Notes:**

1. U.S. Bureau of the Census, *Statistical Abstract of the United States 1998*, Table No. 2, "Population: 1950–1997," p. 8; see also "State Population Estimates and Demographic Components of Population Change: July 1, 1998 to July 1, 1999," December 29, 1999, at *http://www.census.gov/population/estimates/state/st-99-1.txt*.

Table 6.1

## Population Changes from 1950 to 1998 in the Top 20 U.S. Cities in 1970

| Gainers | | | Losers | | |
|---|---|---|---|---|---|
| 1970 Rank | | Increase | 1970 Rank | | Decrease |
| 3. | Los Angeles | 1,628,000 | 1. | New York City | 472,000 |
| 6. | Houston | 1,191,000 | 2. | Chicago | 819,000 |
| 8. | Dallas | 642,000 | 4. | Philadelphia | 636,000 |
| 11. | Indianapolis | 314,000 | 5. | Detroit | 880,000 |
| 14. | San Diego | 887,000 | 7. | Baltimore | 304,000 |
| 15. | San Antonio | 706,000 | 9. | Washington, D.C. | 279,000 |
| 17. | Memphis | 208,000 | 10. | Cleveland | 419,000 |
| 20. | Columbus | 294,000 | 12. | Milwaukee | 59,000 |
| | | | 13. | San Francisco | 29,000 |
| | | | 16. | Boston | 246,000 |
| | | | 18. | St. Louis | 518,000 |
| | | | 19. | New Orleans | 104,000 |
| | All Gainers | 5,870,000 | | All Losers | 4,765,000 |
| | Net Gain | 1,105,000 | | | |

**Note:** 1970 is used because it is near the midpoint of the postwar era.
**Source:** Data for 1950 from *Information Please Almanac;* data for 1970 from U.S. Bureau of the Census, as presented by the Wendell Cox Consultancy in "Urbanized Areas: Ranked by Central City Population," available on the Internet at *http://www.publicpurpose.com/dm-uacr.htm;* data for 1998 from U.S. Bureau of the Census.

oped and built to their borders, so much of the new construction to house the expanding population occurred on undeveloped land beyond the city limits. These lands, of course, became the suburbs, and they continue to expand as the United States adds more than 2 million new residents—the equivalent population of two cities the size of Dallas—each year.

The magnitude of this population growth and the pressure it places on suburban development can be illustrated by examining demographic trends in the nation's top 20 cities since 1970, which is near the midpoint of the post–World War II era. Table 6.1 shows the 1950–1998 population gains or losses for each of these cities. Although the common perception is that cities in general lose population to

their suburbs, eight of the cities listed in the table *gained* population, while 12 experienced losses. In fact, there was a net population gain for all cities in the list; the increase in the population of the eight gainers exceeded by 1,105,000 people the combined decrease in population for the 12 losers. Such trends are fairly representative of demographic changes in all American cities, both big and small.

According to one government report, two-thirds of America's 539 cities experienced an increase in population between 1980 and 1996.[2] Thus, looking at the changes within all U.S. cities, the city-to-suburb flows of population appear not to be of a magnitude sufficient to reshape the postwar residential development patterns substantially.

**Notes:**

2. U.S. Department of Housing and Urban Development, "The State of the Cities, 1999," Third Annual Report, June 1999, p. vii.

The limited significance of these city–suburb flows is even more apparent when looking at these cities from the perspective of population trends throughout their entire metropolitan areas (city plus suburbs) rather than just within the historical borders of the central city. Between 1950 and 1998, these same 20 metro areas experienced a combined increase of 46.5 million people, while the metro areas of the 12 cities losing population gained a combined 23.7 million people. Comparing the metro areas' gain with the combined net loss for the 12 losers in Table 6.1, it appears that for each individual lost by the city, the surrounding suburbs gained five residents. This suggests that persons leaving the city are a minor factor in the suburbs' rising population.

Just as these broad, postwar population trends demonstrate that the exodus of residents from central cities was not a primary force powering suburban growth, these same trends also demonstrate that policies designed to get people to remain in, or move into, central cities will not do much to slow down in the rate of suburban development. In fact, emerging evidence suggests that a troubled central city will diminish suburban growth as well by casting a pall over the entire metropolitan area. Less metro area population growth means less housing construction, commercial development, and suburbanization.

## Troubled Cities, Troubled Suburbs

Between 1950 and 1998, the populations of the metropolitan areas of the eight cities in Table 6.1 that experienced population increases had average growth rates of 207 percent. In contrast, the metro areas of the 12 central cities that lost population grew by only 60.5 percent. At the extreme end of the growth spectrum is the Pittsburgh metropolitan area, which represents one of several areas surrounding troubled

declining cities, where the population of the entire metro area—city and suburbs—fell between 1990 and 1998. Other examples include Providence, Rhode Island; Wheeling, West Virginia; and Toledo, Ohio. The relationship between poor city performance and diminished metro area growth suggests that central-city social deterioration is a deterrent to sprawl, not a contributor.

The fact that central-city deterioration can have negative effects on all the communities in the metropolitan area implies that suburbs cannot afford to be ambivalent about their neighbor's problems. However much suburbanites may be troubled and inconvenienced by exuberant growth and development in their communities, the implication of slow growth caused by depressed economic activity may be even worse. Thus, suburban residents have a big stake in a central city's well-being that is markedly different from what the new urbanists would claim.

> The relationship between poor city performance and diminished metro area growth suggests that central-city social deterioration is a deterrent to sprawl.

Suburban residents have another reason to be interested in the process of city/community decline and revitalization. The deterioration that now characterizes central cities is not unique to the urban core and could just as easily take place in, or spread to, the suburbs. Indeed, in its 1999 report on "The State of the Cities," the U.S. Department of Housing and Urban Development (HUD) highlights such emerging problems in some older suburbs:

> Some older suburbs are experiencing problems once associated with urban areas—job loss, population decline, crime and disinvestment....The challenges once concentrated in central cities have spread to some "inner ring" suburbs, such as Euclid and Garfield Heights, OH (Cleveland), McKeesport, PA (Pittsburgh), and Cov-

ington, KY (Cincinnati), that are facing such urban ills as crime, poverty, and population loss.[3]

Tellingly, each of the above examples in the HUD report highlights suburbs surrounding cities that have declined in population. This again suggests that suburban prosperity and growth are not necessarily at the expense of central-city decline, but instead may be dragged down by it. Nonetheless, because smart growth advocates have the misconception that the decline of the cities is fostering the growth of the suburbs, they have adopted the idea of unified or cooperative forms of government—metropolitan-wide governments that transcend community borders.

As HUD's recent report claims:

> There is a strong consensus on the need for joint city/suburb strategies to address sprawl and the structural decline of cities and older suburbs. We now have an historic opportunity for cooperation between cities and counties, urban as well as suburban, to address the challenges facing our metropolitan areas.[4]

These views are echoed by some academic analysts who believe that America's system of independent local governments contributes to the problem. According to one such analyst, the problem follows logically from "a public sector that consists of a fragmented maze of local governments and special districts and a private sector that builds mostly unrelated subdivisions rather than integrated communities."[5] President Clinton attempted to convert these kinds of views into public policy initiatives through the "Livable Communities" proposal introduced in January 1999. One of the five goals in the proposal was to "Promote collaboration among

neighboring communities—cities, suburbs, rural areas—to develop regional growth strategies and address common issues like crime."[6]

There is a certain intuitive appeal to treating the diverse elements of contiguous communities as if they were connected parts of an organic whole, but from a practical standpoint it is difficult to establish any meaningful relationship between the emerging inconveniences of suburban living and the deep-seated social and economic problems that plague older central cities. Advocates of a metropolitan-wide agenda who argue that there are such relationships have yet to demonstrate that an anti-fragmentation strategy of regional governance is a meaningful solution.

On the contrary, wherever cities have made progress in retaining jobs, residents, and businesses, this has been accomplished by successful, self-reliant city officials. They, and the citizens they govern, recognize the weakness of claims that there are substantial connections between such disparate issues as traffic congestion at a suburban shopping center and inner-city murder rates, or between the loss of farm land on the "exurban" fringe and low math scores by central-city third-graders.

For the many central-city mayors who have failed to stem the flight of business and residents from their jurisdictions because of incompetently managed schools, police forces, and other public services, the metropolitan agenda gets them off the hook by shifting the blame for city ills, and the responsibility for the solution, to the surrounding suburbs.

Population growth alone suggests that rapid suburbanization would have taken place during the postwar era even if the cities had maintained high standards of public services, including law enforcement and education. Although

## Notes:

3. *Ibid.*, p. ix.
4. *Ibid.*, p. xi.
5. Bruce Katz and Scott Bernstein, "The New Metropolitan Agenda: Connecting Cities to Suburbs," *Brookings Review*, Fall 1998, p. 4.
6. While House, "Clinton-Gore Livability Agenda: Building Livable Communities for the 21st Century," Press release, February 1999.

the populations of most older Eastern cities have declined steadily since 1950, simple arithmetic associated with the numbers in Table 1 will demonstrate that such losses, while undermining the civic and economic health of cities, account for only a small fraction of the population gain in the suburbs during the same period. Indeed, the vast majority of individuals flocking to the suburbs represent individuals leaving small towns and rural areas, not city residents fleeing cities.

In 1940, 56.5 percent of the population lived in urbanized areas (central cities and their suburbs). By 1990, that share had risen to 75.2 percent, as farms and small towns lost population to the metropolitan areas, where more and more of America's economic activity was concentrated.[7] Because most older cities already had been built to their borders, new arrivals had either to take up residence in the new suburbs or endure the escalating levels of population density in the older cities. What such density levels would imply can be illustrated by the following hypothetical examples from some leading U.S. metro areas:

- Had suburban development been thwarted early in the postwar era by the type of urban growth boundaries now popular among some growth-control advocates, an already very crowded New York City would have to find room for another 6 million people—more than two present day Chicagos.

- Shortly after the end of World War II, Washington, D.C., housed 802,000 people. What are now its heavily populated suburbs were

then mostly farms and pastures.[8] By 1998, Washington was home to about 523,000 people, 279,000 fewer than in 1950. If Washington, D.C., was restored to its peak population of 802,000, space would still have to be found for the more than 4 million people now living and working in its surrounding suburbs.

Although many new urbanists and growth-control advocates blame government policies, such as federal mortgage insurance and highway funding, as important factors contributing to the suburbanization of America, data indicate that population shifts from rural to urban areas—as well as the natural growth through births and immigration that added 119 million more Americans since 1950—account for the lion's share of the forces that have shaped America's metro areas and their suburbs.

> The vast majority of individuals flocking to the suburbs represent individuals leaving small towns and rural areas, not city residents fleeing cities.

## THE DYNAMICS OF CITIES AND SUBURBS

With the fortunes of cities and suburbs linked, and with the prospect of economic and social deterioration a potentially serious challenge to any community, avoiding it or curing it requires an understanding of community dynamics and knowledge of what solutions work and which ones do not.

### Suburbanization as Global Trend

Although the population decline in the central cities is often seen as a uniquely American phenomenon, the broad demographic trends confronting America's older cities are similar to those affecting many of Europe's older cities.

## Notes:

7. Data for 1940 from U.S. Bureau of the Census, *Historical Statistics of the United States: 1790 to 1970,* Series A57–72; data for 1990 from *Statistical Abstract of the United States, 1995,* Table No. 44, "Urban and Rural Population 1960 to 1990, and by State."

8. Although formal census estimates are available for only 1940 and 1950, some analysts estimate that Washington, D.C., may have reached a population close to 1 million people by war's end in 1945.

The population of central London peaked at the turn of the last century, a half-century earlier than the older Eastern U.S. cities. This peak-to-present decline represents a 40 percent population loss, roughly on par with the peak-to-present rates of decline in many older U.S. cities. Paris experienced similar trends beginning in the 1920s. Tokyo ran about a decade or two behind American cities, but the same dispersal/depopulation trends and rapid suburban growth are now evident in Osaka, Japan's second-largest city. One reason central London experienced a declining population much earlier than other cities may have been the early introduction of a comprehensive commuter rail system that allowed for population dispersal. London's experience suggests that the new urbanists' emphasis on transit may be more curse than blessing for many central cities.

The international experience suggests that U.S demographic patterns may be related to a more widespread, late 20th-century phenomenon, rather than to the purely domestic causes described by new urbanists and advocates of the metropolitan agenda. In particular, alleged causes of urban flight (or suburban sprawl) in America frequently include federal highway and homeownership programs, under-investment in public transit, fragmented jurisdictions, single-purpose zoning, and racial animosity.

But many of these factors are uniquely American and much less evident in Europe—certainly not seen in Japan. This suggests that other factors common to all three continents might be the source of declining city populations and growing suburbanization throughout the developed world. These may include increases in population, rising per capita personal income, and the application of new technologies to commerce, manufacturing, and transportation at approximately the same time.

> London's experience suggests that the emphasis on transit may be more curse than blessing for many central cities.

## A History of the Modern City

The cities as we once knew them, and the model that many public officials and urban experts want to recreate, reflect social and economic arrangements unique to the technology available when cities became the dominant economic, cultural, and political force of the nation—roughly from the late 19th century to the outbreak of World War II. Since then, the special (and limiting) circumstances that encouraged their rise have been supplanted by further technological changes that rendered the social and economic structures of the older cities obsolete.

**The Cities Grow.** The industrial revolution dramatically altered economic relationships, and in the process encouraged the concentration of a large workforce within densely populated urban areas. With transport options limited to water, rail, drayage, and walking, it was essential that factories be located near both water and rail, and that workers live within walking distance of the plant or their place of employment, or to a rail line that served them. The concentration of manufacturing within the newly expanding urban areas, in turn, encouraged the development and concentration of other businesses serving both the manufacturers and their employees with convenient access to each other.

Near the end of the 19th century, the development of electricity, telephone, and natural gas delivery systems further enhanced the economic advantage of urban areas. The then high distribution/transportation costs of gas and electricity limited the availability of these new sources of energy and communication to densely populated urban areas, further encouraging businesses and households to remain or locate there.

**The Suburbs Gain.** The comparative advantage of the cities began to diminish when the concentration of economic activity within narrow geographic boundaries began to increase the cost of land and other services compared with other regions. As cost pressures mounted in urban areas, society had an incentive to adopt technological changes that allowed businesses and consumers some relief from rising prices. Such relief came when technological change in transportation caught up with the rapid changes that had been occurring in manufacturing, energy, and telecommunications.

The technological change that revolutionized transportation and undermined the role of central cities was the development of an inexpensive internal combustion engine, which reduced transportation costs and greatly expanded transportation choices. With economic forces no longer favoring, or requiring, dense living and working arrangements, individuals and businesses now had greater freedom to choose where to locate. For many, the preferred choice more closely conformed to that which characterized living and work arrangements prior to the industrial revolution. Free again to exercise their preferences for privacy, greenery, larger and newer houses, and open spaces, individuals moved to the suburbs by the tens of thousands.

With the arrival of the automobile also came a substantial improvement in family income beginning in 1940. This allowed many families to afford more living space—the average number of persons per room fell from 0.74 in 1940 to 0.48 in 1987[9]—and houses incorporating modern conveniences.

Retail establishments were the first to adjust to these changing demographics by following their customers to the suburbs. And while established businesses created suburban satellites, newly created retail and service establishments increasingly chose to begin life in the suburbs rather than in the central cities, thereby undermining cities' dominant role as an incubator of commercial creativity and innovation. In a process described by Joel Garreau in his provocative book, *Edge City: Life on the New Frontier*, suburbs increasingly became self-sufficient in jobs, commerce, culture, and entertainment, supplanting cities throughout the nation in these activities.

By becoming good places to live, suburbs also became good places to do business; entrepreneurs and commercial establishments responded positively to the availability of high-quality public services for low taxes. Significantly, cities that avoided or reversed population and employment declines did so primarily by focusing on the provision of quality services that are of primary benefit to their residents, namely education and good public services.

**The Cities Decline.** While suburbs were becoming more practical and desirable places to live, rural unemployment and falling agricultural wages that began during the Great Depression caused tens of thousands of unskilled farm hands, many of them African–American, to leave the South to take better paying jobs in northern urban communities. The migration of unskilled African–Americans to the urban areas exacerbated existing racial animosities and accelerated the movement to the suburbs that already was underway in most older cities.

These economic and social changes in older cities became an object of national concern in the early postwar era and the subject of numerous national policy initiatives designed to either mitigate the loss or restore to the cities the prominence they once had. Indeed, shortly after World War II, Congress enacted the Housing Act of 1949, which created the much maligned urban renewal programs that would become the federal government's primary vehicle for urban revitalization.

Unfortunately for the cities, these federal programs and initiatives hastened their demise by undermining their historic role of fostering the upward mobility of newly arrived residents,

## Notes:

9. Robert Rector, "How Poor Are America's Poor?" Heritage Foundation *Backgrounder* No. 791, September 21, 1990, p. 10.

replacing it with welfare dependency, and thereby exacerbating many of the emerging urban social problems. Violent crime, educational decline, welfare dependency, illegitimacy, drug addiction, infant mortality, or family dissolution represent measures of societal dysfunction that often reached their extreme within declining cities. Despite the existence and growth of costly federal programs, these trends worsened through the mid-1990s and continue to exist at destructively high levels in many older central cities.

Today, America's older central cities are in trouble, and for some cities the trouble is getting worse. Notwithstanding the much ballyhooed urban renaissance that some contend is sweeping the land, once leading cities such as Baltimore, Cleveland, Detroit, New Orleans, Philadelphia, and St. Louis consistently lost population through the decade of the 1990s, continuing a trend that for most began in 1950.

## SOME FEDERAL POLICIES MAKE URBAN PROBLEMS WORSE

Mounting evidence suggests that five decades of active federal efforts to "help" cities and older troubled suburbs have seriously undermined them—not by seducing families to live in the suburbs, but by driving people, jobs, and businesses out of the cities. Chief among the early federal culprits is the Urban Renewal Administration, which attempted to improve housing and social conditions in the inner cities by acquiring, through eminent domain, entire neighborhoods that were mostly poor, mostly black, and mostly residential. The population was relocated to newly constructed public housing (a federal program created during the 1930s), and the land was cleared for new development that often included more public housing, commercial structures, highways, or public buildings.

Although the Urban Renewal Administration no longer exists, its approach is alive in today's federal urban economic revitalization policies and programs, many of which are operated by HUD. These programs still emphasize costly and infrastructure-intensive redevelopment

schemes that are designed to bring more visitors and employees downtown and maintain the importance of the city as a cultural and business center. But such programs are often implemented at the expense of city residents, whose quality of life frequently is diminished by these schemes.

Even though these programs of intentional neighborhood destruction have largely been abandoned, their replacements continue the pattern of favoring visitors over residents. The urge to build highways through cities also has diminished, but federal policymakers have shifted their emphasis to capital intensive mass transit systems, such as light rail and subways, whose construction disrupts neighborhoods for extended periods of time just to provide convenient, subsidized transit to suburban commuters.

Although light rail systems increasingly are seen as substitutes for the urban highways of the past, the modern versions of the urban renewal strategies of the 1950s are publicly funded convention centers and stadiums, subsidized hotels, reconstructed public housing projects, and financial incentives to large employers to remain in a city or relocate there. While different in intent, these new strategies are comparable in effect, providing most of the benefits to visitors and commuters and generating just a small number of low-wage, unskilled service-oriented jobs for city residents. These schemes also force city residents to endure inconveniences such as higher taxes, misallocated public funds, increased congestion, and a diminished quality of life to pay for these acts of corporate welfare.

In spite of the fact that publicly funded stadiums and arenas are often sold to the community as vital investments in a city's economic development, virtually all studies of their impact indicate little or no economic benefit. Indeed, one of the more recent academic studies, which examined 37 metropolitan areas, found that "some professional sports franchises reduce the level of per capita personal income in metropolitan areas and have no effect on the growth in per capita income, casting doubt on the ability of a new sports franchise or facility to spur economic growth."[10]

Despite four decades of federal and local efforts to revitalize urban economies through such costly infrastructure projects and increased social service spending, the objects of all of this attention and munificence, the older cities and suburbs, are often worse off than ever. And the real casualties of this failure are not just the taxpayers whose money has been squandered, but the most vulnerable of the hapless urban residents whose hopes and dreams have been dashed and whose lives have been diminished, prematurely ended, or relegated to permanent subsistence and dependency.

The creation of the U.S. Department of Housing and Urban Development in 1966 may have made things worse. Established as the federal government's lead agency to address and resolve the urban problems that began to get worse in the early 1960s, HUD embarked upon an ambitious and costly series of housing construction programs that offered government subsidies to buyers, renters, and builders. Within a few years, these generous subsidies for low- to moderate-income housing stimulated the building industry to achieve record levels (from 1971 to 1973) of new housing and apartment construction that have yet to be surpassed.

> **Despite four decades of federal and local efforts to revitalize urban economies, older cities and suburbs are often worse off than ever.**

But as has happened too often with HUD programs, this record performance was riven with fraud, excessive costs, shoddy construction, and poor management. HUD now confronts multibillion-dollar exposures in deferred maintenance and accumulated losses in many of its project-based programs. Unfortunately, the older cities now find themselves home to vast deteriorated housing projects that concentrate the poorest and most vulnerable urban residents into some of the most dangerous communities in the nation.[11] As Mayor John Norquist of Milwaukee recently observed:

> Federal intervention in housing has been a disaster for cities and the people who live in them. After a succession of fiascoes associated with attempts to eradicate slums, build housing for the poor, and pursue other seemingly noble goals, it should be obvious that government efforts often make urban conditions worse rather than better.[12]

Former Clinton HUD official Bruce Katz, now Director of the Brookings Institution's Center on Urban and Metropolitan Policy, acknowledged the checkered history of government housing policy when he recently wrote: "Perhaps the worst thing that federal and state policies have done to cities and older suburbs has

**Notes:**

10. Dennis Coates and Brad R. Humphreys, "The Growth Effects of Sport Franchises, Stadia and Arenas," University of Maryland, Baltimore County, January 22, 1999, unpublished manuscript. See also Ronald D. Utt, "Cities in Denial: The False Promise of Subsidized Tourist and Entertainment Complexes," Heritage Foundation *Backgrounder* No. 1223, October 2, 1998.

11. Most of the nation's public housing is located in the East and Midwest, and thus concentrated in older cities subject to the severest deterioration. Moreover, most of the public housing was built prior to 1975. See John C. Weicher, "Privatizing Subsidized Housing," *AEI Studies in Policy Reform* (Washington, D.C.: American Enterprise Institute, 1997), pp. 3, 27.

12. Mayor John Norquist, "How Government Killed Affordable Housing," *The American Enterprise*, July/August 1998, p. 68.

been to concentrate populations of poor people within their borders."[13]

High crime rates also characterize these central-city housing projects, and the festering crime in HUD subsidized projects spreads throughout the city. As the dysfunctional social culture of these federally sponsored public housing projects spills over into surrounding neighborhoods, existing city residents and businesses have one more incentive to move elsewhere. A recent study of the impact of HUD housing programs on urban neighborhoods found that "project-based assistance programs do little to improve the quality of recipients' neighborhoods relative to those of welfare households and, in the case of public housing, appear to make things significantly worse."[14]

Although the adverse effects of public housing historically have affected central cities, where most of this housing was built, government efforts are underway to require that such housing also be built in the suburbs. This is an effort to disperse the problems and diminish the extent to which the concentration of public housing in the central city contributes to racial segregation. In recent years, the suburbs of Baltimore, Pittsburgh, and Dallas have been under government pressure to build public housing. Given the crime and social problems generally associated with the concentration of poor households in public housing projects, this government effort, if successful, will undermine the quality of life in the targeted suburbs and encourage some residents to move further away. Chapter 7 discusses an alternative way that HUD can provide housing assistance to the poor without undermining neighborhoods.

Federal transportation programs have also diminished the cities. Recognizing the importance of convenient low-cost transportation in the decision of where to locate, cities attempted to remain competitive in transportation by holding down fares for buses, trains, and trol-

leys. Through the 1950s and early 1960s, most of the urban transit systems were privately owned and operated. When private transit systems went bankrupt, cities took them over and subsidized their fares from local taxes and federal grants. Despite such growing subsidies, public transit systems continued to lose both ridership and money.

Convinced that attractive and convenient transit systems with low fares were a key to reversing the cities' decline and revitalizing their economies, Congress in 1965 enacted the Urban Mass Transit Act. The act created and provided funding for the Urban Mass Transit Administration (now the Federal Transit Administration) and tasked it with helping local systems to upgrade their services. Despite an estimated $385 billion (in 1999 dollars) in federal, state, and local funds lavished since 1960 on (mostly) urban transit systems—including buses, trolleys, subways, and other rail—the program has also done little to improve the cities and may in fact have exacerbated their problems by subsidizing the transportation needs of suburban commuters.

Within the focus on urban transit systems has emerged a disproportionate emphasis on new light rail systems to attract suburban commuters from their cars or suburban shoppers from their malls. Because such systems are costly to build and operate, they invariably divert resources away from ordinary transportation services, such as improved streets or more frequent bus service that would better serve urban residents. For example:

- In Washington, D.C., the high cost of maintaining the rail system has forced a 27 percent cutback in bus service and reductions in road repairs.[15]

- In Los Angeles, a group of minority residents contend that the city's transit agency has neglected the bus routes that serve them by spending 70 percent of its budget

**Notes:**

13. Bruce J. Katz, "Urban Solutions: Beyond City Limits," *Brookings Policy Brief*, No. 33 (June 1998), p. 3.
14. Sandra J. Newman and Ann B. Schnare, "'...And a Suitable Living Environment': The Failure of Housing Programs to Deliver on Neighborhood Quality," *Housing Policy Debate*, Vol. 8, No. 4 (1997), p. 703.

on a rail system that carries only 8 percent of the transit system's riders, most of whom are white and well-to-do.[16] In response to the threat of a lawsuit, Los Angeles has put a hold on light rail construction.

Although suburban commuters may be the greatest beneficiaries of new costly rail systems, the evidence suggests that even they are not much impressed. For the nation as a whole, the decade of the 1980s saw a 17 percent decline in market share of transit, and between 1970 and 1990 the share fell by 42 percent.

This across-the-board failure has not deterred the same transit advocates, now asserting that they are advancing a "metropolitan agenda," from claiming that whatever now ails the suburbs can be cured through heavier doses of transit investment and spending. As Angela Antonelli of The Heritage Foundation reports in Chapter 10, Atlanta's failure to meet the government's Clean Air standards led the U.S. Environmental Protection Agency in 1998 to force Georgia to create the Greater Regional Transportation Authority and task it with the responsibility of getting Atlantans out of their cars and onto buses.

As the cities declined during the postwar era and their suburbs expanded in both population and prosperity, many critics of suburbanization came to view this dynamic process as a zero-sum game in which one community's gain was another's loss. Because of the simultaneous occurrence of decline and growth, these critics viewed, for example, the emergence of Webster Groves, Missouri, as taking place at the expense of St. Louis, while Shaker Heights, Ohio, pulled wealth and talent out of Cleveland, and so on for metropolitan areas throughout the country.

> Many critics of suburbanization came to view this dynamic process as a zero-sum game in which one community's gain was another's loss.

## REVIVING THE CITIES

Although the more than five-decade decline in most older American central cities led to an escalating level of federal intervention, the results were universally unsuccessful and may even have worsened the decline. For the most part, these programs focused on public housing, commuters, businesses, tourists, and other transitory visitors, and did little to enhance the diminished quality of life that challenged the remaining residents every day. All the while, city taxes increased, public services declined, and residents and businesses continued to flee.

That misplaced focus began to change in the late 1980s and early 1990s. A new breed of mayors took office in several major cities and began to use their authority and the cities' resources to stress those quality of life issues that discouraged families from living in cities. These mayors aggressively used their authority to confront entrenched special interests and reform unresponsive bureaucracies to improve public services, restore quality education, and reduce crime.

Rudolph Giuliani in New York City, Stephen Goldsmith in Indianapolis, Richard Daley in Chicago, and John Norquist in Milwaukee are among the many such mayors who exercised firm leadership to improve city services. As a result of these efforts, New York and Indianapolis were the only two major Eastern cities to

**Notes:**

15. Amanda Ripley, "Missing the Bus," *The City Paper* (Washington, D.C.), January 23, 1997, p. 25, and Stephen C. Fehr, "D.C. $1 Billion Short of Funds to Fix Streets," *The Washington Post*, December 18, 1997, p. D1.

16. "Los Angeles Proposes Rail Construction 'Indefinite Hold,'"*Urban Transportation Fact Book,* December 17, 1997, at *http://www.publicpurpose.com.*

experience a population gain during the 1990s, while Chicago experienced its first population gain in 1998 after experiencing a 900,000-person loss between 1950 and 1996.

By emphasizing the provision of quality public services that are important to families—particularly public safety and education—these pioneering mayors have demonstrated that older, troubled cities and inner suburbs can be revitalized and that the solutions lie within their offices, their departments, and their council chambers, not in Washington, D.C.

## Making the Cities Safer

America's older cities in particular have been subject to high crime rates for decades. Until recently, this sustained escalation in violence seemed to defy every effort to stop it. Many people came to view serious urban crime as a natural and inevitable side effect of modern society, and this fatalistic belief took the pressure off public officials to do anything about the problem. For those city residents who did care about crime, a move to the safer suburbs was a swift, certain, and inexpensive solution.

- In 1992, when America's crime rate was near its peak, one's chance of being murdered in any one of the 12 top cities that lost population since 1970 was nine times that of its suburbs, while in the eight cities whose populations increased over the same period, the murder rate was not quite five times greater than that in the suburbs.

- Between 1991 and 1998, 6 of the cities that lost residents during the decade saw their murder rates fall by less than the decline in the national average, while the 9 cities that gained population saw their murder rates decline faster than the national average.

While in 1998 the national murder rate was 64 percent of the rate in 1991, that of the 6 population losers was 73 percent of their 1991 rates, and the 9 population gainers averaged murder rates that were 52 percent of their 1991 rates.

- By 1998, the population gainers had a murder rate 4.4 times higher than their suburbs, while population losers had murder rates that were 11 times higher than their suburban rates.[17]

America's fatalistic approach to urban crime came to an abrupt end in 1994 when newly elected New York City Mayor Giuliani made rapid and substantial crime reduction a high priority and appointed William Bratton the Police Commissioner of New York City. Bratton changed the NYPD's approach to crime from one that was basically *reactive* (responding to 911 calls, for example) to a *proactive* policy stressing problem-solving and crime prevention, and he adopted a community policing strategy that emphasized partnership with the community.

The program was stunningly successful.[18] In 1998, New York experienced 633 homicides, compared with 2,262 in 1992—the lowest number of murders since 1967.[19] New York's murder rate is now near the national average, and less than four times its estimated suburban rate, compared with an eightfold difference between all cities and suburbs in 1991.

Although the crime rate has begun to fall nationally and in several older cities, it is still too high. For most cities, it remains well above the levels that triggered the exodus of residents in the 1970s. As the various findings indicate, defeating crime is critical to urban renewal. Cities must reduce their crime rates to levels

## Notes:

17. Because FBI murder rate data are incomplete for some suburbs, data for nine of the 10 gainers were used, while only six of 10 complete datasets were available for the population losers.
18. See William J. Bratton, "Cutting Crime and Restoring Order: What America Can Learn From New York's Finest," in Edwin Meese III and Robert E. Moffit, eds., *Making America Safer: What Citizens and Their State and Local Officials Can Do to Combat Crime* (Washington, D.C.: The Heritage Foundation, 1997).
19. U.S. Department of Justice, Federal Bureau of Investigation, *Crime in the United States: 1998, Uniform Crime Reports*, October 17, 1999, p. 98.

approaching those of their suburbs if they are to be competitive in offering an attractive community to working families.

## Restoring Quality Education

In addition to crime, the other most important factor determining whether families stay in the city or move to the suburbs is the quality of public education. Unfortunately for most city residents and their children, today's urban public schools are the most troubled in the country, and year after year they fail to impart even the most basic elements of knowledge to their students. This has encouraged middle-class families to choose the suburbs over the city. As a result, the majority of students in urban schools are disadvantaged racial minorities. The absence of an opportunity to receive a decent education robs these children (and their families) of the most important chance they have to become productive, self-reliant citizens and achieve the American dream. Moreover, poorly educated graduates lead to a low-quality workforce that discourages business from staying or opening in the city.

Notwithstanding claims to the contrary, a shortage of funds cannot account for the poor quality of urban schools. According to the annual survey of public schools conducted by the U.S. Department of Education, per-student school spending for 12 of the 20 cities listed in Table 6.1 was higher than the national average, and for 16 of the 20 was higher than the level of spending for the average of all of the schools within a city's state.[20]

Recognizing that the quality of the public education system has an important influence on where families and businesses choose to locate, several cities have recently taken significant action to improve their schools through a variety of programs based upon parental choice, competition, and top-to-bottom shake-ups. Milwaukee, Cleveland, and the state of Florida have implemented voucher and scholarship programs, which are designed to give low-income children in central cities an alternative to their failed traditional public schools. Chicago, Detroit, and Washington, D.C., have taken over their public education systems from inept school boards.

The state of Maryland threatens to do the same in Baltimore if performance does not improve. Indeed, the Maryland Board of Education voted in September 1999 to seek bids from private firms to run failing public schools.[21] Charter schools are also being permitted in several urban centers; in Washington, D.C., one of every 11 students is now enrolled in a charter school, which have been permitted only since 1997.[22] Because only 20 new charter schools are allowed to open each year and because applications to charter schools have exceeded available space, charter school enrollment likely would be higher if more charters were granted.

Starting from scratch in 1991, charter schools numbered about 1,128 nationwide as of the spring of 1999. More recent estimates put the total at 1,700 at the start of the 1999–2000 school year.[23] Charter schools are making inroads in more and more communities and have been endorsed by President Clinton.

Although voucher/scholarship and charter school reforms have been in place for only a few years, studies by independent experts report impressive results:

- A study of the Milwaukee program by professors Paul Peterson of Harvard University and Jay Greene of the University of Texas at Austin found that the gap in test scores between whites and minorities narrowed by 33 percent to 50 percent. Professor

## Notes:

20. U.S. Department of Education, *Digest of Education Statistics 1998*, Table 92 and Table 168.
21. Amy Argetsinger, "State Firm on School Takeover Plan," *The Washington Post*, September 22, 1999, p. B4.
22. Debbi Wilgoren and Valerie Strauss, "1 in 11 D.C. Students Opt for Charters," *The Washington Post*, October 9, 1999, p. A1.
23. "Charter School Expansion Continues," *School Reform News*, March 1999, from *http://www.heartland.org/education/mar99* (August 30, 1999).

Cecilia Rouse of Princeton University found that the program significantly increased mathematical achievement of participating students.[24]

- A 1998 joint study by Harvard's Program on Education Policy and Governance and Mathematica Policy Research, Inc., found that students in New York City's privately funded scholarship program scored higher on math and reading tests after only one year in the program.[25]

Although there are many innovative proposals and successful reforms that a public school system could implement to improve the quality of education, many central-city school systems have failed to take advantage of any of the options. As a consequence, these school systems continue to deny their students the opportunity to improve their lot in life in this knowledge-based economy, which demands better educated workers, and this, in turn, discourages families from living in cities and businesses from locating there.

Mayor Daley of Chicago, Mayor Giuliani of New York, Governor Jeb Bush of Florida, and concerned parents in Milwaukee and Cleveland are examples of effective leaders who contributed to the successful overhaul of their public schools. Repeating these successes elsewhere is the challenge for policymakers of the future, and federal and state education policies should be revised to give greater incentives to local leaders who make meaningful improvements in their public schools.

## CONCLUSION

Although many believe that the declining fortunes of older central cities contributed to the rapid development of suburbs during the postwar era, analysis of U.S. demographic trends during this period indicates that urban decline had a marginal influence, if any, on suburban growth and sprawl after 1950. Indeed, even where cities continued to gain population, such central-city growth coincided with even stronger growth in its suburbs.

To the extent that there is one overarching cause of postwar suburbanization, it is the growth of the U.S. population that added 119 million people since 1950 and necessitated the construction of more than 50 million new homes and apartments to shelter them. Because most older cities had long since built to their borders, this new construction had to take place in the surrounding areas, which at that time mainly consisted of farms, woods, and undeveloped land. Because America's population is expected to continue to increase well into the future, any growth control effort that relies on central city revitalization, or metropolitan-area coordination and cooperation, is likely to be ineffective.

The fact that efforts to revive central cities will have little or no effect on suburban growth does not imply that such efforts should not be undertaken. Many of America's older central cities are deeply troubled, and the low quality of life that troubled cities harbor contributes to a variety of costly problems, such as crime, drug addiction, long-term unemployment, family dissolution, illegitimacy, and poverty. Efforts to improve the cities will closely parallel efforts to reduce these social problems, which in turn will provide benefits to all of society.

There is evidence to suggest that serious urban problems diminish the attractiveness of the entire metropolitan area. This discourages new businesses from locating in that area, and encourages existing residents—urban and suburban alike—to seek a more attractive quality

## Notes:

24. Jay P. Greene and Paul E. Peterson, "The Effectiveness of School Choice in Milwaukee: A Secondary Analysis of Data from the Program's Evaluation," presented at Panel on the Political Analysis of Urban School Systems, American Political Science Association, San Francisco, California, August–September 1996.

25. Paul E. Peterson, David Myers, and William G. Howell, *An Evaluation of New York City School Choice Scholarships Program: The First Year*, Harvard University Program on Education Policy and Governance and Mathematica Policy Research, October 28, 1998.

of life in another metropolitan area. As a result, successful efforts to revive a city may contribute to suburbanization—just the opposite of the claims made by many new urbanists.

This is not necessarily bad, however. Although more growth may lead to more "sprawl," the benefits of enhanced metropolitan areas should be recognized as well. And, as other chapters of this book indicate, there are many ways to achieve "smart growth" in our metropolitan areas.

# 7

# THE FEDERAL ROLE IN SMART GROWTH

## By Ronald D. Utt

The federal government's impact on sprawl is the subject of much contention. Until the introduction of Vice President Al Gore's Livable Communities initiative in January 1999, the federal government had no formal policy regarding the rapid development of the suburban fringe of the country's metropolitan areas. However, many people, including advocates of strong growth controls, have long argued that federal policies ranging from mortgage insurance programs to the interstate highway program encourage sprawl and suburbanization.

The Livable Communities initiative assumes that the vast majority of people really want to live in the suburbs, and that a variety of new federal initiatives can correct the problem of traffic congestion and preserve more open space within developing communities.[1] The Gore plan is relatively limited in scope, yet it marks a sharp break with growth-control advocates, who tend to propose coercive, limiting, and proscriptive regulations to deal with suburban growth.

For example, under the Gore plan, spending by the U.S. Department of Transportation would increase to help alleviate traffic congestion and to beautify streets in suburban neighborhoods. A new federally subsidized loan program would be created to subsidize community purchases of undeveloped land that might otherwise be lost to commercial development, and funding for the U.S. Department of Housing and Urban Development (HUD) would increase to allow it to assist communities in developing regional smart growth plans.

Although Congress rejected the Vice President's plan, other parts of the federal establishment—notably, the U.S. Environmental Protection Agency (EPA)—are beginning to use their authority under existing federal laws to force communities to adopt coercive limits on regional growth and development of the sort promoted by growth-control advocates. In Feb-

## Notes:

1. White House, Office of the Vice President, "Clinton-Gore Livability Agenda: Building Livable Communities for the 21st Century," January, 1999.

ruary 1999, shortly after the introduction of Gore's plan, EPA officials announced their intention to implement more restrictive measures on regional growth and development. EPA's Administrator for the New England region, for example, announced in Boston that the agency would aggressively use its statutory authority to oppose and re-shape development and infrastructure projects that contribute to sprawl and to require mitigation measures where appropriate.[2]

The metropolitan area of Atlanta, Georgia, has become ground zero for EPA's promised involvement in the suburban growth debate. The EPA interpreted its statutory authority under the Clean Air Act as allowing it to mandate a new direction for the Atlanta region's future development. Because Atlanta's air quality fell below the act's mandated level (as revised by the EPA), the federal agency required the communities in the region to limit growth by cutting back on road construction and commercial development and by forcing new residential construction toward denser housing arrangements, such as townhouses and apartments.

If the Atlanta metro area communities fail to implement such plans, the EPA has the power to withhold the federal funding they would receive from several programs, including federal highway money. (See Chapter 10 for details on the Atlanta growth-control effort.) Should the EPA extend such mandates to other metropolitan areas, it would become a *de facto* federal suburban renewal program that could rival past federal urban renewal programs in scope and intrusiveness.

As this chapter will show, historically, the contribution of most federal policies to sprawl

> **Historically, the contribution of most federal policies to sprawl has been limited or non-existent.**

has been limited or non-existent. However, many of these same programs could better address suburban needs if they were modified to allow for greater state and local discretion in the decision-making process. As discussed in Chapter 6, many of the federal policies designed to aid cities have actually tended to undermine them. These deteriorated central cores often have an adverse impact on the quality of life and economic vitality of the entire metropolitan area. In this regard, the key to any federal effort to assist suburbs is to avoid repeating the counterproductive federal efforts that were inflicted upon central cities over the past half-century. Unfortunately, the Livable Communities proposal fails to meet this standard.

## THE FEDERAL GOVERNMENT'S ROLE IN SPRAWL

Growth-control advocates claim that many federal programs and laws have contributed to sprawl. They cite the mortgage insurance programs of the Federal Housing Administration (FHA) and the Veterans Administration (VA), the deductibility of mortgage interest payments from taxable income in determining one's federal income tax, the federal highway program, HUD's low-income housing programs, federal grants for water supply and treatment facilities, the Clean Air Act, the EPA's regulations regarding redevelopment of "brownfield" sites, and its program of "environmental justice."

Environmentalists and anti-growth advocates are not alone in this view. The mayors of some large cities argue that these programs have undermined the economic health of the central cities by encouraging suburban growth. Mayor Stephen Goldsmith of Indianapolis stated that:

**Notes**:

2.  Martha Kessler, "EPA to Take on Problem of Sprawl Using Legal Authority, Regional Chief Says," Bureau of National Affairs, *Regulation, Law & Economics,* February 4, 1999.

"Federal urban policy drives wealth out of the cities. In fact, if we specifically designed a 'suburban policy' to drive investment out of our cities, it would look a lot like the current system."[3] Mayor John Norquist of Milwaukee echoed those sentiments when he noted:

> The federal government, through trillions of dollars, subsidized a superhighway, and undermined the basic value of cities and their advantage of close proximity....The net effect of this is to make it very difficult for cities to survive economically.[4]

Although the federal government has never had a formal policy on suburbanization and regional development, critics of suburban development have argued that many existing federal programs reflect a pro-sprawl/pro-suburb policy that encourages decentralized living arrangements at the expense of what they deem to be the more desirable goal of concentrating regional populations in or near central cities. Among the many programs they cite, the federal highway program and federal mortgage insurance programs have long been viewed as the chief culprits.

Indeed, a recent survey of 240 members of the Society for American City and Regional Planning History, at the behest of the Fannie Mae Foundation of the Federal National Mortgage Association (FNMA), indicates that many urban experts see suburbanites as having been seduced into choosing the suburban lifestyle. According to the survey by Rutgers University Professor Robert Fishman, these experts see the 1956 Interstate Highway Act and the FHA mortgage program as the top two of 10 leading

factors influencing the American metropolis over the past 50 years.[5] As noted, critics believe that federal grants for water and sewage treatment, HUD's public housing programs, and EPA's regulations on brownfields and environmental justice also foster suburbanization.

## Little Evidence of a Federal Role in Suburbanization

Reflecting the widespread belief that the federal government contributes to suburbanization, Senators James M. Jeffords (R–VT) and Carl Levin (D–MI) asked the U.S. General Accounting Office (GAO) in late 1998 to describe the evidence that exists on the influence of current federal programs and policies on "urban sprawl." After months of reviewing the academic literature on sprawl and various federal programs, the GAO could not find any definitive impact and concluded that *the extent of federal influence on "urban sprawl" is not well documented or quantified.*[6] This conclusion is at variance with popular perceptions and prejudices, but consistent with the factual evidence on metropolitan area growth trends.

**Federal Housing Policy.** Federal mortgage insurance programs first appeared in 1934 with the creation of the Federal Housing Administration (FHA). Because the Great Depression put a damper on family income and home buying, it was not until the emergence of postwar prosperity in the late 1940s and early 1950s that homeownership took off and FHA mortgage insurance, as well as the newly enacted VA mortgage guarantee for returning war veterans, became more widely used by American households.

As Chart 7.1 reveals, in the 50 years prior to World War II, the homeownership rate in the

## Notes:

3. Stephen Goldsmith, *The Twenty-First Century City: Resurrecting Urban America* (Washington, D.C.: Regnery Publishing, Inc.), p. 89.

4. William D. Eggers, ed., "Revitalizing Our Cities: Perspectives from America's New Breed of Mayors," Washington Institute for Policy Studies, *Policy Study* No. 185, March 1995, p. 3.

5. Robert Fishman, "The American Metropolis at Century's End: Past and Future Influences," in *Legacy of the 1949 Housing Act*, Fannie Mae Foundation, September 30, 1999.

6. U.S. General Accounting Office, *Community Development: Extent of Federal Influence on "Urban Sprawl" Is Unclear,* GAO/RCED–99–87, April 1999, p. 19.

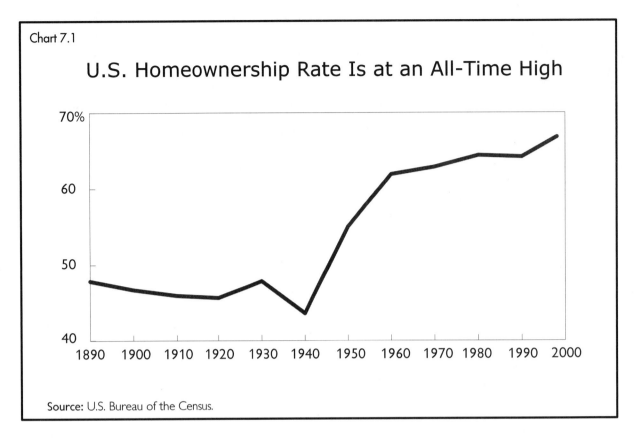

Chart 7.1

## U.S. Homeownership Rate Is at an All-Time High

Source: U.S. Bureau of the Census.

United States fluctuated between 45 percent and 48 percent, except for the 1930s when widespread economic adversity reduced it to 43.6 percent. It accelerated past 60 percent in the decade and a half after the war, and remained within the mid–60 percent range from 1960 through the present.

It is doubtful that the FHA is responsible for this surge, given its relatively modest, and declining, role in mortgage finance during the postwar era. In 1950, FHA mortgages amounted to only about a third of the volume of outstanding conventional mortgages. By 1955 FHA's share had fallen to 29 percent and has remained well below 20 percent since 1980. By 1997, outstanding FHA mortgages amounted to just 12 percent of the volume of conventional mortgages.[7] Thus while suburbanization was surging, the FHA mortgage program

was diminishing rapidly as a factor in the U.S. housing market, although, ironically, it was of growing importance in central cities.

An April 1999 GAO study of the impact of federal policies on suburbanization found that fully 41 percent of federally assisted mortgages were made on central-city houses, and that 37 percent of conventional mortgages purchased by the Federal National Mortgage Association were on houses located in central cities.[8] Inasmuch as both these "market" shares exceed the share of the U.S. population residing in central cities, the activities of FHA and FNMA cannot be viewed as pro-suburb or anti-city. Indeed, the federal government's behavior in this arena suggests quite the opposite.

The period of rising homeownership and suburbanization also coincides with the rapid growth of metropolitan areas, largely the result

**Notes:**

7. The White House, *Economic Report of the President* (Washington, D.C.: U.S. Government Printing Office, February 1999), p. 416.
8. U.S. General Accounting Office, *Community Development*, p. 33.

Table 7.1

## Housing Profile of Selected Metro Areas, 1990

| | Density (People per Square Mile) | | Year Housing Was Built | |
| --- | --- | --- | --- | --- |
| | Central City | Suburb | Central City | Suburb |
| Boston | 11,862 | 454 | 1939 | 1956 |
| Chicago | 12,251 | 378 | 1944 | 1966 |
| Cleveland | 6,564 | 307 | 1939 | 1960 |
| Detroit | 7,410 | 279 | 1945 | 1964 |
| New York | 23,702 | 555 | 1946 | 1958 |
| Philadelphia | 11,734 | 320 | 1939 | 1962 |

Source: John D. Kasarda, Stephen J. Appold, Stuart H. Sweeney and Elaine Sieff, "Central-City and Suburban Migration Patterns: Is a Turnaround on the Horizon?" *Housing Policy Debate*, Volume 8, Issue 2 (1997), p. 315.

of major demographic shifts from the country-side to more urbanized areas. In 1940, 56.5 percent of the population lived in urbanized areas, but by 1990 that share had risen to 75.2 percent as rural areas and small towns declined in population.[9] Although this period also coincides with the gradual decline in central-city populations, the growth of the suburbs was vastly greater than the corresponding decline in cities, largely as a result of the rural-to-urban migration and the increased birth rates that characterized the postwar "baby boom."

Much of this shifting and growing population chose to live in the suburbs, not the central cities. In 1950, the central cities of the 10 largest metropolitan areas held 60 percent of these areas' populations, while 40 percent lived in the suburbs. But because suburban populations in 1950 were growing 10 times faster than central-city populations, these shares drew even by 1960, and by 1990 had reversed themselves, with the suburbs now claiming a 60 percent share.[10] This period also coincides with a rise in household formation, family size, personal income, and growth in metropolitan area populations as rural and small town residents moved in.

It is important to recognize that most of the major central cities, particularly those in the East, had been fully built to their borders by the early 1950s. Therefore, the growth in the postwar population could be accommodated only by developing the surrounding areas. At the same time, 1950 marked the peak population for many of the older central cities, and the exodus of city residents, which continues today, also contributed, albeit modestly, to the growth of population and housing in the surrounding suburbs.

Another way of looking at the impact of population change is to imagine what American cities would be like if an extreme wing of the new urbanist faction had gotten its way in 1950 and was able to thwart any further suburban development in all metropolitan areas. Under such a scenario, an already very crowded New York City would have to find room for another 6 million people—an amount equal to more than

## Notes:

9. Data for 1940 from U.S. Bureau of the Census, *Historical Statistics of the United States: 1790 to 1970*, Series A57–72, "Population in Urban and Rural Territory, by Size and Place." Data for 1990 from U.S. Bureau of the Census, *Statistical Abstract of the United States, 1995*, "Urban and Rural Population 1960 to 1990," and by State," No. 44.

10. U.S. General Accounting Office, *Community Development*, pp. 1–5.

two present day Chicagos. Atlanta, which the EPA recently forced to adopt stiff growth controls, actually experienced an increase in population of 72,000 since 1950, but a 2.2 million increase in the population of the metro area. Had this growth been forced to remain within city limits, Atlanta would have a central-city population nearly as large as Chicago's (2.4 million) and with a density (21,757 persons per square mile) second only to New York City (24,245), but three times more than Los Angeles (7,415).[11]

Of course, no one would seriously contemplate establishing growth boundaries as oppressive as those suggested above. But the exercise reveals the magnitude of the population pressures that induced suburban development at a time when homeownership was becoming a popular, and affordable, option for more and more Americans.

Another important income-related factor contributing to homeownership and suburbanization was the growing obsolescence of central-city housing relative to what the postwar middle class could now afford in terms of both size (house and lot), privacy, and quality. Table 7.1 illustrates the age and density difference between the central cities and suburbs of select metro areas.

Given the age and obsolescence of central-city housing, it is not surprising that newly prosperous postwar households were attracted to homes that were bigger and better.

**Federal Highway Programs**. Many critics of suburbanization cite the federal highway program as the chief culprit in the decline of cities and the rapid growth of suburbs. The program was created in 1956 to build a limited access, high-speed interstate highway system to link America's cities coast to coast and border to border. Such criticism emerged in the system's earliest days, even when only a fraction of

today's network was completed, and it continues today. As noted earlier, a survey of "leading urban historians, planners and architects" ranked "Interstate highways and dominance of the automobile" as number one among the 10 key factors affecting the American metropolis over the past 50 years.[12] Federal mortgage programs were ranked second. Nowhere on the list were such items as population growth, poor schools, or high central-city crime rates as contributing factors of locational choice.

Such conclusions are fairly typical of America's urban experts, and the sheer weight of their opinion, as well as the intuitive appeal of their theories, gives any effort to blame highways for what ails America a compelling patina of credibility. Unfortunately for this popular theory of metropolitan development, it gets little support from the facts.

Most older American cities hit their population peaks in 1950 and declined steadily through the decades that followed. This indicates that the decline was underway even before the interstate highway program became law in 1956. By 1960, when all the older Eastern cities were losing population and suburban development was well underway, only 5,135 miles of the planned 41,000 miles of the interstate highway system were completed, mostly in rural areas.[13] Indeed, because of the difficulty and political controversy associated with land acquisition and road construction in densely populated areas, it was not until the 1980s that residents in many older cities had convenient access to interstate highways..

By then, however, the process of urban decline and suburban growth was well underway, and the segments that were completed to or through the cities had very little influence on the patterns of suburban development that followed. In the Washington, D.C., area, for example, much of the postwar suburban growth took

**Notes**:

11. See *http://www.publicpurpose.com*.
12. Fishman, "The American Metropolis at Century's End."
13. Federal Highway Administration, "Development of the Dwight D. Eisenhower System of Interstate and Defense Highways," unpublished table provided by the U.S. Department of Transportation in 1999.

place due east and due west of the city center, although there were no interstate highways serving either area. Philadelphia's suburbs, too, grew steadily through the postwar era, even though Interstate 95 terminated five miles southwest of the city line until the 1980s. When completed, the interstate route traveled past suburban communities whose existence predated World War II. In fact, their location and the stubborn resistance of their residents were among the major obstacles to the completion of the highway to the city.

As the postwar evidence suggests, the patterns of suburban development in communities across the country bear little or no relationship to the absence or presence of federally funded highways. Rather, these patterns were influenced largely by a growing population, and to a lesser extent by the decline in the quality of life and public services and the aging housing stock characteristic of most older communities.

Although there is little convincing evidence to connect the growth of highways with the growth of the suburbs, automobiles and the federal funding of highways continue to be cited as the chief cause of central-city decline and the major contributor to rapid suburbanization. In turn, critics of suburbs go on to assert that the greater availability of subsidized public transit—whether rail, buses, subways, or trolleys—will discourage auto use and in the process prevent sprawl and suburbanization, while also revitalizing the central cities.

This line of thinking led to the creation of the federal Urban Mass Transit Administration (UMTA) in 1965. UMTA, later renamed the Federal Transit Administration, was rolled into the U.S. Department of Transportation when that cabinet department was created in 1966. Since

> Today, nearly as many people walk and bicycle to work as take all forms of transit.

1960, federal, state, and local governments have invested over $385 billion (in 1999 dollars) in transit programs. Moreover, 2.86 cents of the federal fuel tax paid by motorists, as well as additional funds from general federal revenues, is spent each year on transit projects around the country.

Despite these generous subsidies from motorists and taxpayers in general—fares paid by transit users cover only 25 percent of their costs[14]—transit systems throughout the country serve a declining share of commuters. Today, nearly as many people walk and bicycle to work (2.76 percent) as take all forms of transit (3.19 percent).[15] Even cities with new and costly state-of-the-art light rail systems have failed to stem the decline in transit ridership, and new transit systems in places such as Atlanta, Portland, and Washington, D.C., have lost market share over the past decade. Moreover, major transit investments and upgrades in older Eastern cities have done little to stem the exodus from declining cities, as Baltimore, Maryland, and Washington, D.C., illustrate. (See Chapter 4.)

## The Historical Role of Mass Transit

Although the evidence suggests that federal transit spending has done nothing to deter the decline of central cities, other evidence actually suggests that mass transit systems, whether subsidized or not, may have contributed to the suburbanization process by facilitating and subsidizing commuting patterns that bring suburban workers to their central-city jobs. The history of America's turn-of-the-century trolley systems, whose origins pre-date the mass production of the automobile, is often intertwined with the history of suburban real estate development because many such trolley lines and transit systems were created by real estate

**Notes:**

14. See Chapter 4 for a discussion of transportation-related issues.
15. See the U.S. Census of Transportation, as reproduced on *http://www.publicpurpose.com*.

developers to promote the sale of land and houses.

An interesting example of transit-induced suburbanization occurred in the Washington, D.C., area in the late 19th century. U.S. Senators Francis G. Newlands and William Stewart, both representing Nevada, were two of several partners in the Chevy Chase Land Co., which owned thousands of acres of undeveloped farmland just over the District of Columbia's border in Maryland. At that time, most of northwest Washington and nearby Maryland was farmland. Using his influence in the Senate, Stewart was able to get the federal government to buy 2,000 acres in northwest D.C. to create a "green belt" that would serve as a wooded buffer (now known as Rock Creek Park) between a planned housing development in Maryland and the emerging urban congestion the Land Co. investors believed well-to-do District residents would want to escape. Stewart also used his influence to obtain a charter for a trolley franchise, and Newlands and other partners secretly acquired farmland in Washington's northwest quadrant for the trolley's right-of-way. The trolley line was built in 1892, and by 1901, 49 homes had been built in Chevy Chase to a site plan created by the design firm of Frederick Law Olmsted, the designer of New York's Central Park.[16]

This process of private construction of trolley lines to induce suburban development was repeated in other parts of the Washington area, as well as in other cities around the country. Many other older suburbs originally were part of this national trend of trolley/land development projects created and funded by private entrepreneurs who recognized an emerging market of city dwellers longing for the suburban lifestyle. But within a few short years, the advent of inexpensive mass-produced automobiles induced residents of Chevy Chase to abandon the trolleys, and by 1935—more than 20 years before the creation of the interstate highway program—the Chevy Chase trolley line was shut down for lack of riders. This occurrence was repeated in city after city, ultimately leading to the public ownership of virtually every mass transit system in the country.

Although the automobile would emerge as a key form of personal transportation in the 1920s, it was the availability of mass transit that largely facilitated the move to the suburbs throughout the 1950s. It continues to play an important role today, particularly with the growing emphasis on more attractive—and more costly—light rail systems that in many metropolitan areas connect central cities with distant suburbs.

**Has Anything Changed in 100 Years?** Ironically, the federal government justifies its ongoing subsidies to public transit on the grounds that convenient transit programs will yield a result that is precisely the opposite of what was seen during the first half-century of suburbanization. President Bill Clinton best illustrated this view in 1996 when he announced that "Investment in critical mass transit projects is key to rebuilding our cities and stimulating economic development throughout the Nation."[17]

## Notes:

16. Olmsted's role in shaping America's then emerging suburbs stretched beyond helping to design one here and there; it also extended to establishing a series of design principles still in use today, but which are subject to vigorous criticism by new urbanists in general and the "Main Street" faction in particular. Developers of the early suburbs sought to achieve a "rural ideal," and the design and zoning principles that were utilized attempted to exclude anything that smacked of "urbanization," including mixing commerce with housing. In Olmsted's view, civilization would be enhanced by separating "business premises from domestic premises." Today's rigid adherence to single-use zoning, which excludes retail from suburban developments and concentrates all commercial activities in site-specific shopping centers and business parks, can trace its origins to these late 19th century design principles and the favorable reception to them shown by prospective homebuyers.

17. U.S. Department of Transportation, "President Clinton, Secretary Peña Announce $2 Billion Federal Commitment to Transit," Press Release FTA 05–96, March 13, 1996.

Today's federally subsidized transit systems, with their growing emphasis on rail rather than buses, continue the process of facilitating suburbanization by making commuting from distant suburbs more convenient and less costly. With an efficient and comprehensive rail system, urban workers can now reside far from their place of employment. The metro and light rail systems recently built in Atlanta, Baltimore, San Francisco, and Washington, D.C., to name just a few, represent "hub-and-spoke" designs that connect a ring of distant suburban communities with central-city jobs. They thereby facilitate a degree of population dispersal that might otherwise have been deterred by growing traffic congestion.

This misplaced federal effort continues at ever escalating levels of spending. Thanks to the increased interest among Members of Congress in programs that benefit their growing suburban constituencies, the FY 2000 transportation appropriation bill includes $980 million to design or explore new or extended commuter rail systems in 104 communities. These include cities as small as Girdwood, Alaska; Montpelier, Vermont; Santa Fe, New Mexico; and Calais, Maine.

**Federal Subsidies of Other Infrastructure.** Critics of suburbanization also cite a history of federal financial support for public infrastructure other than roads that may have tipped the balance in favor of suburbs compared with cities. This favoritism, they argue, has led to costly and wasteful expenditures on water supply and treatment facilities that would be unnecessary if individuals had not been seduced into moving to the suburbs.

Historically, the federal government has provided financial grants to communities—both cities and suburbs—to offset some of the cost of wastewater treatment facilities to meet increasingly strict water quality guidelines encouraged or established by the federal government. Grants were made as early as 1956, but became more common following the enact-ment of the federal Clean Water Act. Through the mid-1980s, the federal government provided grants for upgrades, but this assistance subsequently was replaced by federally supported, state-operated revolving funds.

Although such federal financial support currently amounts to about $2.4 billion per year, or 15 percent of what all levels of government are spending on the construction and renovation of water supply and treatment plants, federal law requires that these funds be used for the replacement or upgrade of an existing plant, and not for adding capacity where none had previously existed.[18] As a result of this requirement, federal financial support for wastewater treatment facilities is largely targeted to existing communities because it cannot be used to assist new development.

Facilities to add capacity to accommodate development must be funded from a community's own resources, which means that new developments must pay to build the facilities. Federal water programs do not encourage additional suburbanization. If anything, the federal focus on existing communities could be viewed as biasing the program in favor of older cities and suburbs and against new development. Regardless, both the evidence and the current program's guidelines suggest that federal support for water treatment is not a significant inducement to suburbanization.

## CREATING A MORE ACCOMMODATIVE FEDERAL ROLE

Although an analysis of federal transportation, housing, and infrastructure policies suggests that they have done little or nothing to foster suburbanization, it is also true that they offer little to help communities deal with rapid growth. This need not be the case. A number of reforms in existing federal housing and transportation programs could make them more effective in helping communities to address the problems associated with population growth.

**Notes**:

18. U.S. General Accounting Office, *Community Development*, p. 51.

Even with such reforms, however, federal programs will not necessarily be an important tool for community improvement. The history of federal programs that were created to "benefit" cities and communities has been checkered at best, and counterproductive at worst (see Chapter 6). Urban renewal programs, low-income housing assistance, mass transit subsidies, and generous welfare payments may very well have worsened the plight of many older central cities by undermining the quality of urban living. At the same time, by creating the impression that urban revitalization is a federal responsibility, these programs also discouraged local elected officials from taking the kind of initiative that recently has been so successful in New York City and Chicago.

Like cities in the past, fast-growing suburbs run the risk of embracing new or restructured federal programs at the expense of home-grown solutions that rely on local leadership and community preferences and accommodate the unique characteristics of each community. Community leaders must recognize that proposals to improve federal programs do not translate into solutions to community growth problems, nor can they substitute for local initiative and leadership.

**Reforming Federal Transportation Policy.** As part of the Livable Communities agenda, President Clinton and Vice President Gore in early 1999 proposed a few modest changes in the federal highway program to help communities better deal with escalating traffic congestion and related problems caused by population growth that exceeded the capacity of the existing transportation infrastructure. Although these proposals were not enacted into law, the recognition that the existing federal highway program needs some changes—if not a major overhaul—is an idea that should be pursued by states and local communities in search of relief from worsening traffic congestion.

The federal highway program, which began in 1956, represented a significant break from past practices of funding roads and highways. Through much of America's history, the federal role in roads and highways was limited, and mostly involved Depression-era relief efforts during the 1930s. This changed in 1956 with the creation of the federal highway program, and its dedicated trust fund, with the original purpose of constructing a 41,000-mile interstate highway system linking every state and major cities throughout America. The system was largely completed by 1980 when 40,252 miles were opened for traffic. Yet advocates of the program were reluctant to see its termination, so a new mission was created in 1995; the National Highway System added 161,000 miles of roads that would be eligible for dedicated federal funds, thereby assuring the program's existence for another several decades. An earlier change to broaden support and perpetuate the program was to set aside 2.86 cents of the federal fuel tax for transit spending including trolleys, trains, subways, and buses.

At present, the federal highway program raises and spends approximately $35 billion each year. Although these federal funds are spent by each state's department of transportation, the federal government determines how these funds are allocated among the states and between broad transportation objectives—i.e., highways, bridges, or mass transit—as well as for individual projects earmarked by Members of Congress. As such, it is something of a one-size-fits-all program. This may have been appropriate when the program's task was to build the interstate system, but today, when most transportation "problems" are local and/or regional in nature and vary dramatically from one community to another, such a universal approach is of limited value.

Also undermining the program's ability to deal with suburban traffic congestion are the regional inequities that characterize the state-by-state distribution of the federal highway and transit funds. Federal funds are allocated by mathematical formulae based in part on each state's auto and fuel use, miles and condition of road, and other factors. Although this system would seem to be fair, other factors that influence the formula can bias federal highway spending in favor of states in which population growth is slower than average, and against those that are growing faster than the average.

As a result, the more money you need, the less you get; and the less you need, the more you get.

The failure of the federal highway program to address emerging local and regional mobility problems adequately suggests that the federal highway program, whose original goals have been met, is in need of a fundamental overhaul. Such an overhaul should ensure that the taxpaying motorists end up with a program that best serves their regional and local needs, and that the process of deciding how to spend resources is in the hands of local officials, the best judges of local priorities.

One way to achieve these objectives within the framework of the existing federal highway program is to return to each state, in a block grant, an amount equal to the total federal fuel tax revenue raised in that state. States then should be allowed to spend these funds on transportation projects that meet their priorities, not Washington's. This transportation block grant would be restricted in use only to the extent that it would have to be spent on transportation-related projects (rather than, say, on housing programs, welfare, or higher salaries).

A less complicated alternative would be to allow each state simply to keep the proceeds of the federal fuel tax raised within its borders and to spend them according to its own transportation priorities.

Both of these plans preserve the federal fuel tax and ensure some base level of transportation spending. To address concerns that the maintenance and modernization of the completed federal interstate highway system might be jeopardized by a state's parochial focus, a few cents of the federal fuel tax could remain in Washington and be devoted exclusively to maintenance of the 41,000 miles of roadway in the existing interstate system. Alternatively, states could be required to maintain their segments of the system using the fuel tax funds retained or provided by way of the block grant.

The remaining transportation funds then would be allocated according to a state's own priorities, with no unnecessary federal interference, regulation, or mandates. The advantages of such a reform for each community would be significant:

1. **Fast-growing states** would no longer be financially penalized by a flawed federal allocation formula. Such states would now receive a greater share of transportation dollars to meet their escalating transportation needs.

2. **States** would be free to allocate the funds according to their own transportation priorities, not Washington's.

3. **States** would be free to dispense with costly federally imposed non-transportation objectives and regulations, such as prohibitions on charging tolls; a required union wage scale for highway workers; costly federal contracting rules and preferences; environmental enhancements, such as bicycle paths, noise abatement, historic preservation, landscaping, and hiking trails; set-asides for transit; and specific earmarks for influential constituents, such as developers seeking an interchange or parking garage to serve their property.

4. **Total transportation spending** could no longer be withheld by the federal government to meet other budgetary objectives, such as deficit reduction or increased spending elsewhere in the federal bureaucracy.

**Federal Housing Policy.** Although there is no measurable connection between federal policies that favor homeownership and the suburbanization of metropolitan areas, there is growing evidence that many of the federal housing assistance programs have harmed the central cities by concentrating low-income families in the cities (see Chapter 6). To the extent that these programs have undermined the quality of life in central cities and older suburbs, they also have driven some portion of the central-city population to the suburbs and deterred others from moving in.

About two-thirds of HUD's housing assistance to the poor is delivered by way of government-subsidized housing projects, such as public housing, to serve low-income households. Such projects concentrate the poor in specific neighborhoods, which in turn leads to higher crime rates, diminished economic activity, and community deterioration.[19] Although these low-income projects generally are associated with crumbling inner-city neighborhoods, projects also can be found in older close-in suburbs, and the effect on those communities is similar to that of the central cities. Efforts to introduce such projects to suburban neighborhoods often lead to acrimonious conflict, racial hostility, and court orders that require some communities to take their "fair share" of such subsidized housing.

Recognizing that federal reliance upon such subsidized projects has done more harm than good to both the assisted individuals and the communities in which they are placed, many housing analysts have recommended policy alternatives that avoid concentrating the poor in single projects. One of the leading proposals is to rely more on federally provided rent certificates or vouchers that provide low-income individuals with the funds they need to rent a decent, affordable apartment from a private-sector landlord. Such programs allow the poor to integrate themselves into the community at large, and avoid their segregation and concentration in certain neighborhoods. In turn, this leads to greater neighborhood stability.

Former Secretary of HUD Henry Cisneros, who served in the Clinton Administration from 1992 to 1998, proposed just such an approach in 1995, but Congress rejected it in favor of providing more money for the status quo. Revisiting such a policy, and implementing it, could go a long way toward improving the quality of life in many older cities and suburbs.

Another major HUD program that could be redirected to help communities searching for solutions to congestion and rapid development is the Community Development Block Grant (CDBG) program, which each year spends between $4 billion and $5 billion on a variety of community-based projects. The CDBG program is an entitlement, and cities and counties in designated metropolitan areas receive money according to a formula based upon population and other factors. Non-metropolitan counties receive their federal CDBG allotment by way of their state government.

Although CDBG money generally is used for housing rehabilitation and economic development, many environmental improvements and quality-of-life enhancements related to smart-growth objectives could also be made eligible for CDBG funding. Thus, as community and county governments determine their priorities, they should recognize that the federal CDBG program can be used to meet some of their growth objectives. This also implies that efforts by some Members of Congress and the Administration to create a new federal land purchase/preservation program as part of the Livable Communities plan is redundant, because a federal program to provide such financial support on a more flexible basis already exists.

## EFFECTIVE GOVERNANCE

Notwithstanding the conventional wisdom within the community planning profession and among other urban analysts, there is little evidence to suggest that federal programs have contributed to or encouraged suburbanization or sprawl. Instead, the chief culprit appears to be the postwar population growth that added 119 million new Americans to the nation's cities and suburbs and rural communities since 1950. However, although the suspect federal programs—namely federal highway and housing programs—appear to have done little or

**Notes**:

19. See Ronald Utt, "What to Do About the Cities," Heritage Foundation *Backgrounder* No. 1216, September 1, 1998, p. 31, and Sandra J. Newman and Ann B. Schnare, " '...And a Suitable Living Environment': The Failure of Housing Programs to Deliver on Neighborhood Quality," *Housing Policy Debate*, Vol. 8, No. 4 (1997), p. 703.

nothing to induce sprawl, it also appears that they do little to alleviate some of the adverse effects of rapid suburbanization. This need not be the case. A number of reforms could be made to reconfigure these programs and provide communities with more effective tools to enable them to preserve parkland and overcome traffic congestion.

# THE MARKET RESPONDS TO SMART GROWTH

8

## By Donald R. Leal

"**S**mart growth" has become synonymous with government intervention to deal with the problems of sprawl. Yet as pressure mounts for such intervention, private developers and builders are trying out new concepts that offer more choices.

Even with their faults, suburbs remain the number one choice among the majority of homebuyers. Americans want the privacy, the large lots, and the open space that suburbs provide. At the same time, there is little question that residential development in the suburbs could stand some variation and new ideas.

For those who need or aspire to a lifestyle less dependent on the automobile, the conventional suburban development has little to offer. And for those who desire a stronger community setting, suburbia may be inadequate. As one family stated in *Time* magazine, "We want our four children to grow up in a community, not at a highway exit."[1] Furthermore, like the cities they border, some older suburbs are experiencing deterioration, with increasing traf-

fic congestion, pollution, crime rates, and lost amenities. Such problems have set the stage for another wave of flight from older suburbs that have fewer resources to maintain public services and quality schools.

The good news is that across the country entrepreneurs are capitalizing on the rising demand for social and environmental amenities with innovative ideas for residential development. The innovations can be grouped into three categories:

1. **Traditional neighborhood developments (TNDs).** Sometimes called "new urbanist" or neo-traditional developments, developments such as Kentlands in Maryland and Southern Village in North Carolina are attracting homebuyers who want a stronger feeling of community.

2. **Environmentally sensitive developments.** Sea Ranch in California and River Run in Idaho are examples of

**Notes:**

1. Tim Padgett, "Saving Suburbia," *Time*, August 16, 1999, pp. 50–51.

developments that appeal to homebuyers who desire a natural, rural setting while maintaining all the conveniences of modern life.

3. **Cutting-edge residential designs**. Examples of these are underway in areas around Minneapolis, Indianapolis, and Madison, Wisconsin. They mitigate the unpleasant aspects of sprawl while satisfying homebuyer preferences for privacy, large lot sizes, and open space at a price that is within the range of a large number of homebuyers.

## TRADITIONAL NEIGHBORHOOD DEVELOPMENTS

Traditional neighborhood developments emerged during the 1990s partly in response to the calls for an end to urban sprawl and partly as an attempt to restore a sense of community. These planned communities are designed to reflect the style and patterns of development that existed in many small towns during the first half of the 20th century.

Ironically, these developments also reflect the original design plan used for the oldest sections of many major cities in America—a design that failed to prevent the migration to the suburbs in the latter half of the century. Characteristics of these urban communities included tiny lots with homes situated close to one another; narrow streets connected to form a grid pattern of blocks; commercial use intermingled with residential use; and virtually everything necessary for typical city life—stores, churches, schools, homes, and jobs—within walking distance. Such designs generally preceded the advent of zoning.

**Entrepreneurs are capitalizing on the rising demand for social and environmental amenities with innovative ideas for residential development.**

Today's "new urbanism" movement is seeking something similar. According to the *New Urban News*, a popular newsletter for new urbanists, in order to be classified as a TND a development must include "a mix of uses and housing types, a compact, interconnected street and block pattern, a clearly defined center for each neighborhood, and pedestrian-oriented design."[2]

Several examples illustrate this pattern.

**Seaside, Florida.** Built in the late 1980s, Seaside is one of three contemporary TNDs prominently featured in the media.[3] With this 80-acre beach community, developer Robert Davis hoped to offer a viable alternative to mainstream suburbia. Judging from the extensive coverage Seaside has received in recent years, he appears to have succeeded. Descriptions in a host of popular magazines have conveyed the small-town simplicity of Seaside's housing and the charm of its shops and restaurants.

To help design Seaside, Davis enlisted the services of internationally recognized urban architects Andres Duany and Elizabeth Plater-Zyberk. Their design is definitely "small-town"—people "gather on porches, walk to the market every day, and come together for concerts on the grass; a town where all streets lead to the beach,"[4] writes correspondent Judith Kirkwood in *Attaché*. The travel corridors are pedestrian-

**Notes:**

2. Robert Steuteville, ed., "Nationwide Survey," *New Urban News* (Ithaca, New York), September/October 1999, p. 5.
3. The other two TNDs are Disney's Celebration in Florida and Kentlands in Maryland.
4. Judith Kirkwood, "Endless Summer," *Attaché*, October 1999, p. 66.

friendly. Narrow red brick streets discourage vehicle traffic—"cars are so out of scale that they look like monstrosities, " says Kirkwood—and the layout of the town brings everything within easy reach of foot traffic.[5] Seaside contains 325 homes; about 30 are occupied by the town's permanent residents and the rest are available for rent for vacationers.

Real estate in Seaside is expensive, not only because of its unique design and architecture but also because it is a resort community on a Florida beach. Three-story "cottages" range in price from $750,000 to $985,000; two-bedroom townhomes range in price from $650,000 to $785,000; and one-bedroom "penthouse" condominiums range in price from $250,000 to $385,000.[6]

**Kentlands, Maryland.** Seaside helped to popularize the TND concept, but a host of other developments are proving the concept is applicable in a variety of settings. One of the best known is Kentlands, a development planned for 1,500 homes  located in Gaithersburg, Maryland, near Washington, D.C.

Kentlands recently celebrated its 10th anniversary. This 352-acre development has a colonial village atmosphere; the 200-year-old Kentlands mansion is an integral part of its landscape. There are narrow alleys, some brick sidewalks, and a village green. Most of the detached homes and townhomes have garages located in the rear of the lots with alley access.

Homebuyers pay a premium for choosing a home in Kentlands over nearby areas. Prices in Kentlands for detached homes range from $310,000 to $500,000 or more.[7] Based on home sales data from 1994 to 1997, Kentlands homebuyers paid a premium of about $24,603 per home over home prices in conventional developments.[8] Even so, the sales volume at Kentlands tends to equal or exceed that of competing neighborhoods.

Kentlands also offers a host of modern facilities for recreation, entertainment, and social gatherings. The two-story recreation or community youth center has places for meetings and facilities for such activities such as weightlifting, aerobics, tennis, swimming, basketball, and volleyball. In addition to the youth center, there is a cinema, music store, pizza parlor, and skating rink—all within walking or biking distance of the homes. According to resident Diane Dorney, Kentlands has much to offer children: "I was worried that my kids wouldn't want to hang out so close to home like that until I noticed how often their friends from outside Kentlands keep coming here."[9]

Kentlands is completing construction of a town center called Midtown. In spite of its name, Midtown is not in the center of Kentlands, where the majority of customers for its shops would be walking residents. Instead, to encourage higher customer traffic, Midtown is located on one side of the development where it can be easily reached by people on foot or driving in from the surrounding neighborhoods and businesses.

**Southern Village, North Carolina.** Unlike typical suburban subdivisions, which have many streets that end in cul-de-sacs, none of the streets of the 312-acre Southern Village in Chapel Hill, North Carolina, are dead ends. They all lead to places such as the hilltop village square, which has a church and soon a four-screen cinema, a grocery, and a restaurant, or

**Notes:**

5. *Ibid.*, pp. 66–67.
6. See Seaside Community Realty, Inc., "Properties for Sale in Seaside," at *http://www.seasidefl.com/scripts/re/realtypage.asp.*
7. See "Buying a Home in Kentlands, Montgomery County, Maryland," at *http://www.homes-mont-county-md.com/kentlands/index.html.*
8. Sheila Muto, "'New Urbanism' Seen Lifting Home Prices," *The Wall Street Journal*, California edition, August 4, 1999, p. CA2.
9. Quoted in Padgett, "Saving Suburbia."

the recreation center complete with soccer field and tennis courts.

Home prices at Southern Village range from $90,000 for condominiums to a high of $600,000 for custom-built houses.[10] Nearly all homes are within a five-minute walk of the village square. As with other TNDs, the lots in Southern Village are smaller than is typical in other developments and the community theme is strong. Rather than offering an escape from the suburbs, Southern Village represents a way of reinventing them.

**Civano, Arizona.** Most TNDs offer a range of housing types and prices, including rental units, but few are marketing moderately-priced units as is Civano, a development located along the urban fringe of Tucson, Arizona. Prices for single homes start at $99,000.

Designed by Moule & Polyzoides, Duany Plater-Zyberk, and Wayne Moody, this development offers homes based on Sonoran adobe architecture—the first units of this style built in Tucson in many decades—combined with southwestern bungalows. As with other TNDs, small-lot homes are grouped around a neighborhood center that includes commercial uses intermixed with residential use.

## Prospects for TNDs

There is little question that traditional neighborhood developments offer an option for American homebuyers who want to feel part of a close-knit community and be less dependent on their cars for transportation. Five years ago,

> TNDs are an option for homebuyers who want to feel part of a close-knit community and be less dependent on their cars.

there were probably no more than a handful of these communities in the nation. At the end of 1999, more than 100 were operating, with an additional 200 on the drawing board.[11]

Still, these developments face several challenges.

First, it is difficult to get zoning approval. TNDs require variances to allow intermixing of commercial and residential buildings and building-code changes to allow new designs, such as garages built at the rear of the houses. Robert Daigle of River Ranch, Louisiana, was successful in obtaining all the variances needed to accommodate his mixed uses and narrow roads. However, many others are fighting to get changes in local laws to make TNDs legal.[12]

Second, it is difficult to create an economically viable commercial town center when one of the objectives of a TND is to discourage high vehicular traffic flows. Fortunately, this problem is not insurmountable. As noted above, siting the Kentlands commercial center at the edge of the development may attract enough people from other neighborhoods to maintain a viable retail area.

And while many environmentalists embrace the compactness of TNDs as a way to save open space, there are environmental trade-offs. Such developments often result in as much as 20 percent more linear feet of paved road than do conventional developments,[13] because the curvilinear streets of conventional developments eliminate the alleys and collector streets of

**Notes**:

10. *Ibid.*
11. Steuteville, "Nationwide Survey."
12. *Ibid.*
13. Rick Harrison, "Sensible Solutions for Smart Growth, a Publication for Municipalities and those Impacting Public Policy and/or Housing Funding," published by Rick Harrison Site Design and Software Services, St. Louis Park, Minn., n.d., p. 4.

TNDs. The Environmental Protection Agency and environmental groups point to the expansion of paved roads as a major contributor to deteriorating watershed quality.

Finally, perhaps the biggest challenge for TNDs is affordability. Many of the most successful TND developers rely on custom builders to design the complex architectural home styles that will attract homebuyers willing to give up large lots. The higher design and construction costs as well as the cost of common-area infrastructure result in more expensive homes. Moreover, TND developers who use mass-production builders to lower construction costs have experienced problems. For example, the Walt Disney Company used mass-production builders to construct Celebration, its TND near Orlando, Florida. But there was a rash of complaints over construction quality. Although the main problems were related to labor shortages, subcontractors, and the pace of construction, the complex architectural guidelines also proved too much for the builders to satisfy.[14]

## ECO-DEVELOPMENTS

Another innovation emerging in the marketplace is the environmentally sensitive development. Farms, ranches, forests, wildlife, wetlands, and trout streams are hallmarks of rural life. But now abundant signs of nature can be found in one's backyard (see Chapter 3). Environmentally sensitive developments, or "eco-developments," have created a new niche in the real estate industry, one that harmonizes home sites with the protection of nature and rural amenities.

Typically, a large portion of the eco-development is maintained as community space or a nature preserve. The remaining portion is divided into lots for homes. These can be as small as a half-acre or as large as 500 acres, as in the case of Wildcat Ranch near Aspen, Colorado. Preserving such open space close to urban areas is expensive. The costs are partially offset by eliminating sidewalks, golf courses, paved streets, and manicured landscapes. Even so, because these developments are at the top of the residential market, homes are not cheap. In some eco-developments, family homes are selling for $200,000, while others start at $1 million.

**Environmentally sensitive developments harmonize home sites with the protection of nature and rural amenities.**

**Sea Ranch, California.** Located about 100 miles north of San Francisco, along 10 miles of the scenic northern California coast, Sea Ranch is internationally recognized as one of the best examples of environmentally sensitive residential developments. In 1991, one architectural awards committee noted that Sea Ranch is "profoundly conscious of the natural drama of its coastal site" and has "formed an alliance of architecture and nature that has inspired and captivated a generation of architects."[15] The 5,200-acre site includes a 1,500-acre forest preserve and a 200-acre county park and campground, and more than half of the 3,500-acre building site is permanently dedicated open space. The development offers visitors and permanent residents a 40-mile private road system for bicycling, more than 75 miles of private hiking trails, and a host of other outdoor activities. A design committee ensures that all homes blend into the natural landscape and have a minimal impact on the surrounding environment.

Sea Ranch started as a sheep ranch called Rancho Del Mar. When architect and planner Al Boeke came upon the ranch, he envisioned the

**Notes**:

14. Steuteville, "Nationwide Survey," p. 12.
15. See Sea Ranch Village, Inc., *History of the Sea Ranch Area*, 1996, at *http://www.mcn.org/searanch/history.html*.

possibilities of a second-home community built in harmony with the coastal environment. In 1963, he convinced Hawaii-based developer Castle & Cooke, Inc., to purchase the entire 5,200 acres for $2.3 million through its California subsidiary Oceanic California, Inc. Upon change of ownership, the developer set about funding extensive restoration of the land, based on thorough studies of the native plants, animals, soils, and the climate. Logging slash and debris were removed from the forested areas and thousands of acres of logged and grazed areas were replanted with native trees and grasses, both to reverse the effects of erosion and to provide habitat for wildlife.

The only drawbacks to this exemplary development are high house prices and a location remote from a major job center. Luxurious ocean-front homes are priced from $445,000 to $2.4 million and lots are priced from $175,000 to $575,000. Redwood forest retreats are priced from $145,000 to $575,000 for homes and $27,000 to $65,000 for home sites. Because the community is a long distance from urban areas, those who have been able to make Sea Ranch their full-time residence are primarily self-employed professionals, including authors, artists, and composers, as well as people in aviation, consulting, or other professions that do not require their regular presence at an urban office.

**Prairie Crossing, Illinois.** Prairie Crossing is a residential development in Grayslake, Illinois,[16] a town positioned between Chicago and Milwaukee. Prairie Crossing, which broke ground in 1994, is designed with the goal of preserving the open landscape and encouraging residents to live in harmony with the environment. It is virtually unique in incorporating agricultural production with residential development and open space preservation.[17]

The development's landscape and architecture are inspired by the prairies, marshes, and farms of central Lake County, Illinois. Field lots, for example, are located along the major interior roadways, with rear yards opening to acres of cropland. Prairie lots, in contrast, are grouped together like spokes in a wheel, eight lots per wheel. Each wheel is surrounded by a re-created prairie. House designs hark back to Midwest homesteads, with open-air porches and spacious floor plans.

The houses and streets are situated so that they do not disturb existing natural contours, native vegetation, or wildlife. Streets are named after native prairie plants and the early settlers who frequented the site. Community buildings include the Byron Colby Barn, a restored barn more than 100 years old that serves as the community center and a site for special events, an early schoolhouse, and an old farmhouse, intentionally included to connect new residents with those of the past.

When completed, Prairie Crossing will include 317 home sites within a 668-acre development. Approximately 60 percent of the land will be protected as open space. The development includes 150 acres of agricultural land and community gardens and 228 acres of lakes, wetlands, meadows, and prairies linked by 15 miles of hiking trails. To maintain native prairie vegetation, periodic fire and replantings are necessary. Volunteers conduct these activities under the supervision of the Liberty Prairie Conservancy, an organization that conducts stewardship programs throughout the nearby 2,500-acre Liberty Prairie Reserve.

Prairie Crossing offers more than a dozen different home styles. Homes range in size from 1,140 square feet to 3,428 square feet, with prices ranging from $239,900 to $427,900.

**River Run, Idaho.** River Run, located on the east side of Boise, Idaho, next to the Boise

**Notes:**

16. The development is located one hour northwest of Chicago by train or car and an hour south of Milwaukee, Wisconsin.
17. Prairie Holdings Corporation, *Prairie Crossing: A Conservation Community*, n.d., at *http://www.prairiecrossing.com/index.htm*.

River, exemplifies what developers can do to help restore natural beauty on degraded land and waterways. Most of River Run's property had been heavily grazed by livestock when Peter O'Neill began to develop it as a residential community in 1977. From the beginning, O'Neill emphasized enhancing the property's natural amenities. He recognized that this would increase the values of the homes. A brochure on River Run describes his intentions: "River Run has been designed and built with a sensitivity to the natural environment found here. The plan has always been to create and ensure premium value for homeowners and residents."[18]

River Run's 120 acres contain single-family homes (including custom homes) and condominiums built to capitalize on the river setting. The property's potential for natural amenities was enhanced with the construction of seven-acre Heron Lake and the creation and rehabilitation of free-flowing streams.

Perhaps the most innovative feature of this development was the transformation of an ugly flood-control channel into an attractive year-round trout stream. Between 1984 and 1989, the channel was reshaped, using concrete and log structures, to create a meandering flow with pools, riffles, and spawning beds for trout. Similar modifications were made to other streams in the River Run system. Heron Lake was deepened and over two miles of new streams were created throughout the residential complex. Finally, to help trout from the Boise River enter the River Run system, a fish ladder was constructed at the irrigation gate at Loggers Creek and another at the outflow of Heron Lake. The restoration project has been good for trout: "It's obvious that trout are thriving in the channel now,"[19] says state biologist Scott Grunder.

Has the effort been worth it to O'Neill and residents? Apparently so. Upon completion of the project in 1990, 600-square-foot condominiums were selling for $50,000, homesites for $70,000 to $150,000, and custom homes for upwards of $1 million. The project sold out within a year.

Because the River Run project was the first residential development in the country to create a productive trout habitat from its waterways, O'Neill's development is cited by the Idaho Department of Fish and Game as an example of what developers can do to help restore urban rivers. The Urban Land Institute awarded O'Neill its Design Excellence Award in 1990.

**Dewees Island, South Carolina.** In 1992, developer John Knott came to Dewees Island, a privately owned barrier island 12 miles northeast of Charleston, South Carolina, to help a friend decide how to develop it. Seeing the palmettos and craggy live oaks and other distinctive vegetation, Knott concluded that as little as possible should be done to change the island. He believed he could demonstrate that people could live there with nature without disrupting it too much. He thought that he could leave a good portion of the 1,206-acre island undeveloped and still make a profit. Bill Savage, the Washington, D.C., developer, agreed; Knott became one of the 25 partners in the development group and chief executive officer.[20]

Dewees Island, which is accessible only by boat, eventually will have 150 home sites ranging from one to three acres in size. More than 65 percent of the island is already permanently set aside from development. Home site prices begin at $375,000, and home prices start at $830,000. By 1998, Dewees Island had 104 property owners and 32 completed homes.

## Notes:

18. River Run Development Company, *River Run: The Program for Improving Trout Habitat* (Boise, Idaho: River Run Development Company, 1991).

19. Interview with Scott Grunder, environmental staff biologist, Idaho Fish and Game Department, June 29, 1994.

20. Lyn Riddle, "Nature's a Principal in an Island Project," *The New York Times*, May 29, 1994.

To minimize disturbance to the land, the homes are restricted to a maximum of 5,000 square feet, and the construction of each home must not disturb more than 7,500 square feet of land. Trees must be moved, not cut down. Only indigenous plants may be used in landscaping and exterior materials must be selected to suit the humid subtropical climate. In addition, the 46 oceanfront homes must be built within the maritime forest, situated well back from the sand dunes. No bridge will be built to the island, since cars are not allowed.

Among the island's features are three miles of beaches, boat access, an environmental education center staffed by a full-time naturalist, nature trails, a 200-acre tidal lake, a 120-acre impoundment, a swimming pool, two tennis courts, a community pavilion, fishing docks, and a guest house. Golf carts, bicycles, and walking are the primary means of getting around the island. However, there is no golf course, nor are there plans for one.[21]

### Similar Developments

In other areas of the country as well, "eco-developers" are responding to the demands of an affluent population to build communities that combine conservation with residential real estate.[22] In the early 1970s, for example, Forbes, Inc., the parent company of *Forbes* magazine, acquired the gigantic Trinchera Ranch, which stretches across 400 square miles of southern Colorado. A Forbes subsidiary, Sangre de Cristo Ranches, sold residential sites of varying sizes on selected areas of the ranch to people seeking vacation or retirement homes with access rights to Trinchera's common lands. Forbes subsequently sold the ranch to a real estate developer, who continues to protect the ranch's private wilderness area that is home to abundant elk, deer, bear, grouse, wild turkey, and waterfowl.

Similarly, the AuSable Club in Michigan, the Phantom Canyon Ranch and Wildcat Ranch in Colorado, Eagle Rock Preserve in Montana, the Rocking K Ranch in Arizona, the Farmview in Pennsylvania, the Preserve at Hunter Lake in Wisconsin, and Hilton Head Island in South Carolina combine residential living with exclusive rights to privately owned open spaces that boast abundant wildlife and other natural amenities. All in all, wherever natural surroundings can be "packaged" and a demand for them exists in the marketplace, eco-developers are responding.

### Prospects for Eco-Developments

Eco-developments, however, can face regulatory hurdles in addition to zoning and local land-use laws. For example, before developer Peter O'Neill could break ground at River Run, he needed approval for the project from the Idaho Department of Water Resources, the Boise Parks Department, the U.S. Bureau of Reclamation, and the U.S. Army Corps of Engineers. Fortunately, after O'Neill presented his plan for creating additional trout habitat for the Boise River, Idaho wildlife officials became strong supporters of the project and helped him to get the necessary approvals from the other agencies.[23]

Environmental sensitivity, like traditional neighborhood development, comes at a high price. The 660-acre Triple Tree Ranch near Bozeman, Montana, is something of an exception. Developer Mike Potter chose to leave 330 acres of the ranch as open space, most of which is arranged as buffer zones between clusters of houses. This allowed him to offer lots at $45,000. Although this represents a premium over nearby subdivision lots that sell for

### Notes:

21. Dewees Island, "Facts and Figures on Dewees Island," 1998, at *http://www.deweesisland.com/homeSet.html*.

22. See Terry L. Anderson and Donald R. Leal, *Enviro-Capitalists: Doing Good While Doing Well* (Lanham, Md.: Rowman & Littlefield Inc., 1997), pp. 12–16 and 109–120; see also Stephan Fatsis, "New Communities Make It Easy Being Green," *The Wall Street Journal*, November 10, 1995, p. B16.

23. Anderson and Leal, *Enviro-Capitalists*, pp. 117–120.

$25,000 to $30,000, the price remains within the reach of many Bozeman families.[24]

Missing from this development, however, is a large contiguous block of open space, which state biologists believe would be better for the elk that winter in the area. Bill Ogden did incorporate such a block for elk habitat at Eagle Rock Reserve, which is also near Bozeman. Fully 90 percent of the 650-acre Eagle Rock Reserve is dedicated to open space. But such preservation makes homes more costly. Prices for lots at Eagle Rock are two to three times higher than for lots at Triple Tree Ranch. As a consequence, Eagle Rock is out of the price range of most Bozeman families.[25] Ogden is hoping that his development proves attractive to out-of-state professionals who want to retire to Bozeman or own a second home with outdoor amenities.

## FACELIFTS FOR SUBURBIA

Suburban development is popularly identified with monotony—"cookie cutter" homes on streets and intersections designed for the automobile, not pedestrians. In addition, suburbs have acquired large paved areas and extensive utility infrastructure, which require costly maintenance and grow more unsightly with age. For the most part, the design changes that address these problems make suburban houses expensive.

Two recent design innovations, however, add variation to suburban living with promising benefits. Both offer more open space, less costly roads and utilities, safer travel, and greater variety than do traditional suburbs, and in many cases do so within the price range of a large number of potential homebuyers.

> Coving and bay homes offer more open space, less costly roads and utilities, safer travel, and greater variety than do traditional suburbs.

### Innovation #1: Coving

- Coving is a site-planning method that offers an antidote to many of the problems of urban sprawl. The term "coving" refers to coves of green space that are created in front of houses through varied setbacks (the distance from the street curb to the home fronts) and winding streets (see Chart 8.1).

- Conventional developments position homes parallel to the street, with a specified setback. The problem with this placement is that to achieve affordable density, more lineal feet of road are needed, which requires more paving. The additional road costs are passed on to the consumer.

- Coving removes the assumption that homes must be parallel to the street. Homes are positioned to form a curve that is separate from the pattern of the streets. This allows more homes for a given length of road. Compared with a conventional layout, coving reduces the lineal feet of paved street by an average of 20 percent, sometimes as much as 40 percent. Thus, a coved development should be less expensive to build than a conventional development having similar housing quality.

Because home and street positions are not as rigid in coved developments as they are in TNDs and conventional developments, a developer is better able to place the streets so they conform to the natural topography. So, although housing density generally remains the same as with the conventional layout, there is more open space adjacent to the homes, and walking paths are positioned to follow an efficient curvilinear route independent of the street.

## Notes:

24. *Ibid.*
25. *Ibid.*

Chart 8.1

# Example of a Coved Housing Development: Allen, Texas

Before: 124 Lots

After: 119 Lots

Coving results in 4% fewer lots, but 70% less land for infrastructure, 48% less public paving and the added value of living in an open neighborhood instead of a "subdivision"

Source: Rick Harrison, 1999.

The combination of open space and independent walking paths increases "beauty and safety" at less cost, says coving's inventor, site planner Rick Harrison. He points out that conventional sidewalks are parallel to the street and "bring vehicles in unsafe proximity to people."[26] He notes that his design "utilized street frontage better than standard platting by winding the streets a bit more than usual."[27] In addition, by varying the setbacks so the positioning of houses is curved, he not only improved curb appeal but also reduced the length of roads and utility lines used in a development. "Lots were bigger and I had the same number of houses, but I was saving about 20 percent on infrastructure," he says.

Coving has appeal for a variety of reasons:

**First,** it increases lot size by 15 to 20 percent without sacrificing the number of houses that can be built. In effect, the extra land that is spared from use as roads is added to front yards.

**Second,** by reducing roads, coving cuts maintenance costs for cities and reduces run-off and erosion, protecting water quality.

**Third,** coving allows houses to be positioned individually on lots so they do not face each other. Not only does this enhance individuality among home sites, it creates greater privacy. Says one Minnesota homeowner in a coved development, "I like it that when I look out my

## Notes:

26. *Achieving Sustainability with the Community Planning Techniques of Coving and the Bay Home Concept* (St. Louis Park, Minn.: Rick Harrison Site Design, Inc., n.d.), p. 5.
27. Susan Bady, "Coving Creates New Site Design," *Professional Builder*, March 1999, p. 24.

Chart 8.2

# Example of a Bay Home Housing Development

In a "bay home"-style development, the land and and all items outside the home are not owned by the individual homeowners, b ut held in common by a homeowners association.

Since homes are linked by meandering walkways instead of streets, infrastucture savings can reach 50% when compared to the "traditional neighborhood development" rigid grid pattern of streets.

Source: Rick Harrison, 1999.

window, I'm not looking into someone else's window. There's more privacy. When you drive down the street, it's not just one house after another."[28]

Coving also makes natural amenities more accessible; open space is interwoven with housing rather than located far away, as is typical of conventional developments. And coving is applicable to lower- and middle-income family subdivisions as well as high-end developments. Because it does not rely on expensive architecture or landscaping, as the new urbanist designs do, coving allows homeowners to buy moderately priced homes on varied lot sizes. In contrast to a local government's minimal setbacks, coving allows the distance from the street curb to the home fronts to be increased sufficiently to make an even modestly priced home appear estate-like.

## Innovation #2: The Bay Home Concept

A more recent site-planning method developed by Rick Harrison is called the "bay home" concept (see Chart 8.2). Like coving, the bay home concept uses less infrastructure. It differs from coving, however, in that a coved development is designed primarily around single-family homeownership of land, while in a bay home development, the land and all items outside the house are held in common by a homeowners association. Without the constraints of individually owned lots, bay home designs can achieve even greater savings in infrastructure than can coving.

Most bay home units front other units without a dedicated street in between. Meandering walkways connect the fronts of the units, creating a pedestrian-oriented community. Unlike coved developments, bay home units have an entrance and garage in the rear of the home,

## Notes:

28. Robert Sharoff, "Creating a New Concept in Subdivision Layouts," *The New York Times*, February 15, 1998, p. 11-5.

with the front entrance facing open space. Bay home units also have inviting open porches, creating a more neighborly environment.[29]

The previous descriptions of bay home communities indicate their strong similarities with the traditional neighborhood design. Indeed, the bay home concept offers housing densities as high as TNDs. There are key differences, however. The bay home concept offers much more open space than is available in a comparably sized TND. Compared with TND's rigid grid pattern of streets, the bay home concept's street design cuts infrastructure by about 50 percent while creating a safer pedestrian-oriented environment. Because bay home developments do not require expensive architecture, they can more easily accommodate moderately priced units, including units in inner-city renewal development areas.

## Prospects for Coving and Bay Home Developments

The prospects appear bright for both coving and bay homes. As of December 1999, three coved developments have been completed, 40 are under construction, and over 50 are in the approval process.[30] Coved communities are appearing in major housing markets in Atlanta, Chicago, Dallas, Detroit, Houston, Indianapolis, Minneapolis, Bismarck, and parts of Wisconsin, Iowa, and Florida. In addition to small home builders, such giant companies as Pulte, Centex, and D. R. Horton are developing coved communities. The first bay home project was recently approved in Minnesota, and there are five more in the approval process.

Potential stumbling blocks can occur, however, due to rigid restrictions on setbacks and streets and the approval process itself. Harrison has noted that a quirk in Minnesota's statutes effectively requires builders to seek design approval for coved projects first as planned unit developments (PUDs), rather than merely submitting them to a vote under the municipal zoning ordinances. This adds another step and more expense to what already can be a lengthy process, further complicated by the fact that the use of PUDs varies widely among localities. Some cities routinely approve these developments to encourage construction at hard-to-develop sites; others are reluctant to issue the special-use permit. Generally, however, once a planning board sees the design and the potential benefits, it usually will embrace both designs. Says Harrison, "Coving's claim to over twenty-five approved communities and sixty now in the planning process over a brief two-year period, speaks for itself."[31]

## FREEING THE MARKET TO INNOVATE

Concern over urban sprawl has smart growth advocates calling on government to limit suburban development, even though the suburbs remain quite popular among homebuyers. Suburban communities do have their limitations and to some extent have been stuck in a conceptual rut. However, entrepreneurs are developing innovative design alternatives, as the examples in this chapter show. Smart growth advocates can help suburban communities to evolve by making sure that zoning and planning ordinances are flexible enough to accommodate such innovations.

### Notes:

29. *Achieving Sustainability*, pp. 7–8.
30. Information from Rick Harrison, in correspondence to the author dated December 7, 1999.
31. *Achieving Sustainability*, p. 20.

# LESSONS FROM THE PORTLAND EXPERIENCE

### 9

*By John A. Charles*

For more than decades, officials in Portland, Oregon, have been implementing a growth management agenda that is specifically designed to shape patterns of land use. Although the "urban growth boundary" (UGB) around the metropolitan area is the best-known feature of Portland's approach, its agenda also includes creating a strong regional government, emphasizing government-built light rail rather than highways, and funding programs that contain urbanization by increasing population density in the metropolitan area.

Smart growth advocates frequently cite Portland as a model of what all communities should be doing to control sprawl. They claim its style of growth management offers many potential benefits: It will protect rural farm and forest land from development, reduce the costs of development by encouraging more efficient use of urban infrastructure, and reduce traffic congestion through mass transit serving higher population densities. Moreover, this approach will provide affordable housing while preserving open space and scenic vistas.[1]

Notwithstanding their praise, Portland's 20-year commitment to smart growth has failed to achieve most of these predictions. Its approach has been ineffective in limiting suburban development, and it actually has intensified several of the city's most troubling problems, such as traffic congestion and a lack of affordable housing.

Other cities and regions across the country that consider looking to Portland for guidance would do well to pause and examine its experience.

## PLANNING A NEW METRO AREA

In 1978, voters in Portland's tri-county region approved the creation of an elected regional government, known as Metro, to address issues that transcended traditional city and county

**Notes:**

1.  See, e.g., Carl Abbott, Deborah Howe, and Sy Adler, eds., *Planning the Oregon Way: A Twenty-Year Evaluation* (Corvallis, Ore.: Oregon State University Press, 1994). See also, Oregon Land Conservation and Development Commission at *http://www.lcd.state.or.us*.

boundaries. An amendment to the state constitution increased Metro's powers during the 1990s, giving it jurisdiction over all matters of "metropolitan concern" as set forth in its charter, subject to voter approval. In November 1992, voters approved Metro's charter, and regional planning became reality.

Before Metro's charter was adopted, however, the regional government had begun a 50-year planning process called the Region 2040 Project. This ongoing project became Metro's forum for developing specific land use and transportation planning policies that would implement the smart growth vision of constrained urban land supply and more compact urban development, with a heavy emphasis on building and subsidizing fixed rail transit.

**Planning Tools.** A key tool in the Metro 2040 plan is the strict management of the *urban growth boundary*, a line that Portland drew around its metropolitan area, including the surrounding suburbs, in 1979. The area inside the boundary—approximately 364 square miles—makes up less than 0.4 percent of the land mass of Oregon.

Portland's urban growth boundary has attained near-mythic status among urban planners. One admirer has written:

> [C]ontainment of urban sprawl has been a fundamental objective of the American planning profession since World War II. All approaches at discouraging urban sprawl have either failed or led to perverse outcomes, save one. The sole technique that has been found to be effective is the urban growth

> Portland's urban growth boundary has attained near-mythic status among urban planners.

boundary, which was pioneered in Oregon.[2]

Metro's other fundamental growth management tool—committing massive amounts of public funds for light-rail transit—also garners enthusiastic support. In 1985, Portland opened a 15.5-mile line running east to west between the suburb of Gresham and downtown Portland. A 17.6-mile extension to the western suburbs opened in 1998. Efforts to expand the system with a north–south line, however, were thwarted by three successive ballot measure losses: the first in 1995, when residents of Vancouver, Washington, rejected a taxation plan to build the Washington portion of the north–south line; the second in 1996, in a statewide Oregon vote; and the third in 1998, when voters of the Portland tri-county region rejected a local bond measure.

Such strong grassroots opposition forced the local rail proponents to take a more incremental approach. Instead of seeking large transit expansions that require funding from the sale of bonds, the latest proposals would build small spur lines financed by a combination of local payroll taxes, property taxes, capital grants from Congress, and real estate transfers to private developers. This approach is working. Currently, a 5.5-mile line to the Portland International Airport is under construction and a 5.5-mile spur to North Portland is in the final stages of gaining local political approval and congressional approval for federal grants.

Portland is also building a trolley line, which is functionally almost the same as light rail but which would fall under the jurisdiction of the city of Portland, not the regional transit agency (Tri-Met).[3] The trolley will run from the Pearl

**Notes:**

2. Arthur C. Nelson, "Oregon's Urban Growth Boundary Policy as a Landmark Planning Tool," in Abbott *et al., Planning the Oregon Way*, p. 25.
3. Tri-Met is a tax-supported government monopoly that runs transit services over a 364-square mile area (roughly comparable to Metro's boundaries).

District, a heavily subsidized urban renewal project in northwest Portland, along 10th Avenue just west of the city center, and then southeast to Portland State University. In late 1999, plans suddenly emerged to extend the trolley to the North Macadam District, an area under development just southwest of the city center. However, this extension is not yet formally part of the plan.

## PORTLAND'S PROGRESS

Portland's growth management approach may have been well-intentioned, but it has become a political battleground that pits one community against another, empowers well-heeled developers and affluent homeowners, and fails to achieve some of the plan's most often-stated goals. Evidence of such problems is mounting.

**Controlling Density.** The first analysis should involve Portland's legendary urban growth boundary. Unfortunately, the "model" UGB has done little to change traditional development patterns.

In the early 1990s, the Oregon Department of Land Conservation and Development, which is charged with administering the statewide planning program, commissioned a study of development patterns in four different metropolitan areas in Oregon. The study, conducted by the consulting firm ECO Northwest, looked at Portland, the largest metropolitan area; Medford, a medium-sized city in southern Oregon; Bend, a small but rapidly growing city in central Oregon; and Brookings, a small city on the coast.

The consultants found that the specified goals behind the UGBs had not been met in any of these cities. In each case, land inside the boundaries had been developed at densities *below* the zoning specifications, while land outside the boundaries had been developed at densities *higher* than the zoning specified. In each city, "residential development resulted in low-density housing outside and around most or all of the UGBs."[4]

**Farmland Protection.** Because the philosophy behind growth boundaries is that urban development should only take place within the UGB, the system does not have the flexibility to consider factors other than proximity to the urban core. As a result, the land-use bureaucracy channels development onto prime Willamette Valley farmlands while thousands of acres of non-productive rural lands are deemed off-limits to development simply because they are beyond the UGB.

Thus, Metro's 2040 plan actually calls for the total conversion of the last 10,000 acres of urban farmland left in the region into high-density development, even though most of that land is very productive. If farmland protection were really the goal, land-use regulators would provide incentives for owners of high-value farmland to continue farming—regardless of location—while encouraging owners of non-productive farmland to convert their lands to other uses. But farmland protection, *per se*, is not really the goal; the real agenda is simply "urban containment,"[5] and calling it farmland protection just happens to be a politically useful strategy.

This is not a problem limited to Portland. According to the Department of Land Conservation and Development, more than 600,000 acres of prime Willamette Valley farmland have been converted to other uses through changes in the urban growth boundary and designation of land for residential development.[6]

## Notes:

4. Wayne A. Leeman, *Oregon Land, Rural or Urban? The Struggle for Control* (Ashland, Ore.: Millwright Press, 1997), p. 72.
5. Richard P. Benner, director of the Oregon Department of Land Conservation and Development, in an oral briefing to the joint meeting of the Land Conservation and Development Commission and the Oregon Transportation Commission, spring of 1995.
6. Leeman, *Oregon Land, Rural or Urban?* p. 72.

**Taxpayer Costs.** Portland's growth management plan has failed to reduce the cost of infrastructure, even though advocates claim that urban sprawl raises the cost of roads, sewers, parks, and other utilities. Extensive construction within Portland's UGB is subsidized by the taxpayer. And Portland appears to have some of the highest priced infrastructure in the state.

Consider two of Portland's major "transit-oriented developments." The Pearl District urban renewal project and the conversion of a former state office building to low-income housing along the eastside light-rail line will cost the public more than $171 million in grants, tax abatements, free infrastructure, and other subsidies.[7] Nevertheless, planners and their allies continue to argue that building within the city is inherently cheaper than building on the urban fringe.

When the level of subsidies was debated at a city council hearing on the Pearl District project, Commissioner Jim Francesconi asked one developer why such corporate welfare was necessary. The developer responded, "because density costs money."[8] These costs arise from such factors as more stringent building codes and the need for elevators and off-street parking.

According to a recent report from the Portland City Club, a local civic organization, the costs of development are about $62 per square foot for densities of 0 to 20 units per acre, but rise steadily to a high cost of $126 per square foot for densities above 200 units per acre.[9]

There is also evidence that increased density raises the cost of public services, rather than decreasing them as smart growth proponents suggest. For instance, if urban development were such a bargain, one would expect Portland's public schools to educate their students at lower costs per pupil than suburban schools could. In fact, representatives of the Portland school district have testified before the state legislature that their district has higher costs than do the districts in the suburbs and therefore should receive more state assistance.[10]

Other infrastructure services are costly in Portland as well. The city council has initiated a $1 billion "Combined Sewer Overflow" project to keep raw sewage and stormwater runoff out of the Willamette River during rains with high accumulations (a fairly common occurrence in the Pacific Northwest). This project is almost entirely a function of Portland's relatively high density: If the buildings and roads were not crammed together in the city, more natural land would be available to absorb rainwater.

**The Beaverton Round.** Perhaps no project illustrates the pitfalls of smart growth better than the Beaverton Round, the "poster project" of Portland's growth management plan. This 8.5-acre site near the center of Beaverton (a suburb of Portland) had once been a beaver marsh and then a horseradish farm, and later developed for a sewage treatment plant from the 1950s to the mid-1970s. For the next two decades, the land lay dormant as the Beaverton City Council mulled the various development options. When light rail for the west side entered the planning agenda, Beaverton's political leaders saw an opportunity to design a state-of-the-art "new urbanist" village along its track.

The Beaverton Round was to include a mix of high-density land uses, with multimodal access (rail and sidewalks as well as streets) and various innovative design features. In 1996, a developer was selected, and construction commenced soon thereafter.

## Notes:

7. Personal communication with Melvin Zucker, Yale Corporation, Portland, Oregon, June 1999.
8. Author's notes from a city council hearing, fall 1997.
9. Portland City Club, "Increasing Density in Portland," November 1999, p. 53.
10. James Scherzinger, Chief Financial Officer, Portland Public Schools, briefing book for the Oregon legislature, February 1999. The primary factor in the higher costs is simply higher salaries necessary to attract and retain workers in a competitive urban economy.

Light rail to the area opened in September 1998, but after just two months, the general contractor for the Round declared bankruptcy. The project remains half-completed today. The Beaverton City Council, which originally promised constituents that the Round would be built without government subsidies beyond those needed to fund the light rail line itself, has committed more than $17 million in tax revenues to bail out this project.[11]

The transit system itself is supported by the huge subsidies given to Tri-Met. In addition to light rail construction grants from Congress, Tri-Met relies heavily on a regional payroll tax to subsidize operations and maintenance. Revenues from that tax now exceed $150 million annually and have been increasing rapidly due to Portland's robust economy. Most payroll tax revenues originate from suburban employers, but Tri-Met utilizes a hub-and-spoke transit system oriented toward downtown destinations. Thus, although many suburban employers pay substantial amounts in payroll taxes that subsidize the system, they receive no Tri-Met service.

## LIMITS OF URBAN GROWTH BOUNDARIES

Portland's most prominent planning feature, its urban growth boundary, is also its biggest planning problem. However well-intentioned its designers were, creating such a boundary laid the foundation for a political process that could be easily abused and corrupted.

The inability of an urban growth boundary to live up to its billing as a flexible growth management tool arises from several factors:

1. **It is difficult to know where to set such a boundary.** Planners simply do not have enough information to know for certain where a growth boundary should exist. The setting of a boundary is thus purely a political exercise. As Oregon's experience shows, UGBs when first adopted tend to be set far from existing

urban borders to minimize opposition. This may be good politics, but it means the boundary will have virtually no effect on development in the early years of implementation. The slow initial impact explains why one can drive 30 miles in any direction from downtown Portland and encounter development outside the city center that looks remarkably like suburban development elsewhere in America.

2. **Once established, the boundary creates a political constituency that fiercely opposes any future boundary changes.** Thousands of development decisions are made based on where the boundary is at any given point in time. Many of those making the decisions have a vested interest in maintaining the status quo. This is especially true of homeowners who live just inside or outside the boundary. They have easy access to the service amenities of urban centers, while at the same time enjoying the scenic views and open space found in areas outside the boundary. Since this group tends to have above-average incomes and education, its members can and do form organizations to oppose the expansion of the boundary in their neighborhoods.

3. **To the extent that the boundary succeeds in containing growth inside its limits, it leads to higher home prices.** A number of indicators suggest that Portland's UGB is pushing up housing prices and making it difficult for families to find homes in the city. Most notably, a Metro study found that in 1996, land zoned for single-family housing just inside the UGB was priced at $120,000 per acre, while land just outside the boundary was selling for approximately $18,000 per acre.[12] This difference makes it considerably more challenging to lower the

**Notes:**

11. Susan Misra, Cascade Policy Institute, Portland, Oregon, forthcoming paper.
12. Metro, *Housing Needs Analysis*, Portland, Oregon, 1997, p. 26.

cost of new home construction inside a UGB. Developers can adjust by building at higher densities, but they risk losing customers who want larger yards; and if they build too much, the density itself creates cost problems, as noted above.

Of course, other rapidly growing cities in the West experienced rapid appreciation in housing price during the past decade, an indication that numerous factors are at play. But even compared with such growth centers as Denver, Las Vegas, Phoenix, and Tucson, Portland has experienced the largest increase in the median price of homes for the period from 1990 to 1996.[13] Affordable housing for those with modest incomes is rapidly slipping out of reach in Portland. For example, in the first quarter of 1998, a family making Portland's median household income could afford to buy only 35 percent of the houses sold, while in the United States overall, a family making the median household income could afford almost 68 percent of the houses sold.[14] According to the National Association of Home Builders' Housing Affordability Index, four of Oregon's largest cities—Eugene, Medford, Portland, and Salem—are all in the bottom 10 percent of affordability when ranked against other cities in the country.[15]

**The Boundary Today.** As a result of political conflicts, since 1994, Metro has been in the process of determining where and when the boundary should be expanded. Although Metro

has attempted to be highly analytical by commissioning dozens of technical reports on the "needs" of the region and convening multiple citizen advisory committees, the actual decisions about expansions to the UGB have been mired by lobbying and litigation. Each proposed boundary change requires a public vote by Metro's seven-person elected board. For weeks and months (even years) before a scheduled vote, individual councilors are lobbied in private by representatives of various interest groups, and public hearings are dominated by well-paid lawyers, lobbyists, and consultants representing the affected parties.

Economist Anthony Downs, though a public supporter of Oregon-style land-use regulation, has described these political elements as a fatal flaw. He points out that the factors that lead to the adoption of an urban growth boundary—specifically, large size and fast growth—also make it extremely difficult to maintain rigid urban growth boundaries drawn tightly around the periphery of built-up areas. Where rapid growth is occurring, such tight boundaries would soon require significant increases in residential densities in built-up neighborhoods. But attempts to increase residential densities there would provoke hostile political reactions from residents.[16]

> As recent events demonstrate, when increased densities are forced on individual neighborhoods, citizens will resist strenuously.

**Notes:**

13. Committee to Study Housing Affordability, *Oregon Housing Cost Study*, Portland, Oregon, 1998, p. 5.
14. *Ibid.*, p. 6.
15. National Association of Home Builders at *http://www.nahb.com*. The affordability index is the NAHB's "Housing Opportunity Index" score and represents the share of new and existing homes that could be purchased by a family earning the metropolitan area's median-family income.
16. Anthony Downs, *New Visions for Metropolitan America* (Washington, D.C.: The Brookings Institution, 1994), p. 197.

This is exactly what has happened in Portland. In the abstract, such as when they are responding to polling questions, Portland residents seem to support the general proposition that urban densities should rise in order to avoid a major UGB expansion. However, as recent events demonstrate, when increased densities are forced on individual neighborhoods, citizens will resist strenuously.

For example, in the suburban community of Milwaukie southeast of Portland, the three city council members (including the Mayor) who supported the Region 2040 plan were voted out of office mid-term through a successful recall campaign in 1996. According to the 2040 plan, Milwaukie was to receive a light rail line, along with "upzoning" in the rail corridor to build up to the high densities that rail transit requires. When Milwaukie residents fully understood what this plan was going to do to their community, they rebelled, and the rail proposal eventually was defeated.

Similarly, Metro planners attempted to designate the low-density town of Oak Grove near Milwaukie as a "Town Center" under the 2040 plan. This designation would have gradually increased Oak Grove's population density from about eight people per acre to 31. Existing neighborhoods would be rezoned to encourage increased housing units in what are now open spaces and large backyards. Local opposition was so fierce that Metro eventually dropped the planned designation.[17]

Citizen opposition is not just a suburban reaction. During the mid-1990s, the Portland planning bureau undertook exhaustive citizen involvement processes in North Portland and Southwest Portland neighborhoods, with the goal of rezoning for higher densities. Despite years of negotiations, the city eventually abandoned the plans in the face of broad neighborhood opposition.

In spite of these reactions, Metro officials continue to emphasize the goals outlined in the Region 2040 plan. They are fond of raising the specter of Los Angeles as their rationale for using urban growth boundaries to increase density in Portland. Ironically, Metro's own analysts are on record as stating that Los Angeles represents "an investment pattern we desire to replicate."[18] It turns out, somewhat counterintuitively, that the Los Angeles metropolitan area has the highest population density of any region in the nation, despite its public image as a low-density, sprawling metropolis. Los Angeles also has the fewest number of per capita freeway lane-miles of any region in the country.[19]

Ultimately, despite the immense resources Metro put into its analysis of potential UGB additions during the 2040 process, the Oregon Court of Appeals found Metro's plan for designating urban reserves (land identified for possible inclusion within an expanded UGB) so badly flawed that it ordered Metro to start over.[20] This decision, handed down in January 2000, was an enormous setback for Metro and cast doubt on whether the UGB would ever be able to function as a rational planning tool.

## PORTLAND'S TRANSIT LESSONS

The second major growth management tool in Portland is its major expenditures for developing a fixed-rail transit system. It is conventional wisdom among the new urbanists who consider Portland their model that higher urban densities would increase transit ridership. Although they are correct in determining that transit is more viable in higher-density areas, they are wrong to assert that traffic congestion will go down as transit ridership goes up.

**Notes:**

17. Randal O'Toole, *The Vanishing Automobile and Other Urban Myths* (Portland, Ore.: The Thoreau Institute, 1996), p. 23.
18. Metro, "Metro Measured: Transportation, Housing, and Regional Growth," Portland, Oregon, 1994, p. 7.
19. *Ibid.*
20. Oregon Court of Appeals, January 2000; full decision available at *http://www.metro.dst.or.us/*.

Any rise in transit ridership resulting from higher density almost inevitably will be overwhelmed by the increased number of vehicular trips arising from the expanded population. Since more than 90 percent of American adults own cars, and the rate of vehicle miles traveled has been rising steadily for decades, the increase in transit ridership resulting simply from an increase in density would have to be huge in order to offset the rise in auto trips.

In a typical city, for example, if urban population densities doubled (as desired by many smart-growth advocates), the percentage of residents using transit would have to increase more than tenfold in order to bring about a net reduction in local traffic (see Chapter 4). Trends of urban transit use show no evidence that this will occur. In fact, the trends are moving in the opposite direction of declining market share.

More important, traffic congestion is not caused by a lack of mass transit. It is caused by the failure to price travel correctly on particular roads. If drivers were charged direct user fees based on when, where, and in which direction they were driving, traffic congestion could be reduced substantially. Because most highways are funded primarily through gasoline taxes, motorists do not know how much time and cost they add to the trips of everyone behind them on a crowded highway.[21] Paying for access at peak times would cause drivers to alter their behavior.

> ## Traffic congestion is not caused by a lack of mass transit.

By ignoring these basic facts, Portland transportation officials failed to solve the region's growing congestion problems. But then, perhaps that was not their goal. Early in the 2040 planning process, Metro conducted an opinion poll to discern the issues of greatest concern to the public. Citizens named traffic congestion as their number one problem, even when big issues such as public safety or education were also choices.[22] Yet, in spite of this response, Metro designed its regional transportation plan to allow an increase in the number of congested lane-miles of roads by 200 percent by the year 2015. Specifically, Metro projects that the number of congested lane-miles of roads in the region will increase from 187 in 1994 to 562 in 2015. Metro also predicts that the number of peak hours of delay in the afternoon will rise from 10,052 in 1994 to 34,213 in 2015.[23]

Metro planners do not seem to think that this is a problem. Their documents describe congestion as a "sign of positive urban development."[24] As City Commissioner Erik Sten said upon voting to expand the light rail system, "Maybe if congestion gets bad enough, people will take light rail."[25]

### The Light Rail Obsession

To understand the reasons for the almost obsessive attachment to light rail in Portland, it is necessary to know something about how the rail system came to fruition.

### Notes:

21. Clifford Winston, Carol Evans, and Ken Small, *Road Work* (Washington, D.C.: The Brookings Institution, 1988). See also, Anthony Downs, *Stuck in Traffic* (Washington, D.C.: The Brookings Institution, 1992).
22. Decision Sciences, Inc., *Telephone Survey for the Region 2040 Project: A Quantitative Research Report*, April 1992, p. 3. Respondents were asked what they disliked about living in their part of the metro area. The factor most often mentioned was "too much traffic/congestion" (22.6 percent), followed by "lack of parking" (17.6 percent) and "public safety" (12 percent). The issue of "urban sprawl" was mentioned by only 3.1 percent of respondents.
23. Oregon Transportation Institute, 1999; at *http://www.hevanet.com/oti/metrocongestion.htm*.
24. Metro, "1995 Regional Transportation Plan," Portland, Oregon, cited in O'Toole, *The Vanishing Automobile and Other Urban Myths*, p. 28.
25. Portland City Council hearing, June 14, 1999.

The first light rail line was the result of a major political fight in the 1970s that defeated an urban freeway. It is likely that light rail never would have emerged as a viable option in Portland had it not been for the political necessity of freeway opponents to put forward an alternative. Combined with the willingness of Congress to let Portland build the rail with 83 percent federal financing and, as part of the "freeway for rail" trade to give the Portland region additional funds for dozens of less-controversial highway improvement projects, the deal satisfied both transit advocates and bureaucratic highway builders.

Since the line opened in 1986, costs have been extremely high and benefits uncertain. At the time the decision was made to build it, Tri-Met estimated that construction would take three years and cost $135 million, but the line would carry 42,500 people per day within five years of its completion. The actual figures turned out to be four years and $214 million to build and only 21,000 riders per day after five years. In other words, the line had 55 percent higher costs, yet achieved only half the projected ridership. By 1996, 10 years after opening the line, ridership was still below 75 percent of projections for 1991.[26]

This should have been a clear indication that light rail was not a wise policy choice, but Tri-Met, Metro, and the local jurisdictions decided to expand the system with a 17.6-mile western line running from downtown to the suburb of Hillsboro. In fact, the planning for the westside rail line began before construction on the eastside line had even started.

In 1979, Metro estimated that a westside light rail line would cost $175 million, carry more than 92,400 riders per day, and open in the fall of 1997. In fact, the line opened a year later (fall 1998) with a price tag of $963 million (including 75 percent federal funding), and ridership has not come close to projections.

Despite more than 60,000 free tickets distributed by Tri-Met prior to the grand opening, and the cooperation of major employers like Intel—which gave 10,000 free transit passes to its employees—surveys of passengers during the first week of operation found that the westside light rail drew just 416 additional new riders during the peak morning hours (all other riders were previous bus riders who were forced to take the train due to the cancellation or re-routing of the bus lines). Since the average number of passengers per vehicle in Portland is 1.12, the number of vehicles removed from the road by the addition of 416 new rail riders was a mere 371. Thus, the westside light rail cost $963 million to remove 371 cars from the road during the heavy commute period—an astounding $2,595,687 per car.[27] Ridership has gone up since then, but most riders continue to be current or former bus passengers.

As construction on the westside line began, Metro and Tri-Met were mobilizing political forces to help them obtain funding for a 29-mile north–south extension that would run from Vancouver in Washington State to Oregon City. A local ballot measure in 1994 to authorize a property tax increase for bond financing received a "Yes" vote from 63.5 percent of Portland-area voters.

The plan approved by the voters in 1994 would have had Portlanders pay one-third—or $475 million—of the non-federal costs (the federal government would pay only about 50 percent of the cost due to the changing politics in Washington), the state another third, and Vancouverites the rest. However, Vancouver voters overwhelmingly rejected, by a 2–1 margin, a local bond measure to pay their share, and the Oregon state legislature chose not to ask downstate Oregonians to pay for Portland's system. Thus, state funding did not emerge during the 1995 legislative session.

Additional efforts, including several ballot measures that ended in defeat, were made as

**Notes:**

26. O'Toole, *The Vanishing Automobile and Other Urban Myths*, p. 22.
27. Oregon Transportation Institute, 1998, at *http://www.hevanet.com/oti/maxcounts98.htm*.

key interest groups tried to find support for a north–south line. Today, the southern portion of the north–south line seems to have lost all political support. Local rail advocates doggedly pursue a shorter 5.5-mile northern spur that would run from the east side of downtown Portland to the Multnomah County Expo Center in North Portland. Light rail would replace two lanes of a busy four-lane arterial road.

Proponents continue to cling publicly to the notion that this would be the "staging" line for an eventual light rail into Vancouver, Washington, but no one has yet put forward a credible strategy for overcoming the apparent voter hostility in Washington State. Because it would use publicly owned right-of-way and not involve an expensive underground station, this rail line potentially could be built with existing transportation budget dollars that are siphoned away from other uses, along with congressional grants, thus avoiding the need for another public vote on a bond measure. A final decision on this proposal has not been made, but it was endorsed by the Portland City Council by a 4–0 vote, and the project is one of many pending in Congress for capital financing.

In addition, a 5.5-mile light rail spur is currently being built from the Gateway Transit Center (about nine miles east of downtown Portland) to the Portland International Airport. Rail proponents like to describe this as a public–private venture because the international construction giant, Bechtel Corporation, supposedly is building the line with its own funds. But in reality, the entire line is being subsidized by the taxpayers. In exchange for constructing the line, Bechtel will receive 185 acres of prime airport real estate currently owned by the Port of Portland that was purchased originally with tax dollars.

Though rail proponents are happy to see more construction, they have yet to resolve several major problems with the two most recent proposals. First, no provisions are being made on the airport rail line to accommodate the practical needs of air travelers. Overnight parking at the light rail park-and-rides is forbidden, so travelers will not be able to drive to the Gateway Transit Center and leave their vehicles there while they commute. Second, the light rail cars have no luggage racks. Airport users with luggage will find using the light rail extremely challenging at peak travel times. Third, the airport spur seems to be a track in search of a mission. For the past three years, Tri-Met has run free bus shuttles from Gateway to the airport during the peak travel periods of Thanksgiving weekend and Christmas to New Year's Day. The shuttles have three advantages over the trains: They are free, they have plenty of storage space, and they travel non-stop to the airport. Yet they are virtually unused.

**Light Rail's Track Record.** Light rail is often promoted as a strategy for increasing consumer choice, reducing congestion, improving transit commute times, reducing urban sprawl, and encouraging efficient land development. In Portland, none of these expectations are borne out by experience. Consider:

### Assertion #1: Light rail will reduce traffic congestion.

**Reality:** According to the Texas Transportation Institute, Portland has the ninth worst traffic congestion in the nation; it was ranked 16th in 1986 when its light rail system first opened.[28] Between 1982 and 1997, the annual hours of delay per driver in Portland rose from nine to 52, an increase of nearly 500 percent, while average freeway speeds declined by 18 percent.

Portland's oldest light rail line parallels Interstate 84, the major east–west highway leading to downtown Portland. Between 1986 (the year the light rail opened) and 1997, average daily vehicle trips on I–84 increased from 117,928 to 172,721, even though light rail ridership was also rising. I–84 is now the most heavily traveled road in Oregon.[29] Building more light rail will accel-

**Notes:**

28. Texas Transportation Institute, annual mobility survey, at *http://www.mobility.tamu.edu/*.

erate this discouraging trend. Computer projections for the next planned rail expansion into North Portland show that localized congestion will increase significantly due to the loss of two lanes of the major arterial road for the rail track.[30]

## Assertion #2: Light rail is fast.

**Reality:** The average speed of Portland's light rail cars is 14.5 miles per hour, slowing to 5 mph downtown. Despite its name—the Metropolitan Area Express, or MAX—"express" service on the system does not exist. A limited express would be possible on the eastside line, where there are two bypass tracks at Gateway and the Rose Quarter, but Tri-Met refuses to offer such service. (According to one official, "it's not in our plan."[31]) Unfortunately for many transit users on both the eastside and westside lines, the day the trains opened, Tri-Met cancelled express bus service in those corridors. When access time and bus transfer delays are added in, light rail use actually results in a net increase in commute time for the majority of train riders who had taken the bus previously.

## Assertion #3: Light rail is "high-capacity" transit.

**Reality:** Light rail is high-cost, not high-capacity, transit. There are only 72 seats per car (76 in the older cars) and only two cars per train; any additional cars would block traffic in downtown Portland. Furthermore, because of safety and operational constraints, Tri-Met has never been able to run trains at a greater frequency than one every six minutes. Thus, even if widespread consumer demand for fixed rail suddenly

developed, there would be no place to put the new customers because additional train cars could not be added.

Though many claims are made regarding the theoretical superiority of light rail over freeways, actual passenger counts made in 1994 by Tri-Met showed that during the three-hour morning commute period, I–84 (with three lanes in each direction) carries 7.7 times more riders than does the light rail system in peak (downtown) direction, 11.6 times more riders than light rail in both directions, and 90.8 times more riders than light rail traveling away from the central city.[32] And this is with an average motor vehicle occupancy of only 1.12. If the region were to implement peak-hour road pricing or some other policy that encouraged higher vehicle occupancy, the total potential passenger throughput of I–84 could be much higher.

## Assertion #4: Light rail is economical.

**Reality:** Economist John Kain compared the construction costs of new busways, transitways, commuter highway lanes, and light rail and found that rail was anywhere from seven to 252 times more expensive than any of the other options. Kain's analysis showed that, on a cost-per-trip basis, the capital costs of the various modes were: $19,898 (in 1989 dollars) per trip for light rail; $2,790 per trip for exclusive busways; and $79 per trip for highway commuter lanes.[33]

If Portland builds the 5.5-mile rail link approved by the city council on June 16, 1999, the estimated cost per additional transit passenger trip will be approximately

## Notes:

29. Oregon Department of Transportation automatic traffic count data tables, at *http://www.odot.state.or.us*.
30. Metro, "Final Environmental Impact Statement for North Interstate Light Rail," Portland, Oregon, 1999.
31. Personal communication with Tri-Met rail staff.
32. Oregon Transportation Institute, 1997, at *http://www.hevanet.com/oti/*.
33. John F. Kain, "The Urban Transportation Problem: A Reexamination and Update," in Jose Gomez-Ibanez, William B. Tye, and Clifford Winston, eds., *Essays in Transportation Economics and Policy* (Washington, D.C.: Brookings Institution Press, 1999), p. 375.

$31, or $62 per round trip. More than half of this cost will be paid by federal taxpayers as a train construction subsidy.[34]

These costs are completely unnecessary because some of Tri-Met's most cost-effective bus routes already operate in that neighborhood. The average cost of a bus transit trip in North Portland is only $1.61 per passenger boarding. Those buses will be cancelled or re-routed to become feeder buses for light rail if that line is built.[35]

Other forms of road-based transit, such as jitneys, would not cost the public one dime in subsidies if the city council would remove legal barriers to private transit. In the city of Miami, approximately 400 unsubsidized jitneys carry nearly 49,000 passengers each day—approximately the same number of riders carried by its billion-dollar heavy rail system.

### Assertion #5: Light rail is an important tool for economic revitalization.

**Reality:** Development along the light rail lines was so sparse after its construction that Portland adopted a policy of giving 10-year property tax abatements to developers who build high-density projects in the corridor. If the city has to pay people to build near it, MAX cannot be much of a magnet.

### Assertion #6: Light rail will attract large numbers of new transit patrons.

**Reality:** Surveys repeatedly show that most MAX riders had previously ridden the bus, so the net increase in transit use is small. The only reason they are MAX riders is because the transit agency has a policy of eliminating the best bus routes as soon as a new train line opens, and converting others to feeder lines for light rail. This artificially inflates ridership numbers on the trains.[36] Moreover, the extensive use of park-and-rides for MAX means that many people drive long distances to park for free at the MAX stations. Riding the slow MAX is simply what they will pay in exchange for about $7 worth of free parking a day. This also inflates ridership numbers, but it does little to improve environmental quality.

In sum, Portland's investment in light rail has failed to reduce traffic or auto dependency. Between 1980 and 1990, Portland's use of transit for work trips fell from 8.1 percent to 5.4 percent, a drop of 33 percent. During a similar time period (1982–1992), daily per capita vehicle miles traveled increased in Portland from 13.04 to 19.74, up 51 percent. These numbers mirror the trends found in nearly every major city in America. People are driving more because of rising affluence, the declining marginal costs of vehicle use, and the unmatched convenience of their personal automobiles. Although it is possible that public policies could reverse this trend, such policies have not yet been adopted in Portland.

## STRAINING FOR OPEN SPACE

Many of Portland's other goals also have not been achieved. Planning advocates describe a vision of compact cities surrounded by green belts of land, with parks and open spaces sprinkled throughout residential neighborhoods. The reality is that such a vision is impossible to achieve under the Portland strategy, which is based on making the area within the urban growth boundary more dense. The density campaign is a comprehensive assault on urban open space. It involves such steps as:

### Notes:

34. Gerard C. S. Mildner, "Punishing North Portland Commuters and Taxpayers: The Hidden Costs of the Proposed Interstate Avenue Light Rail Line," Cascade Policy Institute, Portland, Oregon, 2000.

35. *Ibid.*

36. Jonathan E. D. Richmond, "New Rail Transit Investments—A Review," Taubman Center for State and Local Government, John F. Kennedy School of Government, Harvard University, Cambridge, Massachusetts, June 29, 1998, pp. 28–29.

- **Promoting** urban in-fill and redevelopment through tax subsidized urban renewal projects and federal grants;

- **Up-zoning** to require high-density development in every rail and transit corridor;

- **Establishing** minimum density requirements that average eight housing units per net acre (an acre minus the land required for such things as setbacks and sidewalks) across the region; and

- **Zoning** ordinances to encourage the complete conversion of all remaining urban farmland (approximately 10,000 acres) to high-density housing.

All of these techniques sacrifice urban open space for vast amounts of "protected" rural farm and forest land. Most of this open space will be inaccessible to urban dwellers (either by virtue of their distance or because they are privately owned and not open to the public). The psychological benefits of all this rural farmland are likely overstated, especially for families. The existence of thousands of acres of privately owned farmland 30 miles from an urban neighborhood offers little help to parents in the city whose children are looking for a place to play ball.

The creation of urban parks would be more useful to most Portlanders. Yet in terms of the number of city-owned park acres per capita, Portland does not fare well against other big cities. Tucson, which is almost identical to Portland in size, population, and density, has nearly 70 acres of park per 1,000 people; Portland has only 21. Other cities not known for urban planning put Portland to shame as well: Dallas has 46 park acres per 1,000 residents, while Phoenix has 29. The bad news for Portlanders is that the situation is getting worse; the city had 24 acres per 1,000 people in 1990.

In 1994, Portland-area voters approved a $135.6 million bond measure for purchasing new parks and "greenspaces." Metro expects to spend this money buying 6,000 acres over a five- to seven-year period. The fund will also be used to provide trails and other facilities. However, few of these purchases will help those who live in the urban growth boundary. By design, the 1994 ballot measure is aimed primarily at buying up green spaces outside the UGB, even though there is no apparent shortage of open space in those areas.

## THE AFFORDABLE HOUSING MYTH

Finally, it should be noted that affordable housing in Portland is rapidly disappearing. Rising prices are not an aberration; they were anticipated—and planned for—by Metro. In a 1994 report entitled "Metro Measured," analysts for the agency compared the Portland region with 54 other cities using dozens of statistical measures. The researchers found that the growth management policies then being considered for adoption by Metro had a high probability of raising housing prices. Specifically, the agency found that pursuing the goals of "increased density, reduced vehicle-miles-traveled and higher nonauto travel" would have some costs. "The downside of pursuing such objectives appears to be higher housing prices and reduced housing output."[37] This turned out to be a remarkably accurate forecast.

In fact, the agency found a distinct relationship between road building and affordable housing. Researchers noted that housing prices went up as road miles went down. "Once we drop below three miles of road per 1,000 population, only two of 10 regions are below $100,000 median value [home price] and those two are above $80,000. Above three miles of road per 1,000 population only three of 36 regions are more than $100,000."[38]

Metro concluded, "interpreting road miles per capita as roughly comparable to land availability, we cannot dismiss the importance of

**Notes**:

37. Metro, "Metro Measured," p. 45.
38. *Ibid.*

transportation investment as a factor in owner occupied housing prices."[39] One might think that these forecasts would have had some effect on the Metro council, but one year later it adopted the Region 2040 plan. A key element of this plan was a proposal calling for only a 13 percent increase in new lane-miles of roads, despite projections of an 80 percent increase in population.

By limiting road building, Metro has ensured that vast tracts of land throughout the region (primarily outside the UGB) will remain landlocked, unavailable for housing. Metro can guarantee this outcome through its bureaucratic control of the regional transportation budget (all transportation dollars available to the region, including federal grants and gas tax revenues) and by its legal authority over any proposed expansions of the urban growth boundary. In essence, under the 2040 plan, Metro is the perfect monopolist, allowing just enough new land and road investments to keep land prices inside the UGB extremely high. This will benefit a select group of landowners at the expense of everyone else.

The "success" of this strategy was documented in Metro's 1997 Housing Needs Analysis. This report found that

> holding neighborhood characteristics, zoning, and development fees constant, price per acre for single-family residential areas declines steadily from about $150,000 per

> **Metro is the perfect monopolist, allowing just enough new land and road investments to keep land prices extremely high, which benefits select landowners at others' expense.**

acre to $120,000 per acre at the edge of the UGB. Beyond the UGB, price per acre falls dramatically to $18,000 per acre which is a combination of the value of land for rural uses and a speculative premium value based on the presumption that it will eventually be used for some urban purpose.[40]

Even the $18,000 is high compared with the cost for more remote land. Metro estimated that moving the UGB out 12 more miles would reduce the cost of land to about $4,000 per acre at the periphery of the region.

Although no one knows what the future holds, one of Metro's many consultants summarized the likely scenario as follows:

> The model incorporates and illustrates many of the impacts that one would expect when one assumes substantial growth and/or limited expansion of land supply: reduced average lot sizes, a greater proportion of households in multifamily housing, decreased percentage of households owning their own homes, increased percentage of household income spent on housing, and increased number of housing units that will require subsidy.[41]

**Notes**:

39. *Ibid.*
40. Metro, *Housing Needs Analysis*, p. 25.
41. Hobson Johnson & Associates, "Task 3 Working Paper: Residential Market Evaluation," 2040 Means Business Committee, November 22, 1996.

# MOVING BEYOND URBAN MYTH

Portland's growth management system is not succeeding. Even Andres Duany, the Miami-based architect generally considered a high priest of smart growth, has reached his limit with the "insufferable sanctimonious tone" of the "Portland cult." In a widely circulated e-mail exchange, Duany recently commented: "An urban boundary and the provision of light rail are not tools sufficient to ensure a sustainable pattern of growth. Yet the 'urban boundary' and 'transit' have become a mantra that is dumbing down the planning profession even further than usual." Reflecting on his gradual shift of views about Portland, Duany said:

> First, my personal experience of Portland…. [M]any of Portland's admirers may have undergone similar experiences, leading to similar deluded conclusions. I have visited Portland five times. All of them were invitations to public speaking and so in all cases I was …shown the many wonderful places that make it a great, livable city. I agreed that Portland was great and livable and praised the city accordingly. This was pleasant to hear and thus the repeat invitations to speak. On the fifth trip, however, before my engagement, I "escaped" my hosts and went out to visit the famous urban boundary on my own. What did I find, to my surprise? That as soon as one left the prewar urbanism (to which all my prior visits had been confined) the sectors all the way to the urban boundary were chock full of the usual sprawl that one finds in any American city, no better than in Miami. So the outcome wasn't that different after all; in Portland most

of the prewar urbanism is excellent and most of the postwar version is junk. But can't we say that, despite that, an urban boundary is an achievement in itself? That depends on where you draw it, and from that point of view, Portland's was not a great achievement. It was drawn 20 years out; which is to say slack enough to include 20 years of future growth. [42]

While the residents of the postwar suburbs that Duany dismisses as "junk" presumably would disagree with his assessment, since they have chosen to live there, it is certainly true that most of suburban Portland looks like other metropolitan areas in America. All the political wrangling and emotional investment in the Portland strategy has produced little significant change. It is time to give the Portland myth a decent burial and move on to strategies that would make a difference.

Oregon's central-state planning approach has relied on false assumptions about shortages of resource land, placed policymakers in the untenable position of having to pick winners and losers in the market, and failed to accomplish its chief goal of containing urban development. Nonetheless, its supporters have argued more strenuously than ever that it can work, if we just improve the quality of decision-making by land-use officials.

This is a familiar refrain in the land-use business. It reflects a naïve hope that the quality of people who serve in government will improve and that a utopian vision will be achieved as a result. But there is no reason to think that local government land-use decision-making will dramatically change in the near future, regardless of the tactics that planning advocates may use. As management guru W. Edwards Deming stated repeatedly during his lifetime, if an organization is not getting the desired result, don't

**Notes**:

42. Andres Duany, posted on the New Urbanism e-mail network, October 8, 1996; full text available at *http://www.dpz.com*. A toned-down version of his critique appeared in the *Oregonian* on December 19, 1999.

blame the workers; blame the system. Oregon's system, when used by ordinary people, clearly does not lead to the outcomes that many of its proponents desire. And that will not change until the incentives within the system change.

As other chapters in this book indicate, there are genuine smart-growth strategies to deal with the unpleasant aspects of suburban growth. These smart-growth strategies of the future will include peak-period road pricing, privatized transit, and less-rigid performance zoning. Unlike the Portland will o' the wisp, these are the policies that will lead to lower-cost infrastructure, personal mobility, and livable neighborhoods.

# 10

# LESSONS FROM THE ATLANTA EXPERIMENT

*By Angela M. Antonelli*

**A**s cities go, Atlanta is thriving. Now one of the nation's largest metropolitan areas, in 1998 its population reached 3.7 million. In population growth, Atlanta was second only to Los Angeles from 1990 to 1998 (see Table 10.1). By 2020, Atlanta's metropolitan area population is expected to exceed 5 million, and its wider commuting region will be home to nearly 7 million people,[1] comparable in size to San Francisco and Chicago today.

Atlanta's postwar suburbanization boom is now known pejoratively as "sprawl." Indeed, Atlanta is accused of being the nationally recognized poster child for sprawl. This accusation is due in part to a 1998 national ranking on sprawl by the Sierra Club. The environmental organization ranked Atlanta the number one "sprawl threatened" large city after looking at trends in population growth, land use, and traffic congestion.[2] Not everyone would agree with this assessment. Another study concluded that, for the years 1970 through 1992, the state of Georgia ranked 38th in the rate of sprawl.[3] This new attention on Atlanta's growth has made it the lightening rod for federal activism and a target of environmental groups.

Washington's involvement became direct after Atlanta failed to meet federal standards for air quality. In January 1998, the U.S. Environmental Protection Agency (EPA) threatened to withhold Atlanta's federal transportation funds

**Notes:**

1. Research Atlanta, Inc, "Deciding Factors for Regional Decisionmaking in Metro Atlanta," at *http://researchatlanta.org/exesum24.htm* (August 10, 1999).
2. Sierra Club, "Dark Side of the American Dream," at *http://www.sierraclub.org/sprawl/report98* (March 7, 2000).
3. Samuel R. Staley, *The Sprawling of America: In Defense of the Dynamic City*, Reason Public Policy Institute, *Policy Study* No. 251, January 1999, pp. 12–13, and Appendix A, available at *http://www.rppi.org/ps251.html*. Staley's sprawl index compares a state's population growth with its rate of urbanization. According to the U.S. Bureau of the Census, an urbanized area is a densely populated area with a population of more than 50,000 and a density of more than 1,000 people per square mile.

because its air quality had not met the federal standards under the Clean Air Act of 1970, as amended, for ozone and other pollutants. Soon thereafter, Atlanta halted its efforts to expand road capacity to deal with mounting traffic congestion. The federal government found cause to act in this traditionally local matter because Atlanta had been unable to demonstrate that its transportation plans would not interfere with its efforts to meet the federal air quality standards.

The issue of growth quickly turned into a "crisis" in need of resolution. In November 1998, Georgians replaced outgoing Democratic Governor Zell Miller with Roy Barnes, a Democrat from Atlanta who had run on a platform that emphasized aggressively managing growth in the Atlanta metropolitan region. By April 1999, the Georgia Assembly had passed and the new governor had signed into law legislation creating what may be the most powerful regional growth management authority in the nation today. The Georgia Regional Transportation Authority (GRTA) has been given considerable power to dictate not only transportation decisions but also land use in a 13-county metropolitan region of Atlanta. In just its first year, the GRTA has focused on expanding light rail and other modes of mass transit.[4] In addition, Governor Barnes, who also acts as the GRTA's chairman, has proposed land set-asides on a county-by-county basis.

> By April 1999, the Georgia Assembly and the new governor had signed into law legislation creating what may well be the most powerful regional growth management authority in the nation today.

By February 2000, within the GRTA's first 12 months of existence, the EPA tentatively approved Georgia's air quality plan; but it conditioned this approval—and the flow of highway funds—on a number of stipulated improvements, including the enactment of legislation or rules to implement some of its air quality control measures.

Atlanta's experience with federal involvement in local growth management efforts is particularly illustrative. The establishment of a super–growth management agency has been greeted with great enthusiasm by Vice President Al Gore and others in the Clinton Administration, making Atlanta the environmentalists' newest symbol of growth management. Although since 1995, state after state has been moving toward growth management policies designed to rein in development,[5] what is unprecedented is the extent to which growth management efforts in Atlanta are being led by the federal government. Atlanta's recent experience reflects a chilling trend toward the federal takeover of metropolitan regions, with unpredictable consequences for the freedom of their citizens to live and work as they choose.

**Notes:**

4. More information on GRTA can be found at its Web site at *http://www.grta.org*.
5. See Michael Dobbins and Peggy Dobbins, "Sprawl Things Considered: Controlling Growth," *American City and County,* September 1997.

## GROWTH'S GAINS AND PAINS

Atlanta's metropolitan region has been one of the fastest growing in the nation. Although most of its growth has occurred since World War II, a substantial portion of this postwar growth has occurred just since 1980. As Table 10.2 illustrates, Atlanta's metropolitan population quadrupled between 1950 and 1998. Between 1980 and 1998, it almost doubled, from about 2.14 million to 3.75 million. It should be noted that most of this growth has not occurred within the city of Atlanta, but rather in its suburbs. Indeed, between 1980 and 1998, the population of the city of Atlanta actually *decreased*.

Metropolitan Atlanta's economy is one of the strongest in the nation. Over the past few years, Atlanta has benefited from the growth of both manufacturing and technology-based industries (see Chart 10.1). Its high-tech workforce is one of the largest in the southeastern United States.[6]

Atlanta's population explosion (see Chart 10.2) has been coupled with an increase in the percentage of workers who live far from their primary place of employment. In fact, metropolitan Atlanta citizens drive more miles per person each day (34 miles) than do Americans

| Table 10.1 |
| --- |

### Atlanta Second to L.A. in Growth, 1990–1998

| | Population Growth |
| --- | --- |
| Los-Angeles-Riverside-Orange County | 1,249,744 |
| Atlanta | 786,559 |
| Dallas-Fort Worth | 765,181 |
| Phoenix-Mesa | 692,506 |
| Houston-Galveston-Brazoria | 676,550 |
| Chicago-Gary-Kenosha | 570,026 |
| New York-North NJ-Long Island | 558,936 |
| Washington, D.C.-Baltimore | 558,811 |
| San Francisco-Oakland-San Jose | 538,522 |
| Miami-Fort Lauderdale | 463,119 |
| Seattle-Tacoma-Bremerton | 454,119 |
| Detroit-Ann Arbor-Flint | 270,412 |

Source: U.S. Census Bureau, 7/1/98 revision.

anywhere else in the country.[7] More than half of the area's employees now live in one county and work in another (see Table 10.3). According to the U.S. Census Bureau, the median commuting time in Atlanta in 1990 was 26 minutes, slightly above the national average of 23 min-

| Table 10.2 |
| --- |

### The Suburbanization of Atlanta, 1950-1998

| | | | | | | | % Change | | |
| --- | --- | --- | --- | --- | --- | --- | --- | --- | --- |
| | 1950 | 1960 | 1970 | 1980 | 1990 | 1998 | 1950–98 | 1980–98 | 1990–98 |
| Atlanta MSA | 727,000 | 1,017,188 | 1,684,200 | 2,138,135 | 2,833,511 | 3,746,059 | 415.3% | 75.2% | 32.2% |
| Atlanta City | 331,314 | 487,455 | 496,973 | 425,022 | 394,017 | 403,819 | 21.9% | -5.0% | 2.5% |
| Atlanta Suburbs | 395,686 | 529,733 | 1,187,227 | 1,713,113 | 2,439,494 | 3,342,240 | 744.7% | 95.1% | 37.0% |

Note: The Atlanta Metropolitan Statistical Area (MSA) is a 20-county region that includes Barrow, Bartow, Carroll, Cherokee, Clayton, Cobb, Coweta, DeKalb, Douglas, Fayette, Forsyth, Fulton, Gwinnett, Henry, Newton, Paulding, Pickens, Rockdale, Spalding, and Walton counties.
Source: U.S. Census Bureau, 7/1/98 revision.

## Notes:

6. Laura Creasy, "Metro Atlanta's Congestion & Air Quality Conundrum: Shuttle Vans to the Rescue?" *Commentary*, Georgia Public Policy Foundation, March 16, 1999, at *http://www.gppf.org/pubs/commentaries/Shuttle-Vans.html*.

7. *Ibid.*

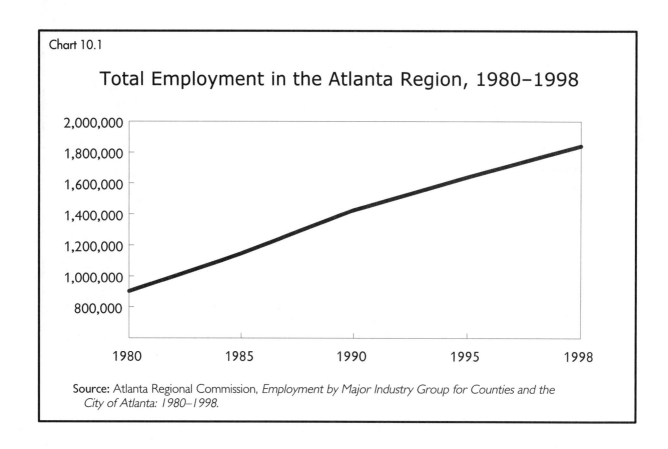

Chart 10.1

## Total Employment in the Atlanta Region, 1980–1998

**Source:** Atlanta Regional Commission, *Employment by Major Industry Group for Counties and the City of Atlanta: 1980–1998.*

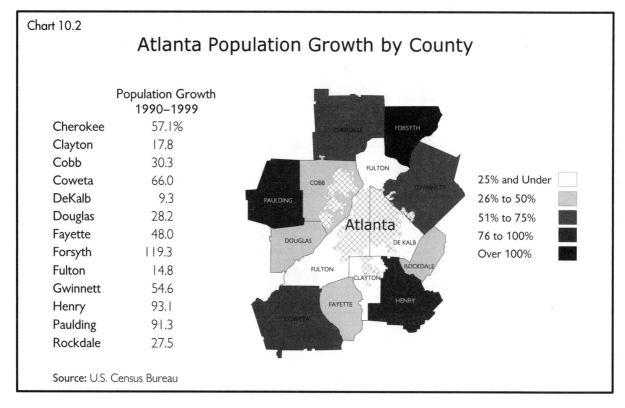

Chart 10.2

## Atlanta Population Growth by County

| | Population Growth 1990–1999 |
|---|---|
| Cherokee | 57.1% |
| Clayton | 17.8 |
| Cobb | 30.3 |
| Coweta | 66.0 |
| DeKalb | 9.3 |
| Douglas | 28.2 |
| Fayette | 48.0 |
| Forsyth | 119.3 |
| Fulton | 14.8 |
| Gwinnett | 54.6 |
| Henry | 93.1 |
| Paulding | 91.3 |
| Rockdale | 27.5 |

25% and Under
26% to 50%
51% to 75%
76 to 100%
Over 100%

**Source:** U.S. Census Bureau

utes, but Atlanta's commuting time is projected to increase to 45 minutes by 2020.[8]

As Wendell Cox explains in Chapter 4, the fundamental cause of traffic congestion in Atlanta is insufficient road space. In Atlanta, congestion is getting worse because the area's booming economy has contributed to population growth that exceeds its highway capacity. Metropolitan Atlanta had the seventh fastest traffic growth rate between 1994 and 1996.[9]

## The Fascination With Light Rail

Over the past two decades, Atlanta's effort to mitigate road congestion through use of light rail has been very expensive and largely unsuccessful; money has been squandered on transit that could have been used to improve the roads. During that period, the Metropolitan Atlanta Rapid Transit Authority (MARTA) built a subway system extending more than 45 miles and connecting 38 stations. This system costs approximately $130 million annually to maintain and operate.[10] In 1997, Atlanta's transit operating cost per passenger mile (31.2 cents) was similar to those in Honolulu, San Diego, and Las Vegas.[11]

Yet, despite the billions the state has invested in public transportation in Atlanta over the past 20 years, only downtown Atlanta has direct, no-transfer service from throughout the area, and less than 1 percent of the metropolitan area is within walking distance of a rail station. Transit passengers pay 27 percent of the cost of their transportation, while mass transit carries only 1.9 percent of the area's overall travel. Between 1980 and 1990, public ridership increased 24 percent; but between 1990 and 1996, it decreased by 1.2 percent.[12] Such numbers cast doubt on mass transit's effectiveness in reduc-

| Table 10.3 | |
|---|---|
| **Many Atlantans Work Outside Their Home Counties** | |
| County | Work Outside County of Residence, 1990 |
| Cherokee | 68.5% |
| Clayton | 54.3% |
| Cobb | 48.6% |
| Coweta | 42.5% |
| DeKalb | 52.9% |
| Douglas | 67.2% |
| Fayette | 67.0% |
| Forsyth | 60.5% |
| Fulton | 29.8% |
| Gwinnett | 52.7% |
| Henry | 70.4% |
| Paulding | 75.3% |
| Rockdale | 60.9% |

**Source:** U.S. Census Bureau, 1990 County-to-County Worker Flow Files.
**Note:** These are the 13 Atlanta counties that comprise the U.S. EPA's ozone nonattainment area.

ing congestion or improving air quality in the Atlanta area.[13]

In 1972, the *Atlanta Journal-Constitution,* in a series of reports entitled "Atlanta 1990," made a number of predictions about what the city would look like in 18 years. One prediction was that by 1990 new office and residential developments would spring up all around MARTA stations. At the time, it seemed obvious that people would want to work and live just steps away from modern, high-speed trains that would "rescue them from the gridlock of the highway commute."[14] But, as the *Atlanta Jour-*

## Notes:

8. U.S. Census data (1990) and Alan Ehrenhalt, "The Czar of Gridlock," *Governing Magazine,* May 1999.
9. The Public Purpose, *Urban Transport Fact Book,* at *http://www.publicpurpose.com/ut-ushyg.htm* (March 6, 2000).
10. If the bus system is included, MARTA's annual budget is $300 million.
11. The Public Purpose, *Urban Transport Fact Book,* at *http://www.publicpurpose.com/ut-us97pm-metro.htm.*
12. *Ibid.,* at *http://publicpurpose.com/ut-us96ride.htm.*
13. Georgia Public Policy Foundation and the Pacific Research Institute, "The Georgia 1999 Index of Leading Environmental Indicators," April 1999.

*nal-Constitution* was forced to conclude in 1997,

> So much for sure things: Not only did these developments fail to materialize by 1990, but also there's little evidence they are ever going to appear, at least not if it's left up to private builders to act on their own... not a single rail station has sparked the expected building boom.[15]

Despite this failure, MARTA continues to encourage transit-oriented developments. For example, it has taken land it already owns around the Lindbergh station, purchased a bit more, and then put together a 46-acre tract on which it hopes newly developed residences and businesses will thrive.[16]

While public transportation fails to meet expectations, traffic congestion continues to get worse. In 1996, Atlanta ranked eighth in the nation's top 10 congested areas and ninth in the top 10 in annual person-hour delays.[17] Needless to say, traffic congestion exacerbates air quality problems because emissions are greater at slower speeds and whenever vehicles accelerate, decelerate, or idle due to heavy congestion. The California Air Resources Board estimates that emissions are 250 percent higher under congested conditions than during free-flowing traffic conditions.[18]

## Atlanta's Air Quality Problem

Under the Clean Air Act, the EPA set National Ambient Air Quality Standards (NAAQS) for six pollutants: ozone, carbon monoxide, particulate matter, sulfur dioxide, nitrogen dioxide, and lead. States are required to monitor these pollutants and to report data to the EPA, which then are used to determine whether a state is in compliance ("attainment"). In developing its air quality implementation plan, the state establishes a baseline measure of air quality and then uses complex computer modeling techniques to determine whether its proposed pollution control programs would achieve the necessary reduction in emissions to meet EPA's standards for each pollutant.

Notwithstanding its recent improvements, the Atlanta metropolitan area for more than 20 years has had ozone levels that exceed the federal air quality standards (no more than 0.12 parts per million during one hour on any day per year). Because of this, 13 metropolitan Atlanta counties are considered "serious" nonattainment areas.[19] Forty-four percent of Georgia's population lives within the 13-county nonattainment area, while an additional 15 percent live in counties within 25 miles of the nonattainment area.[20]

Metropolitan Atlanta's ozone problem is caused mostly by emissions from on- and off-road mobile sources and from stationary sources, such as power plants and manufacturing facilities, which are called "point sources" of pollution.[21] Georgia's plan for improving "seri-

## Notes:

14. "Beginning of a Boom?" *Atlanta Journal-Constitution*, May 20, 1997, p. 12A.
15. *Ibid.*
16. *Ibid.* See also MARTA's *Annual Report 1999,* at *http://www.itsmarta.com/inside/annualreportpg12.html* (March 4, 2000).
17. Texas Transportation Institute, "1999 Urban Mobility Study," November 1999, Table S–1 and Table S–2.
18. Georgia Public Policy Foundation *et al.,* "The Georgia 1999 Index of Leading Environmental Indicators."
19. The counties are: Cherokee, Clayton, Cobb, Coweta, DeKalb, Douglas, Fayette, Forsyth, Fulton, Gwinnett, Henry, Paulding, and Rockdale. The Atlanta Metropolitan Statistical Area (MSA) consists of these counties plus Barrow, Bartow, Carroll, Newton, Pickens, Spalding, and Walton counties.
20. Ken Green, Ph.D., "Innovative Approaches for Meeting the Georgia Ozone Challenge," Georgia Public Policy Foundation, February 8, 1999, at *http://www.gppf.org/pubs/ projects..20Georgia%20Ozone%20Challenge.html* (July 7, 1999).
21. *Ibid.*

ous" nonattainment areas must include such measures as an inventory of actual emissions; a plan for measuring reductions in emissions; mobile source controls, including automobile inspection and maintenance and fuel requirements (including reformulated gas); and operating permits for stationary sources of pollution.[22]

Yet a recent study of Georgia's air quality by the Georgia Public Policy Foundation and the Pacific Research Institute indicates that air quality statewide has been improving steadily over the past few decades. As the study notes,

> even in Atlanta, rapid urban growth has not overwhelmed improving air trends: the EPA reports that between 1992 and 1996, the number of days that exceeded federal air quality standards from the previous five year period decreased 31 percent.... Levels of all six of the pollutants thought to contribute to air pollution have decreased steadily over the past decade.[23]

## HOW ATLANTA LOST MONEY AND CONTROL

Despite Atlanta's improvements in air quality, the federal government decided to inject itself into Atlanta's regional growth management plans through an important tool in the Clean Air Act—the so-called conformity provisions. These provisions address the last requirement of Atlanta's air quality plan—the implementation of transportation control measures. The requirements are a response to concerns that new transportation projects, especially those that add capacity, will increase vehicle travel and jeopardize the progress being made in lowering emissions.

A 1997 report by the National Governors' Association summarizes the relationship between clean air and transportation planning.[24] According to the report:

> The conformity requirements [of the Clean Air Act Amendments of 1990] are intended to integrate air quality and transportation planning by requiring that transportation programs, plans and projects in nonattainment areas be consistent with emissions budgets outlined in the submitted or approved state implementation plan (SIP). Through quantitative analysis, states and metropolitan planning organizations (MPOs) must demonstrate that transportation systems will not exceed the level of motor vehicle emissions allowed in the SIP.

### Notes:

22. See Susan Mayer, "Implementing the Clean Air Act Amendments of 1990: Where Are We Now?" Congressional Research Service, 95–234 ENR, January 30, 1995. For more specific details see, Green, "Innovative Approaches for Meeting the Georgia Ozone Challenge." The latter report lists the specific requirements, which include: enhanced vehicle inspection and maintenance; an inventory of actual emissions from all sources (provided by each facility); implementation of reasonably available control technologies for existing major sources of volatile organic compounds (VOCs) or nitrogen oxides (NOx); new source permits and offset ratios for stationary sources of NOx and VOC emissions; an inventory of current emissions from all sources (a total-area inventory); reporting of actual NOx and VOC emissions by stationary source owners and operators; demonstration of progress toward control of NOx or VOC emissions (reduction of emissions by 15 percent against a 1990 baseline and additional reductions averaging 3 percent a year beginning in 1996); regulation of vehicle refueling; enhanced ambient air quality monitoring; implementation of a clean fuel vehicle program; and implementation of transportation control measures.
23. Georgia Public Policy Foundation *et al.,* "The Georgia 1999 Index of Leading Environmental Indicators."
24. National Governors' Association, Natural Resources Policy Studies Division, "Clean Air and Transportation Planning: An Overview of State Experiences," March 18, 1997, at *http://www.nga.org/Pubs/Issue-Briefs/1997/970318CleanAir.asp.*

To enforce this provision, Congress prohibits federal action to support, approve or provide financial assistance for transportation activities that do not meet the conformity requirements. Failure to demonstrate conformity or to submit a revised SIP by the specified deadline causes a region's transportation plan and transportation improvement program [TIP] to lapse or become invalid. If a lapse occurs, federal highway and transit funds are withheld and federally funded transportation projects in a region's transportation plan or TIP cannot proceed.[25]

Because the Atlanta region fails to meet air quality standards for ground-level ozone, the conformity provisions of the Clean Air Act require regional transportation plans and transportation improvement plans to undergo air quality analyses. They must conform to the state's implementation plan objectives. In mid-1996, the Atlanta Regional Commission, the region's planning and intergovernmental coordination agency,[26] failed to produce transportation plans that conformed to Georgia's air quality implementation plan. Consequently, Atlanta by law had only 18 months—until the end of 1997—to bring its transportation plans into conformity.

Clearly, the conformity provisions of the Clean Air Act increase the significance of air pollution in considering how a metropolitan area like Atlanta will address its transportation problems and manage growth. The threat of federal sanctions—in this case, the loss of hundreds of millions of dollars in transportation funding—is a powerful tool.[27]

The failure of Atlanta's transportation plans to pass muster under the federal clean air laws began a major shakeup in the way the region handled its growth. In the short term, dozens of road expansions throughout the metropolitan Atlanta area were delayed or abandoned. In the long term, the entire region would be forced to curb its dependence on road building to accommodate growth.[28]

When Atlanta's conformity was found to have lapsed in 1996, local and state officials were forced to begin to draft a new transportation plan, which eliminated dozens of proposed road expansions. Only projects that would improve bicycle and pedestrian ways or promote transit programs, traffic management, and/or carpooling could be included in the Transportation Improvement Program.[29] The Atlanta Regional Commission

> The Clean Air Act's provisions increase the significance of air pollution in managing growth. The threat of federal sanctions is a powerful tool.

**Notes:**

25. *Ibid.*
26. In addition to the 20-county MSA and the 13-county air quality non-attainment area, the Atlanta Regional Commission's jurisdiction has covered a 10-county area for 50 years. These 10 counties represent a subset of the 13-county non-attainment area that excludes Coweta, Forsyth, and Paulding counties, See footnote 19.
27. Research Atlanta, Inc., "Deciding Factors for Regional Decisionmaking in Metro Atlanta," at *http://researchatlanta.org/exesum.htm* (August 10, 1999). See also James E. McCarthy, "Highway Fund Sanctions and Conformity Under the Clean Air Act," Congressional Research Service, Report Code RL30131, Updated October 15, 1999.
28. David Goldberg, "Panel to Scrap Several Road Projects; Failed Transportation Plan May Result In Shakeup," *Atlanta Journal-Constitution*, June 14, 1996, p. 01A.

worked to develop a strategy by the end of 1997 that would keep emissions of nitrogen oxides (NOx), the key pollutant in Atlanta's ozone problem, in line with the plan set by Georgia's Environmental Protection Division for 1999 through 2005.[30] The approach the Commission was forced to consider included technology improvements, such as tougher tailpipe standards and emissions testing as well as cleaner burning fuels; more alternative modes, such as regional transit, bicycle lanes, sidewalks, and carpool lanes; reductions in car travel (employee incentives for carpooling, transit use, and telecommuting); and plans that focus growth on developed areas served by transit.

Meanwhile, faced with the loss of highway funding, the Georgia Department of Transportation began speeding up road construction projects and sending them to Washington for approval in the hopes that they would be "grandfathered" and funded.[31] Under a grandfather provision of the Clean Air Act, certain projects that might not otherwise be allowed would be permitted if they were already underway, or if significant investments already had been made. The Clean Air Act would not allow Atlanta to start new road projects without a long-term transportation plan that complied with federal Clean Air standards.

Getting consensus on how to manage growth would not be easy. "You can't manage growth unless people want it managed," observed Barbara Ray, an associate professor of urban studies in the Georgia State University Department of Public Administration and Urban Studies. "Different communities have different value systems. I don't think Atlanta wants to manage growth. Growth is such an embedded part of our value system."[32]

Although the Commission promised to have a new transportation plan completed in 1997, it was unable to achieve a consensus. As a result, it amended its 1995 Transportation Improvement Program in September 1996 and again in June 1997. The amendments were for only a few projects that, because they would have no impact on air quality, were considered to be exempt from air quality requirements.[33]

On December 30, 1997, the Commission adopted an interim Transportation Improvement Program for fiscal years 1998 through 2000. Federal officials continued to approve metropolitan Atlanta road projects, in some cases only after "grueling weeks of negotiations that ultimately involved two members of President Clinton's cabinet."[34] Increasingly, the U.S. Department of Transportation and the EPA disagreed about whether to exempt a project from the clean air laws. With 50 Atlanta projects already having been "grandfathered" by federal transportation officials, the EPA started to draw the line on other projects.

But that would not end the controversy. Environmentalists soon filed notice of a lawsuit over the 61 road projects that state and federal officials had agreed to exempt from the freeze.[35] As the latest Interim Transportation Improve-

## Notes:

29. *Ibid.*
30. David Goldberg and Lucy Soto, "ARC's Job: Plot a Course for Better Air Quality," *Atlanta Journal-Constitution*, December 1, 1997, p. 03E
31. David Goldberg, "DOT Faces Air Quality Challenge: Environmentalists Charge Georgia Highway Builders Are Trying to Evade Pollution Rules," *Atlanta Journal-Constitution*, November 20, 1997, p. 01F.
32. See Dobbins and Dobbins, "Sprawl Things Considered: Controlling Growth."
33. Atlanta Regional Commission, "Interim Atlanta Region Transportation Improvement Program, FY 2000–FY 2002." The Commission's Web site is found at *http://www.atlreg.com.*
34. "Region Can't Duck Clean Air Act," *Atlanta Journal-Constitution*, January 8, 1998, p. 14A; and David Goldberg, "Three Road Projects in Metro Area Get the Nod," *Atlanta Journal-Constitution*, January 17, 1998, p. 01A.
35. "Strategies For New Governor: Barnes Should Focus on Growth First," *Atlanta Journal-Constitution*, January 4, 1999, p. 06A.

ment Program was being finalized in late 1997, the Washington-based Environmental Defense Fund (EDF) charged that the Georgia transportation department was abusing the grandfathering provision of the Clean Air Act in order to proceed with $1 billion worth of highway expansions. "We believe the transportation planning process in Atlanta is in violation of federal law," said Michael Reploggle, federal transportation director for the EDF. "What's happening in Atlanta in transportation is of national significance."[36]

During 1998, Atlanta's transportation plans lapsed again, which left the region without a means to program and implement federally funded projects. Invoking the Clean Air Act, federal officials did what they had long threatened to do and turned off money for all but specifically exempted road projects, many of which remained the target of environmental groups.[37] However, because so many projects were considered exempt, most of the $600 million in annual transportation funds available still flowed to Atlanta.

Because the region was unable to adopt a new 25-year transportation plan that could meet all the federal air quality conformity requirements, it was necessary to develop an interim regional transportation plan, which would remain in effect until a new conforming plan could be adopted in March 2000.[38] The interim plan consisted of only a limited number of projects (exempt and air quality beneficial projects), which allowed the Transportation Improvement Program to be updated in July 1998 to add fiscal year 2001 to the plan and amended in December 1998 to include additional projects.[39]

## Federally Induced Growth Management

In January 1998, with hundreds of new road construction projects halted, Atlanta began to declare war on its urban problems. The EPA gave it no choice. As noted in a May 1999 article for *Governing Magazine*,

> [T]here are worse violators: Los Angeles is in the "extreme" category, and New York, Chicago and several other cities are rated "severe." But those cities have all been given extensions well into the next decade to solve their ozone problems; Atlanta, for reasons best known to the EPA, has not.[40]

Within six months after Washington halted new highway construction, Atlanta's image began to change for the worse. The *Wall Street Journal* on June 18, 1998, published an article entitled "Is Traffic-Clogged Atlanta the New Los Angeles?" that brought it national attention. At about the same time, Atlanta dropped from first to fourth and then fifth in the U.S. real estate market in polls of foreign investors.[41] Not surprisingly, the business community suddenly became much more engaged in what was happening in the metropolitan Atlanta region.

Business and civic leaders formed the Metro Atlanta Transportation Initiative in July 1998. Representing first-time business leaders from across the region, the Initiative came together to tackle transportation or any regional problem. The Initiative included chief executive officers of several of the area's largest businesses, as well as college presidents and government officials.[42] It also hired the consulting firm of McKinsey & Co. to study the traffic and

## Notes:

36. Goldberg, "DOT Faces Air Quality Challenge," p. 01F.
37. David Goldberg, "Region Turns Its Attention to Growth Issues," *Atlanta Journal-Constitution*, March 8, 1999, p. 07E.
38. The Atlanta Regional Commission's 25-year transportation plan drafted in January 2000 was available for public comment at *http://www.atlreg.com/transportation/2000rtplinks.html* (March 15, 2000).
39. Atlanta Regional Commission, "Interim Atlanta Region Transportation Improvement Program."
40. Ehrenhalt, "The Czar of Gridlock."
41. *Ibid.*

growth management problems of the Atlanta region.

The Initiative was doing its work while many of the 1998 election campaigns were in high gear, including the race for governor of Georgia. Roy Barnes, who had served for more than 20 years in the Georgia Assembly, made tackling Atlanta's air quality, transportation, and growth management issues one of the cornerstones of his successful campaign. By November 1998, it was clear that slow-growth candidates had done very well in the local elections. Cherokee County turned out its pro-growth county commissioner, replacing him with a housewife, a bookkeeper who had never run or held public office. Cherokee's population of 90,000 in 1990 is now more than 135,000, and it is projected to surpass 300,000 by 2020.[43]

In December 1998, the Initiative unveiled its recommendations to the public. One recommendation was to create a regional transit authority. Another was to designate a single agency with the power to plan, fund, and implement a regional transportation system. The Initiative convinced governor-elect Barnes that a super-regional authority was both needed and feasible.[44] He told lawmakers that a transportation authority responsible for planning and operating an integrated system—to include commuter trains and rapid rail and buses—was the only way to satisfy federal Clean Air mandates and melt the freeze on the region's federal highway funds.[45]

Barnes's first budget proposed $1 million to create the Georgia Urban Transportation Management Authority. He quickly found support.

"I've changed my mind on rail transport," said House Speaker Tom Murphy (D–Bremen), who said he that foresees Atlanta's commuter rail lines extending 40 to 50 miles out within the next decade. "We may have to force people to do what they don't want to do."[46] Only one metropolitan area in the country, Portland, Oregon, already had an agency with the authority to plan land use and transportation together on a regionwide basis.

## The Georgia Regional Transportation Authority (GRTA)

In January 1999, Governor Barnes's proposal to establish the Georgia Regional Transportation Authority (GRTA) was introduced in legislation.[47] GRTA, which would be responsible for regional growth management, would supervise the Atlanta Regional Commission and Georgia's Department of Transportation. It would do so through its authority to plan, design, and implement mass transit and road construction.[48] The bill was signed into law in April 1999.

The stunning speed with which the powerful GRTA was created was considered an unbelievable step in Georgia, where property rights and local land use control are so strong that county commissioners have been recalled just for advocating zoning. In the words of Jerry Griffin, executive director of Georgia's association of county commissioners, "Zoning in a lot of these counties is right up there with communism."[49] As Governor Barnes would later remark, "Two years ago, the notion that there might be an agency to coordinate planning and transportation, even mass transit in the suburbs, would have been regarded as 'nuts.'" [50] But the idea of

## Notes:

42. David Goldberg, "Panel Finds Consensus for New Transit Plan, *Atlanta Journal-Constitution*, November 24, 1998, p. 01A.
43. Ehrenhalt, "The Czar of Gridlock."
44. *Ibid.*
45. Kathey Pruitt, "Barnes Talks Tough on Transit," *Atlanta Journal-Constitution*, December 9, 1998, p. 01A.
46. Peter Mantius, "Tax Cut, Transit Initiative, Drive Barnes' First Budget," *Atlanta Journal-Constitution*, January 14, 1999, p. 01A.
47. Georgia Senate Bill Number 57.
48. More information on the GRTA can be found at its Web site at *http://www.grta.org*.
49. Ehrenhalt, "The Czar of Gridlock."

a GRTA, or the "Give Roy Total Authority" program, as it is jokingly called, was now the law of the land.

Indeed, the GRTA law was passed, but not without some concern by state leaders. Both the chairman and the director of the Atlanta Regional Commission voiced their opinion about the wisdom of creating the new planning agency and its effect on their organization. Others expressed concern that the authority was producing bigger government while decreasing input from the people. Some feared it would force counties to raise taxes in order to pay for projects the authority deemed necessary, since local jurisdictions would have to pay 20 percent of the funding to supplement federal money.

The law gave the governor the power to appoint a 15-member authority to plan and coordinate all transportation and air quality projects in the 13 counties currently out of compliance with the mandates of the federal Clean Air Act. Additional counties identified by the EPA that are likely to fall out of compliance within seven years also can be brought under GRTA's jurisdiction. If additional counties are added, as much as two-thirds of Georgia's population would be living in a nonattainment area and subjected to GRTA decisionmaking power.

The GRTA can veto planning proposals put forth by the Atlanta Regional Commission and the state transportation department. Adding to its power is its ability to veto any major real estate development, such as a mall, that would affect traffic. However, local governments can override that veto by a three-fourths vote. The 15 board members also make up the Governor's Development Council, which is responsible for land use management. In order to raise money for the projects it advocates, the authority is able to sell up to $2 billion in revenue bonds, half of which is guaranteed by the taxpayers. In addition, it can use the resources of the state transportation and environment departments. It has authorization to fund and operate its own mass transit system.

> GRTA's most controversial power is its ability to deny state and federal funds to any jurisdiction that decides not to comply with its recommendations.

The GRTA's most controversial power is its ability to deny state and federal funds to any jurisdiction that decides not to comply with its recommendations. Except for funds designated for education, health, or public safety, the GRTA can redistribute state and federal money from uncooperative counties to counties that are following its policies to supplement the cost of projects in those counties.[51] The power of the GRTA's fiscal hammer is significant and raises questions as to whether it also can direct federal housing and other funds designated for certain communities; the law also tasks GRTA to protect "federal interests" and to "accept and use federal funds."

### The Authority's One-Year Record

When Atlanta's new media-designated "Czar of Gridlock," Governor Roy Barnes, met with Vice President Al Gore in Washington, D.C, in early 1999, the Vice President embraced the idea of a regional authority to relieve metropolitan Atlanta's gridlock and stated that he would help the GRTA to find a way to pay for it. "He told me he was looking forward to making sure that effort was rewarded," said Governor Bar-

**Notes:**

50. Governor Barnes, quoted in "Georgia Conservancy," *Panorama*, May-June 1999, p. 3.
51. See "Georgia Conservancy," p. 3.

nes. Gore believed the plan would be adopted by other states, because this is "the type of effort that we need."[52]

In June 1999, three environmental groups settled their suit against state and federal transportation officials who agreed to cancel all but 17 of 61 contested Atlanta-area road projects. The suit had been filed in January 1999 against the state and federal transportation departments and the Commission, challenging authorization of the road projects.[53] The projects that were allowed to go forward in June 1999 were those already under construction and worth about $125 million. The rest (from a total of more than $600 million in projects) would do without 80 percent federal funding until they could show that they would help reduce Atlanta's ozone levels, which have been out of compliance since 1995.

## GRTA's Push for Light Rail

The GRTA was determined to redirect state transportation money away from highways and toward public transportation. Governor Barnes made clear his approach would be to begin by building local bus networks—to link up with MARTA or to provide service directly to employers—in each of metropolitan Atlanta's largest counties, and expanding the use of high occupancy vehicle (HOV) lanes, rather than to move to an immediate proliferation of rapid rail. Nevertheless, light rail proposals are definitely in play, including a light rail line from Marietta in Cobb County to Lawrenceville in Gwinnett Country.[54] The GRTA awarded Clayton County a $4 million federal grant to start a bus system that would operate under contract to MARTA.[55]

The GRTA appears determined to create a new transit system in the suburbs north of Atlanta. By law, it cannot decree an extension of the existing MARTA system from the city into another county. This would require a public vote. Only DeKalb County has joined MARTA so far. One reason for this is that county taxes would have to be levied to pay for the system. But the new transportation authority could, for example, dictate construction of a light rail system from Marietta east as far as Lawrenceville, the Gwinnett County seat; and Barnes has given every indication he wants to do this.[56]

The GRTA also is being pressured to extend MARTA from its Doraville station north into Gwinnett County. However, on two occasions the voters of Gwinnett County have rejected referendums to join MARTA. The law creating MARTA requires counties to get voter approval and to levy a sales tax to support MARTA. To get around this, the GRTA could recommend that Gwinnett start its own rail system that links to MARTA. If county officials declined, the law establishing the GRTA has the potential to allow the authority to block funds going to Gwinnett, except those related to health, education, and public safety.[57]

MARTA, with the support of the GRTA, is pushing transit-oriented development to create mixed-use villages of office, retail space, apartments, and condominiums around MARTA stations. In Atlanta, the old Atlantic Steel site is being redeveloped, and the EPA supported the project by granting special permission to build a bridge that had been halted by the funding freeze. This was the EPA's idea of "regulatory

## Notes:

52. Rebecca Carr, "Gore Vows Support for Barnes' Transit Ideas," *Atlanta Journal-Constitution*, February 23, 1999, p. 03A.

53. James Pilcher, "Environmentalists, Transportation Agencies Settle Highway Suit," Associated Press, State and Local Wires, June 21, 1999.

54. Kathey Pruitt, "Barnes Envisions Buses, HOV Lane As Gridlock Cure, *Atlanta Journal-Constitution*, May 12, 1999, p. 5B.

55. Gary Hendricks and Kathey Pruitt, "Clayton Wins GRTA Grant for Bus System, *Atlanta Journal-Constitution*, August 12, 1999, p. 1D.

56. Ehrenhalt, "The Czar of Gridlock."

57. "What Ifs: Here Are Some Hypothetical Issues that the Proposed Georgia Regional Transportation Authority Might Face," *Atlanta Journal-Constitution*, February 22, 1999, p. 08A.

flexibility," because the project was considered an example of smart growth. Other examples include BellSouth, which plans to consolidate dozens of suburban offices into three locations served by MARTA, and will be a major tenant at the Lindbergh station transit-oriented development.[58] Finally, in September 1999, Governor Barnes and Amtrak leaders met to discuss ways in which Amtrak might be play a role in Georgia's commuter rail system.[59]

Unfortunately, the GRTA and the rest of the Atlanta metropolitan region appear unwilling or unable to learn from the experiences of other major metropolitan areas. Public transit commuters as a share of all commuters in Atlanta were cut almost in half—7.94 percent to 4.59 percent—between 1970 and 1990, the period during which MARTA was being built.[60] As Georgia prepares to dedicate millions of dollars to the creation of HOV lanes, mass transit, and park-and-ride programs, among others—in hopes of luring people to alternative modes of transportation—it should consider the cost-effectiveness of these programs. A recent study by the Georgia Public Policy Foundation strongly recommends such an approach. The study shows the cost per ton of various Phoenix, Arizona–based emission reduction policies that would directly affect traffic congestion. Phoenix faces a problem similar to that of Atlanta.[61] (See Table 10.4)

## Land Use Control

The most telling test of just how powerful the GRTA will become is whether it moves beyond just transportation planning and enters the land use debate, as the enabling legislation makes clear it can. It is widely assumed that the creation of the GRTA means the end of mega-mall

| Table 10.4 | |
|---|---|
| **Costs of Emissions Reduction Policies for the Phoenix Area** | |
| | Cost per Ton $NO_x$ |
| Compressed Work Week | Nil |
| Flex Time | Nil |
| Guaranteed Ride Home | $265 |
| Vanpooling | $1,099 |
| Telecommuting (1 day/week) | $2,038 |
| Park and Ride | $2,873 |
| HOV Lanes | $6,133 |
| Bus Service | $32,017 |
| Natural Gas Bus Service | $32,422 |
| Moderate Bus Expansion | $62,992 |
| Rail Transit | $377,333 |

Source: Arizona Department of Transportation, as cited in Laura Creasy, "Metro Atlanta's Congestion and Air Quality Conundrum: Shuttle Vans to the Rescue?" Georgia Public Policy Foundation, March 16, 1999.

construction for the foreseeable future.[62] In late 1999, in Gwinnett County, the Mall of Georgia opened with nearly 500 acres and 3.7 million square feet of retail space, with enough parking for 8,600 cars. The Mall of Georgia will be the largest shopping center in the Southeast.[63]

The anti-growth supporters appeared highly successful in getting counties to place moratoriums on developers in the metropolitan region. Forsyth County declared a 16-month moratorium on rezoning and froze existing land use. DeKalb County declared a 30-day moratorium while it developed an ordinance to preserve fast-declining urban forest. Cherokee County established a 12-month moratorium on rezoning for residential construction.[64] In June 1999,

## Notes:

58. Goldberg, "Region Turns Its Attention to Growth Issues," p. 07E.

59. Don Fernandez and Kathey Pruitt, "Barnes, Amtrak Leaders Meet on Transportation Needs," *Atlanta Journal-Constitution,* September 16, 1999, p. 3E.

60. Ronald D. Utt, Ph.D., and Wendell Cox, "Transit Pork Has Few Passengers," Heritage Foundation *Executive Memorandum* No. 518, March 27, 1998, Table 1.

61. Creasy, "Metro Atlanta's Congestion and Air Quality Conundrum."

62. Ehrenhalt, "The Czar of Gridlock."

63. *Ibid.*

64. Goldberg, "Region Turns Its Attention to Growth Issues," p. 07E.

Fulton County considered dividing itself into a growth area that will allow high-density residential zoning and an area that will remain rural or agricultural.[65]

As land use moratoriums were seemingly proliferating, Governor Barnes sent a strong indication in August 1999 that the GRTA would move into land use planning. He unveiled his green space initiative at the Southern Governors' Conference in St. Louis. This proposal requires fast-growth counties to set aside at least 20 percent of their undeveloped land for open space. Those that failed to include that goal in their land use plans would not be eligible for state money for infrastructure improvements.[66]

Unfortunately, the irony of this type of proposal is that businesses are less and less interested in locating in the 13-county nonattainment area and prefer to locate just outside of it. Efforts to combat sprawl are having exactly the opposite effect and only make it more likely that the GRTA will expand its reach to those areas as well.

## Tentative Federal Air Quality Approval

With Washington looking favorably on the creation of GRTA, Atlanta prepared again to get the EPA's approval of its air quality plan. On October 28, 1999, Georgia's Environmental Protection Division prepared a revised air quality plan to submit to the EPA. This proposal included computer modeling results to show how its control measures would reach attainment status, a request to extend the period for the Atlanta nonattainment areas to 2003, a list of control measures, and regulations to implement them. The state promised to implement the following regulations by May 1, 2003:[67]

- **Require** motor vehicle emission inspections annually, rather than every two years, in the 13 metropolitan counties that failed to meet air quality guidelines, and have cars undergo more rigorous testing regardless of age.

- **Require** an even lower sulfur gasoline, the only type of gas retailers can sell in 25 metropolitan area counties between May and September, in 44 additional counties.

- **Impose** new emission controls on power plants inside the 13-county metropolitan area as well as new permitting requirements in 34 additional counties surrounding the region.

The state hoped these steps would bring the region into compliance with federal rules, thus freeing the frozen federal highway construction dollars. However, state officials were initially told by the EPA that the plan still did not meet its air quality standards. Even though the state Environmental Protection Division received that message, it still voted out the new rules and sent them to the GRTA to give it time to "guide the plan."[68] State Environment Director Harold Reheis said at the time, "There's only so much that we can do. We can affect fuels and how clean cars are that are on the road...but we can't affect people driving in their cars."[69]

On February 28, 2000, the EPA approved Georgia's plan for Atlanta's 13-county nonattainment area. However, the agency indicated that it could not determine "conformity," that is, whether the motor vehicle emissions budget submitted by the state in the plan could be

## Notes:

65. Sandra Eckstein, "Latest Land Use Plan Includes Growth Area," *Atlanta Journal-Constitution*, June 10, 1999, p. 1JK.
66. Kathey Pruitt, "Barnes' Green Space Concept Has Other Governors Intrigued," *Atlanta Journal-Constitution*, September 13, 1999, p. 2C.
67. See *Federal Register*, Vol. 65, p. 10490.
68. Lucy Soto, "Air Pollution Plan Vote Set for Today," *Atlanta Journal-Constitution*, September 16, 1999, p. 1E.
69. *Ibid*.

Table 10.5

# Is Portland a Role Model?

| | Atlanta | Portland |
|---|---|---|
| Urbanized Population Density (population/sq. mi.) | 1,359 | 2,105 |
| Rate of Roadway Construction Compared to 1982 Base[1] | 58.9% | 108.1% |
| Change in Roadway Congestion Index (RCI): 1982-1996[2] | 36.3% | 33.3% |
| Core Service Area Public Transport Ridership per Capita (MARTA vs. Tri-Met): 1997 | 137.3 | 72.3 |

Note: 1. Roadway construction in Portland has occurred at almost twice the rate as in Atlanta.
2. RCI is a density measurement that considers traffic volume (demand) and the number of freeway and major street lanes (supply) in an area. The higher the RCI, the worse the congestion.
Source: Wendell Cox Consultancy using data from the Federal Highway Administration, National Transit Database. Texas Transportation Institute, American Public Transit Association, and U.S. Census Bureau.

attained by the existing transportation plan. Yet, the Georgia Assembly did nothing to stop the annual vehicle inspection program, one of the steps that must be taken to assure final approval. Atlanta is operating under an interim transportation plan with just a few projects approved to move forward.[70]

The EPA's tentative approval was welcome news in Atlanta. The Atlanta Regional Commission finalized its 25-year Regional Transportation Plan on March 22, 2000. It includes changes in vehicle inspections and other steps for reducing on-road mobile sources and emissions overall, by encouraging alternative transportation and mass transit options. But efforts could ultimately have to become more draconian. This plan now goes to the federal government to determine its conformity with the state's air quality plan.

## Federal Implementation Plan Possible

Under the Clean Air Act, if a state's plan for meeting air quality standards has been declared deficient and if the deficiencies have not been corrected, the EPA is required to establish a federal implementation plan within two years. The original plans under the Act were due in November 1994, and in 1996 and 1997 EPA issued determinations that several plans, including Atlanta's, were in nonattainment. Soon after that, several environmental groups filed a notice of a citizen's suit demanding that the EPA fulfill its requirement under the Act and issue a federal plan.

The EPA is under a court-ordered deadline to approve or disapprove these nonattainment state implementation plans during 2000 and to implement federal pollution reduction programs in those areas where plans remain deficient. The 2000 deadline for federal action on the plan is being driven by a lawsuit filed by the Natural Resources Defense Council, the Environmental Defense Fund, and other groups. Thirteen states and the District of Columbia are in these nonattainment areas with deficient plans.[71]

There is a very real possibility that some or all of these states might be subjected to an even greater level of federal control in 2000 and beyond. Of course, for Atlanta, even without a

## Notes:

70. *Federal Register,* p. 10490.
71. Bureau of National Affairs, *Daily Report for Executives*, "Groups Challenge EPA Conditional Approval of Nonattainment SIPs in Major Metro Areas," March 3, 2000, p. A-15.

federal takeover, the threat of federal control already has had an effect.

## PORTLAND IS NO MODEL FOR ATLANTA

Atlanta is looking at Portland, Oregon, as a model for how to manage its growth, but not because it has seen anything about Portland that it finds particularly attractive. Atlanta looks to Portland because the federal government is forcing it to find ways to manage its growth aggressively in the name of improving air quality. Any "solution" the GRTA—Atlanta's federally induced super–growth management authority—might be tempted to impose, be it mass transit, zoning changes, or inducements to density, could have only a marginal impact on the region's air quality, especially during the next five years. The EPA is focusing on this period. At the same time, the quality of life and prosperity of the Atlanta region also is likely to suffer. A hard look at the Portland experience inevitably leads to this assessment.

Aggressive efforts over the past 20 years to manage growth in Portland have had the exact opposite of the intended effect, contributing instead to deteriorating environmental conditions and a diminished quality of life. (See Chapter 9.) Today, as Table 10.5 shows, Portland's population density is higher than Atlanta's and the city is building roads faster than Atlanta to relieve the traffic congestion that contributes to deteriorating air quality. Portland's magnificent obsession and spending on light rail has done little to reduce the growing traffic congestion. Land use restrictions have only limited the availability of affordable housing and forced sprawl to jump the growth boundaries and move into other areas.

*Atlanta has turned from a poster child for sprawl into a disturbing model for federal growth management.*

## THE TREND TOWARD FEDERAL GROWTH MANAGEMENT

What is happening in Atlanta today is of national significance in the debate over smart growth. Atlanta has turned from a poster child for sprawl into a disturbing model for federal growth management. It is the largest metropolitan area in America to be subjected to federal sanctions that interfere with the ability of a community to address growth as it its people see fit.

In Chapter 7, Ronald Utt explores whether or not the federal government has a role in smart growth. He concludes that there is little evidence to suggest that federal policies have either helped or hindered suburbanization or sprawl. But, as we see in Atlanta, it is clear that the federal government has the potential to do a great deal to stunt growth in the future. The ability of the federal government to dictate growth management —by withholding millions in transportation funding and stopping road projects—is a reality. Indeed, the federal government has forced local communities and the citizens of metropolitan Atlanta to cede enormous power to a state authority that seems determined to adopt Portland's smart-growth policies.

Although it is still too early to draw any conclusions about the impact of federal actions on Atlanta, it provides a groundbreaking case study in federally induced growth management. Indeed, it is possible that the EPA, under the provisions of Clean Air Act, might go as far as to take direct control of managing growth in the future.

The lesson from the Atlanta experience is a warning to fast-growing metropolitan regions: If you fail to develop your own growth management plans, today's activist federal government will be more aggressive in dictating those plans. Atlanta would appear to signal a chilling trend toward the federal takeover of metropolitan regions, with unpredictable consequences for the freedom of its citizens to live and work as they choose.

# AMERICA'S COMMUNITIES TOMORROW

*By Jane S. Shaw and Ronald D. Utt*

L ike all popular sound bites, the terms "urban sprawl" and "suburbanization" mean many things to many people. As the authors of these chapters show, such broad terms encompass many problems that are not so easily defined, much less solved. People within the same communities and across the country see these problems quite differently. For some, the difficulty of rapidly growing suburbs is traffic, pure and simple. Others object to the "cookie cutter" designs that characterize some fast-growing towns, while for many more, alarm stems from the development of agricultural land, open space, and wildlife habitat. The challenge is to sort out these problems and delineate the most effective ways to address them.

Where today's touted smart-growth solutions are found wanting, these pages offer fresh ideas. For example, Samuel Staley recommends performance zoning and the overlay of zoning districts to allow developers more opportunities to innovate and still protect residents from harm as their neighborhoods change. Wendell Cox offers a broad array of innovations that could, for example, enable today's crowded highways to carry more cars while traffic flows

more smoothly. Donald Leal introduces us to entrepreneurs who are designing residences today that not only make people feel a part of their community and environs, but that also integrate nature with home.

Taken as a whole, this book offers a dose of realism—with clarity of analysis and reasoned scrutiny of possible solutions—to the debate over sprawl. However, what is most clear after all is said and read is that everyone must begin to think more expansively about suburban growth. Both enthusiasts for smart-growth solutions and their critics face a danger: an over-reliance on solutions already at hand, rather than maintaining an openness to new ideas and new possibilities as they evolve.

The controversy over sprawl can be seen as a debate over two solutions from the past, a 19th century solution and a 20th century one, a debate over railroads and automobiles. One group argues for rail lines in metropolitan areas to keep people in the city, while another argues that we must come to terms with the automobile, making driving in America more pleasant, less congested, and more convenient. But this level of argument demonstrates how easy it is to assume that the solutions we see around us today are all there is.

It is now the 21st century. Surely, there is a way to cut the Gordian knot and come up with something better. We do not suggest that we necessarily know what the answer will be. We can say it will not be a single answer; rather, it will involve many different approaches. The anecdotal evidence we have encountered in researching this subject shows that people indeed are responding creatively to sprawl. Consider: While many people have moved into "edge cities," average commuting times have not gone up very much. Why? Because people are driving slightly longer distances, but driving faster. Rather than allowing themselves to be stymied in traffic, they are finding routes that make their commutes more pleasant.

Other ways of coping with traffic are increasing in use, such as telecommuting—that is, living in one place and using computers and long-distance communications to reduce or eliminate time spent at a central workplace. The recent attempt by the U.S. Department of Labor to enforce safety rules for telecommuters who work in their own homes led to an outcry from businesses, even more than from the telecommuters themselves. Businesses see the flexibility of working from a home base as an important option for the future, and many companies are developing the technological infrastructure to facilitate it. Some businesses already encourage flexible hours to help reduce commuting time. The explosion of Internet shopping, too, is reducing the amount of time people spend driving to stores and malls.

As wealth increases, people find they have more choices, which includes the choice of where to live. In Donald Leal's chapter, we find

that individuals from professional writers to airplane pilots are choosing to live in Sea Ranch, California, because their time is important, and they choose to spend it in a beautiful place, rather than a traditionally convenient one.

Will this increase in choices continue? If history is any gauge, changing technology will continue to expand our options. People will pursue their desires and, as they cope with new challenges, come up with new ideas and new living patterns to improve their quality of life. The lesson for planners, city and town officials, and American citizens is to avoid making decisions today that will eliminate or inhibit their choices in the future.

In the 1920s, it would have been difficult to predict that less than 2 percent of the U.S. population would need to work in agriculture, just as it would have been hard to know that there would be 130 million cars on the road. No one would have guessed that the number of deer in 1890, around 500,000, would rise to over 15 million today. Circumstances change drastically over time, and keeping options open is one of the greatest legacies policymakers can give future generations.

Rather than having government decide where people must live and how their houses must be designed, America will be better off if we take a more humble perspective, recognizing that future paths may veer in entirely unexpected directions and that we do not want to block off those directions forever. America's unique river of freedom to find new paths and places, try out new ideas, and build new communities must not be dammed. By maintaining flexibility and freedom, we as a nation can sustain our greatest strengths and ensure that the future will be better than the past.

# ABOUT THE AUTHORS

### Angela M. Antonelli

Since 1995, Angela M. Antonelli has managed The Heritage Foundation's research on budget, tax, regulatory, labor, and environmental policy as the Director of the Thomas A. Roe Institute for Economic Policy Studies. She also has administrative responsibilities for managing the production of all policy research products produced by the Domestic and Economic Policy Studies Department. A former policy analyst and Assistant Branch Chief in the White House Office of Management Budget (OMB), she specializes in general government and regulatory reform and environmental policy. She is a contributing editor of *Environment and Climate News*, a publication sponsored by The Heartland Institute and circulated to more than 40,000 readers each month.

Antonelli has testified before a number of congressional committees on regulatory reform and environmental issues. Her work has been cited in newspapers including the *Washington Post, Roll Call, Business Week,* and *Investor's Business Daily*, and she has appeared on *CNN* and *Fox News Channel* as well as talk radio.

Antonelli also held positions with the U.S. General Accounting Office, the State of New Jersey and as a senior consultant with Lewin-VHI, a health care consulting firm in Vienna, Virginia. A graduate of Cornell University, Antonelli earned a Master's degree in public affairs from Princeton University.

### John A. Charles

John Charles joined the Cascade Policy Institute in January 1997 as environmental policy director. Cascade is a free-market think tank in Portland, Oregon. The focus of Charles's work is transportation, growth management, and pollution control.

Prior to joining the Institute, Charles was executive director of the Oregon Environmental Council from 1980–1996. Earlier, he worked with the Environmental Defense Fund in New York City.

Charles has written extensively on environmental topics, and has been published in *The Oregonian, The Arizona Republic, The Pittsburgh Courier-Review, The Hartford Courant* and *Natural Resources Law Institute News*. He is also a Contributing Editor to *Brainstorm* magazine. His most recent paper, "Beyond Zoning: Land Use Controls in a Digital Economy," presents a market-based approach to land-use regulation.

Charles received a B.A. degree with honors from the University of Pittsburgh in 1976 and an M.P.A. degree from Portland State University in 1991.

### Wendell Cox

Wendell Cox is principal of Wendell Cox Consultancy, an international public policy firm specializing in transport, economics, labor, and demographics. Among the firm's most notable projects have been an evaluation of proposed growth control proposals in the state of Pennsylvania, a series of performance analyses on major public transport systems in the state of Texas, an evaluation of the state public transit program for the Washington legislature, a performance audit of British Columbia Transit, the New Zealand competitive pricing procedures, and competitive tendering projects in a number of urban areas.

Cox is a member of the Amtrak Reform Council, which has the responsibility to oversee intercity rail passenger policy over the next three years, and serves as chair of its Financial Analysis Committee. He also served as Director of Policy and Legislation for the American Legislative Exchange Council and is a Visiting Fellow of The Heritage Foundation.

Cox was appointed to three terms on the Los Angeles County Transportation Commission by Los Angeles Mayor Tom Bradley. There he chaired the Service Coordination Committee and served on the Finance Review and Rail Construction Committees. In connection with these responsibilities, he also chaired two American Public Transit Association national committees (Governing Boards and Planning & Policy).

### Steven Hayward

Steven Hayward is Senior Fellow and director of the Center for Environmental and Regulatory Reform at the Pacific Research Institute for Public Policy in San Francisco, where he co-authors *The Index of Leading Environmental Indicators*, released each year on Earth Day. During 1997–1998, he was also a Bradley Fellow at The Heritage Foundation in Washington, D.C., and he is an adjunct fellow of the John Ashbrook Center at Ashland College, Ohio. He holds a Ph.D. in American Studies and an M.A. in Government from Claremont Graduate School.

Hayward has extensive experience as a journalist and writer, and has published dozens of articles in scholarly and popular journals. He writes frequently for *National Review, Reason*, and *Policy Review*, and his newspaper articles have appeared in the *New York Times, Baltimore Sun, San Francisco Chronicle, Chicago Tribune*, and many other daily newspapers. He has been a Weaver Fellow of the Intercollegiate Studies Institute of Bryn Mawr, Pennsylvania, and a fellow of the Earhart Foundation, based in Ann Arbor, Michigan. In 1990 and 1992, Hayward was an Olive Garvey Fellow of the Mont Pelerin Society, an international organization devoted to the study of political economy. The paperback edition of his business book, *Churchill on Leadership: Executive Success in the Face of Adversity* (Prima Publishing) was released in October 1998. He is currently working on a major book, *The Age of Reagan: A Chronicle of the Closing Decades of the American Century*.

### Donald R. Leal

Donald R. Leal is a Senior Associate at the Political Economy Research Center (PERC) in Bozeman, Montana, where he has been conducting research in natural resource and environmental issues since 1985. He received his B.S. in mathematics and M.S. in statistics from California State University at Hayward. He is a contributing author of *Taking Ownership: Property Rights and Fishery Management on the Atlantic Coast* (1996), *Multiple Conflicts Over Multiple Uses* (1994), *Taking the Environment Seriously* (1993), and *The Yellowstone Primer: Land and Resource Management in the Greater Yellowstone Ecosystem* (1990). He is co-author with Terry Anderson of *Free Market Environmentalism* (1991) which received the 1992 Sir Antony Fisher International Memorial Award, and *Enviro-Capitalists: Doing Good While Doing Well*, also co-authored with Anderson. He has published extensively on such topics as fisheries, water, recreation, oil and gas, timber, and public land use policy. Leal's studies comparing federal and state management of forests and parks have fostered a new perspective on public land management. His current projects include assessing the impact of individual transferable quota programs in fishery management throughout the world, documenting cases where government programs have harmed the environment, and co-authoring a revision of *Free Market Environmentalism*.

### Jane S. Shaw

Jane S. Shaw is a Senior Associate at the Political Economy Research Center (PERC) in Bozeman, Montana. As director of PERC's Outreach Program, she writes and edits articles and books and directs PERC's conferences for journalists and business executives. She is co-author with Michael Sanera of *Facts, Not Fear: Teaching Children about the Environment* (Regnery Publishing, Inc., 2nd edition, 1999). She edits PERC's quarterly newsletter, *PERC Reports,* and was editor of *A Blueprint for Environmental Education*, published by PERC in 1999. She has lectured around the country on environmental issues and their treatment in the schools and by the media. Shaw received her B.A. from Wellesley College. Before joining PERC, she was an associate economics editor of *Business Week*, and was previously a correspondent for McGraw-Hill Publications in Washington, D.C., and Chicago. She is a member of the Editorial Advisory Panel of *Regulation*, a senior editor of *Liberty*, and a trustee of the Philadelphia Society and the Association of Private Enterprise Education.

### Samuel R. Staley

Samuel R. Staley, Ph.D., directs the Urban Futures Program at Reason Public Policy Institute, a nonprofit research and education organization based in Los Angeles. Active in his community, he is currently a member of his local planning board and former member of its Board of Zoning Appeals. Staley is the author of more than 50 professional articles, reports, and studies on urban development and policy issues, including the books *Planning Rules and Urban Economic Performance: The Case of Hong Kong* (Chinese University Press/Hong Kong Centre for Economic Research, 1994), *Drug Policy and the Decline of American Cities* (Transaction Books, 1992), and is co-editor (with Randall G. Holcombe) of *Land Use Planning for the 21st Century* (Greenwood Press, forthcoming). His research has appeared in professional journals, such as the *Journal of the American Planning Association*, *Planning and Markets*, and *Planning* magazine, as well as the popular press, including the *Wall Street Journal*, *Los Angeles Times*, *Detroit News and Free Press*, the Charlotte Observer, and dozens of other newspapers across the nation.

## Richard L. Stroup

Richard L. Stroup is a professor of economics at Montana State University and a Senior Associate at the Political Economy Research Center. He received his B.A., M.A., and Ph.D. degrees from the University of Washington. From 1982 to 1984, he was director of the Office of Policy Analysis at the U.S. Department of the Interior. Stroup is a widely published author and speaker on economics, including natural resources and environmental issues, and he has written many articles for professional journals and popular media outlets. His work has been a major force in the development of the approach to resource problems known as the New Resource Economics or free market environmentalism. Stroup is coauthor with James D. Gwartney of a primer on economics, *What Everyone Should Know About Economics and Prosperity*, as well as a leading economics principles textbook, *Economics: Private and Public Choice*, now in its ninth edition. His recent research has focused on alternative institutional arrangements for dealing with endangered species, regulatory takings, hazardous waste, and other environmental risks, and he is currently writing a monograph entitled *What Everyone Should Know About Economics and the Environment*.

## Ronald D. Utt

Ronald D. Utt, Ph.D., is currently a Senior Research Fellow at The Heritage Foundation where the focus of his research is on national policies for transportation, housing, infrastructure, urban revitalization, and natural resources. Utt specializes in the application of privatization, restructuring, decentralization, and devolution to federal programs.

Utt has served as a staff director for a subcommittee of the United States Senate; the founder and President of Potomac Renovations, Ltd., a company that buys, renovates, and resells existing residential homes in Northern Virginia; and Vice President of the National Chamber Foundation, where he created and edited the *Journal of Economic Growth* and the *Journal of Regulation and Social Cost*.

Utt also served as the Managing Director for Novecon Ltd., a Washington, D.C.-based company specializing in trade and business development with East Europe and the countries of the former Soviet Union, where he was the L.A. Gear distributor for Bulgaria, Romania, and Macedonia. In 1987 and 1988, Utt served as the first Director of Privatization at the U.S. Office of Management and Budget under President Ronald Reagan.

Dr. Utt holds a Ph.D. in economics from Indiana University, a B.S. in Business Administration from Penn State, and is licensed as a general contractor in Virginia.

## The Honorable Malcolm Wallop

The Honorable Malcolm Wallop is the founder and chairman of the Frontiers of Freedom Institute. He was elected to the U.S. Senate in 1976 and held his seat for 18 years, retiring in 1994. During his tenure, Wallop served on numerous committees, including Energy and Natural Resources, Finance, Small Business, and the Select Committee on Intelligence. As a ranking Republican member of the Energy and Natural Resources Committee, Wallop was an outspoken opponent of increased regulation of the use of federal lands.

Senator Wallop also is the Chung Ju-Yung Fellow for Policy Studies, the first named fellowship in the Asian Studies Center at The Heritage Foundation.

He holds a bachelor's degree from Yale University.

# INDEX